IN PRAISE OF

American Educators

And How They Can Become Even Better

Dr. Richard DuFour

Solution Tree | Press

a division of
Solution Tree

555 North Morton Street
Bloomington, IN 47404
800.733.6786 (toll free) / 812.336.7700
FAX: 812.336.7790

email: info@solution-tree.com
solution-tree.com

Printed in the United States of America

19 18 17 16 15   1 2 3 4 5

Library of Congress Control Number: 2015940396

Solution Tree
Jeffrey C. Jones, CEO
Edmund M. Ackerman, President

Solution Tree Press
President: Douglas M. Rife
Senior Acquisitions Editor: Amy Rubenstein
Editorial Director: Lesley Bolton
Managing Production Editor: Caroline Weiss
Senior Production Editor: Suzanne Kraszewski
Proofreader: Jessi Finn
Text and Cover Designer: Rian Anderson

What the Experts Are Saying About
In Praise of American Educators

"*In Praise of American Educators* demonstrates Rick DuFour's passion for education, and just as important, for educators themselves. From a defense of today's teachers to a call for collective commitment to transform schools, this book offers both inspiration and concrete next actions for educators at all levels."

—Stephanie Hirsh, Executive Director, Learning Forward

"A 'stop the nonsense' manifesto from one of the leading education practitioners in the United States. Rick DuFour convincingly shows how current reform strategies blame the victims with baseless and counterproductive measures. *In Praise of American Educators* then provides the definitive solution. You won't be able to read this book without getting the urge to immediately get down to positive action!"

—Michael Fullan, Professor Emeritus, Ontario Institute for Studies in Education, University of Toronto

"This book pulls together the powerful and decisive arguments that debunk myths of the 'failure' of U.S. schools. It is indispensable for understanding the current political climate and also vital to pointing the way forward. 'Must-read' is overused, but in this case, it is right on!"

—Jon Saphier, Founder and President, Research for Better Teaching

"Had enough teacher bashing? With a mountain of evidence and indisputable logic, Rick DuFour considers the prevailing hypotheses about the ills of American education and knocks them down, one by one. He does not cover up the failings of schools, unions, and education systems. There is much work to be done. But the evidence is solidly on the side of improvements in professional practices, not in sharpening the political swords that perennially inflict damage on the teaching profession. If we expect teaching—the most significant impact on student learning—to improve, then we must consider not only how to improve the current generation of teachers but the next generation as well. The final sentence of this book says it all: 'The greatest generation of American educators is on hand to take on this challenge.' I would add, 'If only we will let them.' This book is Rick DuFour at his best: calm, deliberate, and incisive. His words will influence educators and educational leaders for decades to come."

—Douglas Reeves, Founding Partner, Creative Leadership Solutions

"No one has done more to give educators a voice in discussions on how to improve their profession than Rick DuFour. No one has articulated better how to make that voice heard than Rick does in this book. At a time when we desperately need heroes to tell the truth, confront the critics, and challenge traditions, Rick has again stepped forward to inspire us and lead the way."

—Thomas R. Guskey, College of Education, University of Kentucky

"As a full-time classroom teacher, I have spent the better part of fifteen years wrestling with failed policies, frustrated by the suggestion that practitioners are to blame for everything that is wrong with American schools and paralyzed waiting for meaningful change that never seems to come. Reading *In Praise of American Educators* reminded me that change isn't something that I have to hope for. Instead, it's something that I can create by working together with my peers in service of student learning."

—William M. Ferriter, Sixth-Grade Teacher, Author, Blogger, and Educational Consultant

"With its sharp focus on the facts surrounding the truths about our teaching profession, this book will serve as a catalyst for conversation—both among educators regarding our accomplishments as well as by those planning direction on policies and practices leading to continuous improvement. Rick DuFour rallies a clear call to action for America's teachers to rise to the challenge of making all students successful learners."

—Chris Jakicic, Author and Educational Consultant, Former Principal and Classroom Teacher

"Rick DuFour issues a clarion call that both celebrates the greatest generation of teachers and appeals to that distinguished group to push for more—all with the desired outcome of ensuring our students have an opportunity to successfully transition to the next stages of their lives beyond the public school. This book serves as the proverbial mirror and window, allowing educators to reflect on their significant accomplishments while also seeing through to an even brighter future. Our schools and our teachers deserve nothing less."

—Tom Hierck, Author and Educational Consultant, Former District and School Administrator and Classroom Teacher

"At once a heartfelt tribute to American educators and an urgent call for them to do more—specifically, to establish the kind of collaborative and reflective professional learning communities that are known to have a positive impact on student learning. This thoughtful, well-researched, and well-argued book is sure to influence and inspire those who read it."

—Harvey Silver, President, Silver Strong & Associates and Thoughtful Education Press

"Rick DuFour crafts an aggressive, cogent defense of public schools and the teachers who serve our kids, effectively debunking most of the reforms intended to 'fix' them and offering solutions for moving forward to a better place in education."

—Will Richardson, Publisher, Cofounder, and Editorial Director, ModernLearners.com

"DuFour takes on the world—the world of education—debunking myths and challenging quick fixes. He responds to the critical issues facing educators today and offers practical, time-tested, and concrete advice about how to create amazing learning environments for students to thrive. He builds on his past work, extending the scope of Professional Learning Communities at Work to ensure the success of every student."

—Douglas Fisher and Nancy Frey, Teacher Leaders at Health Sciences High and Professors of Educational Leadership, San Diego State University

"What a rare treasure in these times of declining resources and respect for teachers and school leaders—someone in the position to really know schools is paying tribute to American educators! Unprecedented and so needed. Also rare is a treatise like this one that combines such thorough scholarship with down-to-earth common sense. Rick leaves no challenge to teacher quality unaddressed as he builds his case for their positive impact on schools and student well-being."

—Rick Stiggins, Classroom Assessment Consultant

"Rick DuFour provides an objective and factual analysis of the current state of American education; he separates the facts from the myths. He appeals to all parties involved to place the needs of children at the center of the debate about school improvement and to let go of political jargon and the vilification of educators."

—Anthony Muhammad, CEO, New Frontier 21

"A must-read for anyone who cares about the future of our country, our schools, and our children. The author delivers an honest assessment of where schools are today, explains why our reform efforts thus far have failed, and shows us the way forward toward measurably better schools. The clearest, most coherent piece on public education written in the last decade."

—Thomas Many, Author and Educational Consultant

"This is a book only Rick DuFour could have written. It is panoramic in perspective, yet laser-focused in terms of message. It tells us what we have done well and on what we need to improve in a style and level of honesty that is characteristic of Rick's large body of work and the manner in which he lives his life. We all need to take Rick's message to heart."

—Robert J. Marzano, CEO, Marzano Research

"DuFour deftly uses hard facts and evidence to eradicate the popular perception that American schools are failing and instead builds a remarkable case to the contrary. DuFour goes to considerable lengths to light a pathway of hope for American educators, offering clear and concise research-based and immediately practical strategies to make our schools the very best they can be. This book is a treasure trove for any teacher, administrator, or policymaker who is seeking (1) ideas on how to improve, (2) language with which to help parents understand what's needed, and (3) a foundation with which to challenge and ultimately inform the national agenda in education. This book is a must-have for every educator committed to a better tomorrow."

—Cassandra Erkens, Educational Consultant

"*In Praise of American Educators* is unrelentingly honest, optimistic, and inspiring. Written with poignant elegance, it's a courageous and altogether clarifying call to arms."

—Casey Reason, Author and Consultant, Casey Reason Companies/HighPoint Learning, LLC

"In this well-written, beautifully judged, and moving book, Rick DuFour shows that, despite the many criticisms leveled against them, the current generation of American educators is the best we have ever seen, but, to prepare our young people for a world that no one can imagine, educators need to be even better. Building on decades of work, the book shows how there is really only one way to meet this challenge—creating and sustaining professional learning communities in every single school. Everyone involved in education needs to read and act on the contents of this book."

—Dylan Wiliam, Emeritus Professor of Educational Assessment, Institute of Education, University College London

"Rick DuFour examines the question, 'Why do we not identify the success that is all around us, esteem it, and build a coalition to then become even better?' The method Rick presents to provide a solution, via professional learning teams, acknowledges expertise and is the underlying principle of his call to action. The book sparkles in evidence and stories and is a challenge to the naysayers and to those who wish to distract the development of U.S. students. It is hard to come away with any other view than, 'We can do it!'"

—John Hattie, Director, Melbourne Education Research Institute

This book is dedicated to Robert Eaker, my great friend and colleague. Bob is the last Renaissance man—U.S. Marine, watercolorist, furniture maker, musician, author, speaker, humorist, husband, father, grandfather, and handyman. He devoted most of his life, however, to education. He is an institution at Middle Tennessee State University, where he served as professor, dean of the College of Education, and provost of the university. Throughout his career, he has been passionate about helping K–12 educators apply educational research in their schools and classrooms, and he was cited by *Phi Delta Kappan* magazine as one of the nation's leaders in translating educational research into practice.

Bob served as coauthor of our first book on professional learning communities (PLCs) in 1998: *Professional Learning Communities at Work: Best Practices for Enhancing Student Achievement*. Since then, Bob has made a tremendous contribution to the literature on the PLC at Work™ process. Among his titles are:

- *Getting Started: Reculturing Schools to Become Professional Learning Communities*

- *Whatever It Takes: How Professional Learning Communities Respond When Kids Don't Learn*

- *Learning by Doing: A Handbook for Professional Learning Communities at Work* (first and second editions)

- *Revisiting Professional Learning Communities at Work: New Insights for Improving Schools*
- *A Leader's Companion: Inspiration for Professional Learning Communities at Work*
- *Raising the Bar and Closing the Gap: Whatever It Takes*
- *Every School, Every Team, Every Classroom: District Leadership for Growing Professional Learning Communities at Work*
- *The Journey to Becoming a Professional Learning Community*

Bob was also the coeditor of the anthology *On Common Ground: The Power of Professional Learning Communities* in which the leading educators in North America offered their insights into PLCs.

Bob has been a featured speaker at more than one hundred PLC institutes and summits and has worked with state departments of education, regional service centers, and school districts throughout North America. He is, without question, one of this nation's leading spokespersons on the PLC process.

In addition to his contribution to the field, he has been the greatest friend a person could have.

We first met in 1978 and have worked together ever since. But we are much more than colleagues; we are best friends who now have spent the majority of our lives together as PLC pioneers. His commitment to me and this work has never wavered in more than thirty-five years.

I am forever grateful to be a fellow traveler with Bob on the journey to bring the PLC process to life in schools and districts. As the Grateful Dead put it, "What a long, strange trip it's been." But the trip has been far more enjoyable and filled with fun and laughter because I have had the pleasure of having Bob Eaker as my companion. I am among the many in our profession who are indebted to him.

Acknowledgments

This book could not have been written without the input and support of my wonderful wife, Becky DuFour, and my great friend Mike Mattos. They carefully read every word, challenged my thinking, made suggestions to address key issues and enhance clarity, and worked closely with me through every phase of the writing project. I am indebted to them both.

I also had the benefit of two excellent editors. Mike's wife, Anita Mattos, caught my mistakes and helped me to clarify major points. Suzanne Kraszewski improved this book as she has every book I have ever written for Solution Tree. She has been a wonderful partner and collaborator.

Jeff Jones, the chief executive officer of Solution Tree, has been a passionate advocate for PLCs since he took over the company in 1998. There is no question that his tireless efforts to support PLCs helped to make the process a major force in improving schools in the United States and around the world. He is an amazing friend to whom I am deeply indebted.

Finally, I have had the privilege of working with more than seventy-five of America's finest educational leaders who now serve as PLC associates. They have traveled the globe as missionaries for the PLC process, speaking with conviction because they have brought the process to life in their own schools and districts. I am honored to call them colleagues. It is because of them that I know the number of educators embracing PLCs will continue to grow and flourish long after I am gone.

Visit **go.solution-tree.com/PLCbooks** to download the reproducibles in this book.

Table of Contents

About the Author

Richard DuFour, EdD, was a public school educator for thirty-four years, serving as a teacher, principal, and superintendent. During his nineteen-year tenure as a leader at Adlai E. Stevenson High School in Lincolnshire, Illinois, Stevenson was one of only three schools in the nation to win the United States Department of Education Blue Ribbon Award on four occasions and the first comprehensive high school to be designated a New America High School as a model of successful school reform. He received his state's highest award as both a principal and superintendent.

A prolific author and sought-after consultant, he is recognized as one of the leading authorities on helping school practitioners implement the Professional Learning Communities at Work™ process in their schools and districts.

Dr. DuFour wrote a quarterly column for the *Journal of Staff Development* for nearly a decade. He was the lead consultant and author of ASCD's video series on principalship and the author of several other videos. Dr. DuFour was named as one of the Top 100 School Administrators in North America by *Executive Educator* magazine, was presented the Distinguished Scholar Practitioner Award from the University of Illinois, and was the 2004 recipient of the National Staff Development Council's Distinguished Service Award.

To learn more about Rick DuFour's work, visit www.allthings plc.info. To follow Rick's battle with cancer in his own words, go to www.caringbridge.org and enter Rick DuFour.

To book Rick for professional development, contact PD@ solution-tree.com.

Foreword

By Robert Eaker

Richard DuFour has written a troubling book, and rightly so! It should be troubling to realize that a segment of our society—particularly a segment of politicians and the media—has declared war on America's public schools, and more specifically, on America's public school teachers. It is even more troubling that the war on teachers is based on data that are interpreted incorrectly, manipulated, or simply false.

Particularly disturbing is the fact that the bulk of the attacks have come from elected officials at the state and national levels. Rather than offering support to help make educators even better, they call for increasingly punitive sanctions against educators, the elimination of tenure, the implementation of merit pay schemes, and the incremental and relentless privatization of public schools through charters and vouchers.

Even if we assume that this war on public schools and public school teachers is being waged with the best of intentions (I, for one, am not so generous!), the attacks have not been based on a hard examination of a broad array of accessible facts about America's public schools. Rather, critics tend to carefully cherry-pick the most negative facts and then repeat them again and again in selected media outlets, all in support of a larger political agenda.

In Praise of American Educators: And How They Can Become Even Better demonstrates that there is not a lack of accurate and informative data readily available to those who want to honestly examine our public schools; this book is crammed with facts! It sets the record straight. It does not offer a subjective, romantic defense of public schools and the teaching profession. Rather, the author presents the facts, reminding me of the line Jack Webb made famous in *Dragnet*, the popular television series of the 1950s: "Just the facts, ma'am, just the facts."

This book informs us of the current state of our public schools as they *actually* exist. Do you want to know how teachers are doing based on an array of studies using multiple measures? Do you want to look at America's public schools through the prism of international comparisons? Do you want to know how countries with high student achievement attain such impressive results? How about what the facts tell us about teacher unions? What about the prognosis for current reform efforts? It's all right here. And do you want to know how American educators can become much better? Well, that is all here too!

America's teachers are being asked (in fact, directed) to do more than ever before and reach levels of student achievement that have no precedent in any country in the world while they confront increasingly complex and difficult circumstances. They continue to be besieged by hostile attacks while the unprecedented successes of our public schools are being largely ignored. With a nod to Winston Churchill, it could be said that never have so many been asked to do so much with so little—and been appreciated by so few!

The author presents readers with a stark choice. Will we as a nation choose to accept the evidence that our schools and teachers are doing better than ever before, under increasingly difficult circumstances, and then commit to further improvement; or will we choose to ignore the facts, succumb to despair, and head down the road of systematically destroying the very public school system that has served as our nation's foundation for democracy and our citizens' most reliable tool for upward mobility?

In Praise of American Educators is not a Pollyannaish defense of public schools and their teachers. It is a clarion call for educators to do better—to create schools for *every* child that would be good enough for their *own* child!

Rick DuFour acknowledges his frustration with the unwillingness of too many educators to implement what clearly are proven practices and the tendency to allow the happiness and autonomy of adults to take precedence over practical, common-sense steps that will enhance student learning. He also shares his frustration with teacher unions that cling to positions their own members often find indefensible. He recognizes that unions should advocate for their members but insists there is nothing incongruous about unions being both teacher advocates and champions of proven practices for improving student learning.

At the same time *In Praise of American Educators* is troubling, it also brims with optimism. It is passionate and caring—caring enough to focus on how to make our public schools better, and the good news is that knowing how to improve schools is not a great mystery. Certainly, conditions such as poverty and declining support for public schools affect the difficulty of the tasks at hand. But knowing what needs to be done has never been clearer. In the history of American public education, there has never been such widespread agreement among researchers and practitioners regarding the most promising pathway for improving student learning. Schools and school districts need to function as professional learning communities. The concepts and practices of true, high-performing PLCs form a research-based, proven approach for bringing the disparate elements of best practice under an umbrella of common sense.

The optimism of *In Praise of American Educators* is also reflected in a clearly articulated focus on what teachers *really* need in order to attain systemic and sustained increases in student learning levels. Teachers need to work in schools and in school districts that are led by highly effective leaders who are continuous learners—constantly seeking out and leading the implementation of best practices, relying on the collaborative analysis of student learning data to drive decision making, and fostering a culture of continuous improvement.

Teachers also need the benefit of membership in a high-performing collaborative team—a team that is engaged in the right work; work in which team members collaboratively focus on the learning of each student, skill by skill, and are continually learning from and supporting each other. Additionally, teachers need to work in schools that have developed an effective, systematic, schoolwide plan for providing additional time and support for students when they experience difficulty in their learning and the extension of learning for students who demonstrate proficiency.

Finally, and very importantly, teachers need to be frequently recognized, genuinely appreciated, and respected for doing a difficult and complex job well. In short, teachers need to work in schools that function as PLCs!

Because *In Praise of American Educators* clearly addresses the things teachers and schools need to do to improve, it is a powerful source of inspiration for educators at every level. It helps us realize that in spite of the difficulties and obstacles facing public school educators each and every day, schools can be improved, and more students can learn at increasingly high levels. Rick shows the way and demonstrates that improving schools is undeniably doable.

At its core, this book is a call for commitment to action. Simply put, the author challenges us to take an honest look at our public schools—what they are doing well and the challenges they face—and then commit to making our public schools better by implementing the concepts and practices in the PLC process in every school, in every classroom, and in every team, accepting nothing less, because the stakes are so high!

As I approached the final chapters of this book, I asked myself, "Who should read this book?" It certainly speaks directly to national and state leaders, educators at every level and in every discipline, and every person in a position to affect educational policy. Then I realized that *everyone*—every citizen—should read this book! If we as a nation are not careful, we may one day come to realize that the very institution on which our democracy rests has been incrementally dismantled, and then we'll wonder, "How did this happen, and for what purpose?" Unless we reverse the direction of American educational policy, generations of students and the nation at large will bear an enormous cost. So, read (don't skim), underline, make notes in the margins, "dog ear" the pages, reflect, question, and enjoy, and learn from and become inspired to act by the wisdom found throughout *In Praise of American Educators: And How They Can Become Even Better.*

I must add one final, more personal note: I have often pointed out how much I admire Rick DuFour's leadership, presentation, and writing skills and just how much I treasure his nearly four decades of unwavering and generous friendship. I would be remiss if I did not share a word about Rick's enormous courage. Rick has shown remarkable strength—and humor—as he has been engaged in a tough battle with a serious illness. Even as Rick has struggled with his health, he has continued writing and assisting educators in their school improvement efforts. At first, I asked myself, "Why does he do this—why does he spend his time this way?" Then I realized it is because he is Rick DuFour, and his commitment to and love for educators and students is at the very core of his being. It is who he is, and he cannot stop being himself.

Winston Churchill could have been speaking of Rick when he said, "What is the use of living if it be not to strive for noble causes and to make this muddled world a better place for those who will live in it after we are gone."

Introduction

"Rick, you have lung cancer." That was the message my doctor presented to my wife, Becky, and me in September 2014. The news floored us. I wasn't a candidate for lung cancer. I had never smoked, and there was no history of cancer on either side of my family.

And then the news got worse: The initial diagnosis was that I had stage 2 cancer in one lobe of my right lung. Surgery could remove the lobe and thus free me of the disease. Once the procedure began, however, the surgeon discovered the cancer had spread throughout my right lung. He aborted the surgery, advised us that I had stage 4 cancer (there is no stage 5), and said the goal was no longer seeking a cure but exploring methods to extend my life.

My oncologist was more optimistic. She felt that once I had completed a chemotherapy regimen, I could be a candidate for surgery to remove the entire right lung. This option rested on the hope that the cancer was confined to the single lung. That hope was dashed when we discovered the cancer had spread to my left lung despite the chemotherapy.

Up until this point, my life had been filled with abundant blessings. One of those blessings was that I had spent thirty-four years as a public school educator—as a teacher, principal, and superintendent—a career that I truly loved. I then remained in the profession as an author and consultant. I have written seventeen books and more than one hundred professional articles in an attempt to influence my profession. I have worked with educators in every state and in countries throughout the world to provide concrete suggestions as to how they could implement the Professional Learning Communities at Work™ (PLC) process in their schools and districts.

But as I assessed my career at this crossroads of my life, I felt more frustration than satisfaction. Throughout history, Americans have criticized their schools—it is more of an American pastime than baseball. I am frustrated, however, that politicians and the media seem to be waging an increasingly aggressive war not just on the public school system but also on the educators within it. Their unfair characterization of teachers and principals as lazy incompetents who are unconcerned about the well-being of their students is nothing like the amazing educators with whom I have worked both directly and indirectly. I am frustrated that members of the profession I love are receiving none of the recognition they deserve for what they are accomplishing in the face of incredibly challenging conditions.

I am also frustrated by what I view as the intransigence of teacher unions at the national, state, and local levels. My grand-father was a union organizer in Chicago, my father was a lifelong union member, and I served for a brief period as the president of my local teacher union. I believe that unions have an important place in a capitalistic society, but I am discouraged when I see unions clinging to outdated positions that make little sense to the public or to their members.

And, while I genuinely admire the members of my profession in many ways, I am frustrated by the fact that educational pro-cesses that clearly have a positive impact on student achievement have not yet become the norm in American schools. I recognize that external forces at the state and federal levels have provided teachers and principals with little support for making the necessary changes. I know that the current reform agenda has fostered con-ditions that actually impede school improvement. But I also must acknowledge that there are powerful processes educators could implement to improve student and adult learning—processes that lie within their sphere of influence. Too often, these processes are ignored or applied in a halfhearted way that puts a greater emphasis on preserving the traditional culture and structure of schools than on transforming them.

So, in a very real sense, this book arises from frustration. It represents what is likely my final attempt to influence the profession I have been a part of for more than forty-five years. It is a labor of love and a call to arms.

Our profession will not benefit from either unloving critics or uncritical lovers. I intend to be neither. This book is divided into two parts. The first part offers a vigorous defense of American educators and an objective critique of state and national policies that have attempted (and failed) to improve schools through competition, privatization, and increasingly punitive sanctions. The second part challenges educators to accept individual and collective responsibility for taking immediate steps that are proven to improve student and adult learning. I define those steps in very specific terms and stress the goal is not merely to tweak the existing culture and structure of schooling but to transform them.

Changing the traditional culture of public schools that has endured for more than a century is no easy task, but at no point in American history have the stakes for our students been greater. The words of Martin Luther King Jr. (2001) ring true today for our profession:

> We are confronted with the fierce urgency of now. . . . Procrastination is still the thief of time. We must move past indecision to action. . . . Shall we say the odds are too great? Shall we tell them the struggle is too hard? Or will there be another message—of longing, of hope, of solidarity with their yearnings, of commitment to their cause, whatever the cost? The choice is ours, and though we might prefer it otherwise, we must choose in this crucial moment of human history. (p. 162)

CHAPTER 1

Educators Under Attack

"America's public schools are terrible! And they are getting worse!"

This is conventional wisdom in the United States. The public has heard this proclamation almost constantly since at least 1983 when the National Commission on Excellence in Education issued its findings in a report titled *A Nation at Risk*. The commission asserted that American education had fallen victim to a "rising tide of mediocrity that threatens our very future as a nation and as a people" (National Commission on Excellence in Education, 1983, p. 5). The report was replete with dire warnings of *decline*, *deficiencies*, *threats*, *risks*, *afflictions*, and *plight*. Americans were urged to reverse the "unthinking, unilateral educational disarmament" that had taken hold of our schools and to reestablish the United States as the world leader in educational attainment (National Commission on Excellence in Education, 1983, p. 9).

Six years later, President George H. W. Bush took office and announced his intention to become the *education president*. According to President Bush (1989), educational reform was the key to maintaining America's competitiveness in the world. He convened the nation's governors for an Education Summit to establish Goals 2000—ambitious targets to improve America's schools. By the turn of the century, America would rank first in the world in mathematics and science achievement, the high school graduation rate would increase to at least 90 percent, and students would leave grades 4, 8, and 12 having demonstrated competence in challenging subject matter including English, mathematics, science, history, and geography (North Central Regional Educational Laboratory, 1994).

It was Bush's successor, President Bill Clinton, who was able to enact legislation to make Goals 2000 the law of the land. In his first address to Congress, Clinton insisted the nation must demand more from our schools and called for providing more funding and authority to the Department of Education so it could promote effective strategies for improving schools. When the year 2000 deadline arrived, however, it was painfully evident that schools had been unable to come close to achieving any of the goals that had been established for them (Kirp, 2000).

In 2002, newly inaugurated President George W. Bush was able to persuade Congress to pass legislation to address the first item on his domestic agenda: educational reform. That legislation, No Child Left Behind (NCLB), ramped up testing requirements; mandated annual assessments in reading and mathematics in grades 3–8 and once in high school; called for reporting student test results separately by race, ethnicity, and other key demographic groups; and required schools to demonstrate adequate yearly progress (AYP) on state tests overall and for each subgroup of students. If schools could not demonstrate AYP, they faced interventions followed by increasingly severe sanctions (U.S. Department of Education, 2003).

The law required states to ensure that every teacher was highly qualified, and it mandated detailed reports to parents on school performance and teacher quality. The law also stipulated that students could transfer to better-performing schools or receive tutoring if their schools did not demonstrate sufficient progress. It specifically offered charter schools as alternatives to failing schools, and the Bush administration devoted $1.5 billion to the U.S. Department of Education's Charter Schools Program. As Diane Ravitch (2014) observes, "For the first time in history, federal law decreed that privatization was a viable remedy to improve low-performing public schools" (p. 313).

Finally, NCLB designated annual increases in the percentage of students achieving proficiency on the state assessment until 2014 when the poor performance of a single student would designate the entire school as "failing." In effect, the passage of NCLB ensured that each year the number of public schools labeled as "failing" would increase until every school in the country would carry that designation.

NCLB signaled a major turning point in the effort to reform education in the United States. Now educators were being told they must improve student achievement or else be subjected to increasingly punitive sanctions for failure to do so. Once again, America's very survival was at stake. Advocates of the law contended that the United States faced a stark choice: Would it take bold steps to improve education or "risk jeopardizing the future of our nation's children and our competitiveness in the global economy by maintaining the status quo" (Commission on No Child Left Behind, 2007, p. 11)?

President Barack Obama and his administration continued on the NCLB path of choice, competition, and accountability but ratcheted up the pressure on educators with the Race to the Top program. It offered significant funding to states *if* they would agree to implement the priorities of the Obama educational policy. Those priorities included such things as states agreeing to (U.S. Department of Education, 2009a):

1. Work collaboratively with other states to adopt a common set of high-quality standards that were internationally benchmarked and that ensured college and career readiness. This stipulation was generally

understood to mean that states must embrace the emerging Common Core State Standards.

2. Join a consortium of states to administer rigorous assessments based on the internationally benchmarked standards.

3. Make student growth (or value-added testing) a factor in the evaluation of teachers and principals, including decisions regarding retention or removal of tenured and untenured teachers.

4. Make student growth a factor in a plan to provide additional compensation (merit pay) for effective teachers and principals.

5. Identify persistently low-performing schools (the bottom 5 percent in the state) and develop plans to either close or reconstitute them.

6. Provide alternative routes to teacher and principal certification.

Race to the Top offered federal funding to cash-starved states struggling to deal with the most dramatic recession since the Great Depression of the 1930s. But to receive the funds, states had to compete with one another in demonstrating their willingness to embrace the Race to the Top requirements. Forty-eight states initially adopted the Common Core, two-thirds of the states changed their laws on teacher evaluation, half of the states declared student test scores would be included in teacher evaluations, and eighteen weakened tenure protections (Goldstein, 2014a). While NCLB allowed for punishing schools, Race to the Top provided the tools to punish individual teachers and principals.

Some might call these desperate measures, and a cursory glimpse of the headlines demonstrates that Americans were constantly being reminded that, when it came to education, these were indeed desperate times.

- "The Failure of American Schools." *The Atlantic*, June 2011

- "American Schools in Crisis." *Saturday Evening Post*, September/October, 2011

- "How to Fix the Education Crisis." *Businessweek*, October 13, 2011

- "Report: Half of U.S. Schools Fail Federal Standards." *USA Today*, December 15, 2011

- "The Real Reason America's Schools Stink." *Businessweek*, August 19, 2012

- "Public High Schools Are Not Doing Their Jobs." *U.S. News and World Report*, August 28, 2012

- "Apollo 20: One Man's Plan to Fix Failing Schools." PBS, September 25, 2012

- "Why American Education Fails: And How Lessons From Abroad Could Improve It." *Foreign Affairs*, May/June 2013

- "Parents Revolt Against Failing Schools." *USA Today*, July 1, 2013

- "Public Schools Are Failing, and That's a Healthy Sign for Good Teachers." *Forbes*, September 20, 2013

- "What's Holding Back American Teenagers?" *Slate*, February 11, 2014

- "Why Do Americans Stink at Math?" *New York Times*, July 23, 2014

- "Here's the Real Problem With America's Educational System." *Time*, June 2, 2014

Keep in mind that this is just a small sample of the consistent media message about schooling in America. Plug the phrase "failing schools" into the searchable database Nexis, and it provides 544 hits in newspapers and wire stories for the single month of January 2012 (Farhi, 2012).

We Have Found the Enemy, and It's . . . Teachers

The clarion call sounded by *A Nation at Risk* offered curricular and structural solutions to the problems of American schooling. It proposed more challenging courses that required more homework, higher graduation requirements, longer school days, longer school years, more frequent testing, and higher expectations for and demands on students.

By the time Race to the Top was enacted, however, there was a growing sense that the real problem with schools was teachers and the unions that protected them. Consider the following.

- The Center for Union Facts ran an advertising campaign claiming that teacher unions were the "biggest bullies in schools." It invited people to nominate candidates for the "worst teacher" and promised to offer the top ten nominees $10,000 each if they would leave the classroom (Masterson, 2008).

- In 2010, *Newsweek* published a cover story called "The Key to Saving American Education." The image was of a blackboard, with a single phrase chalked over and over again in a child's handwriting: "We must fire bad teachers. We must fire bad teachers. We must fire bad teachers" (Thomas, 2010).

In explaining the premise of Terry M. Moe's (2011) *Special Interest: Teachers Unions and America's Public Schools*, the publisher writes:

Why are America's public schools falling so short of the mark in educating the nation's children? Why are they organized in ineffective ways that fly in the face of common sense, to the point that it is virtually impossible to get even the worst teachers out of the classroom? And why, after more than a quarter century of costly education reform, have the schools proven so resistant to change and so difficult to improve? In this path-breaking book, Terry M. Moe demonstrates that the answers to these questions have a great deal to do with teachers unions—which are by far the most powerful forces in American education and use their power to promote their own special interests at the expense of what is best for kids. . . . The bottom line is simple but devastating: as long as the teachers unions remain powerful, the nation's schools will never be organized to provide kids with the most effective education possible.

On the Fox television show *Freedom Watch*, host and senior judicial analyst Andrew Napolitano blasted teachers and their unions: "How hard would you work if you couldn't get fired? Teachers know that kids are going to be in the seats, and the taxpayers are just going to be sending in the money, no matter how poorly they do. So they have no incentive to do a good job" (Bruinkid, 2011).

In *Endangering Prosperity*, authors Eric Hanushek, Paul Peterson, and Ludger Woessmann (2013) present the problem of American schools as a struggle between those who want to do what is best for students versus educators who are only interested in themselves. They write:

The battle is a conflict between the needs of school-age children and the interests of those adults who have agreed to educate them in our public schools.

The school workforce—teachers, principals, super-intendents, other administrators, and ancillary personnel—too often favors only those changes to the status quo that enhance their income or lighten their workload. They oppose changes in the organization and structure of the school system that would likely enhance the learning opportunities of those for whom they are educationally responsible. (p. 3)

The cover of the November 3, 2014, edition of *Time* magazine features a gavel preparing to crush an apple with the caption "Rotten Apples: It's nearly impossible to fire a bad teacher. Some tech millionaires may have found a way to change that."

An article in the *Hoover Digest* asserts:

Vested interests have captured control of our school system. The people who are working in the schools are trying to create a system that runs very well for the adults who work there. They are so concerned about that they don't focus on the needs of the students. (Robinson, 2015, p. 120)

If teachers and unions were the problem, the obvious solution was to lessen the power of unions and fire more teachers. By 2011, eighteen states had weakened tenure protections, with Florida and North Carolina ending tenure altogether. Wisconsin, Michigan, and Indiana limited the scope of issues teacher unions could address through collective bargaining. The Hoover Institution's (2011) list of the five best events to occur in education in 2011 includes:

1. The reinvigoration of school choice via opportunity scholarships and vouchers to increase competitive pressure on public school educators

2. The rollback of collective bargaining agreements in states throughout the country

3. California's "Parent Trigger" that allowed parents to demand a school be converted to a charter school or undergo some other transformational remedy

4. The continuation of Washington, DC's, tougher teacher evaluation system

5. Indiana's sweeping reforms, including abolishing collective bargaining for teacher benefits and work rules, allowing all universities to authorize charter schools, removing the cap on the number of charter schools, and providing opportunity scholarships to allow low-income students to attend private schools of their parents' choice

Furthermore, with states moving to value-added testing to evaluate individual teacher effectiveness, data were now available on the performance of specific teachers. The press demanded access to that data. The *Los Angeles Times* defends its publication of the database revealing scores of individual teachers "because it bears directly on the performance of public employees who provide an important public service, and in the belief that parents and the public have a right to judge the data for themselves" (Zavis & Barboza, 2010). The paper came under attack, however, when one of the teachers it listed as less effective based on test scores committed suicide. His family and colleagues alleged he had become depressed after publicly being branded an ineffective teacher.

On the other side of the United States, the *New York Times* and the *Wall Street Journal* sued under the Freedom of Information Act to obtain access to data on value-added test scores of individual New York City teachers. The court ruled in favor of the media, explaining:

> When balancing the privacy interests at stake against the public interest in disclosure of the information . . . we conclude that the requested reports should be disclosed. Indeed, the reports concern information of a type that is of compelling interest to the public, namely, the proficiency of public employees in the performance of their job duties. (Zhao, 2012)

That rationale apparently did not apply to other public employees. Shortly after the teacher evaluations were released to the media, the New York state legislature passed, and the New York governor signed a bill that exempted police and firefighters from having their evaluations released to the public. As the *Washington Post* reporter Valerie Strauss (2012) writes, "What better symbolizes the way teachers have become 'fair game' for public demonization?"

Finally, in August 2014, Judge Rolf Treu ruled that California's tenure laws, dismissal proceedings, and seniority laws violated students' rights to equality of education. The court concluded that the impact of those laws caused California students in general, and poor and minority students in particular, to have such unreasonable exposure to grossly ineffective teachers that it "shocks the conscience" (p. 7).

Teaching has become America's most embattled profession. As the author of *The Teacher Wars: A History of America's Most Embattled Profession* concludes:

> Today the ineffective tenured teacher has emerged as a feared character, a vampire type who sucks tax dollars into her bloated pension and health care plans, without much regard for the children under her care . . . the media repeats, *ad nauseam*, anecdotes about the most despicable examples of this type of person. . . . As a result, the public has gotten the message that public school teaching—especially urban teaching—is a broadly failed profession. (Goldstein, 2014a, pp. 5–6)

If this narrative about the state of education is true—that our schools are terrible and getting worse because of the uncaring educators who work in them—then there should be ample evidence to support it. In reality, a fair and balanced review of the facts paints a very different picture. In the next chapter, we present such a review.

CHAPTER 2

The Phony Crisis

In 1998, Tom Brokaw presented the premise that the American men and women who survived the Great Depression, led the nation to victory in World War II, and created the postwar economic engine that provided the United States with the world's strongest economy were "the greatest generation any society has ever produced" (p. xxx). That bold statement is clearly subjective. If, however, we ask which is the greatest generation of educators America has ever produced and we answer the question based on the evidence, the answer is irrefutably clear. No generation of American educators has ever accomplished what our teachers and administrators are achieving today. Consider the evidence.

Record-Setting High School Graduation Rates

According to *Education Week* (2014):

- The graduation rate for the high school class of 2012 exceeded 80 percent for the first time in our nation's history. Forty-seven states showed gains, two held steady, and only one (Rhode Island) declined by 2 percent.

- The improved graduation rate for Latino students was twice the national increase.

- Gains in graduation rates for African American students exceeded the national average.

More Students Succeeding in a More Rigorous Curriculum

The College Board (2014) found that:

- For the first time in American history, 20 percent of the high school graduating class scored honor grades of 3 or higher on the College Board's Advanced Placement (AP) exams in 2013.

- The number of students participating in the AP program exceeded one million students for the first time.

- Since 2004:

  - The number of students participating in the AP program has nearly doubled.

  - The number of AP exams written by high school students has more than doubled.

  - The number of low-income students participating in the AP program has more than quadrupled.

- More students earned honor grades in 2013 than attempted exams in 2003.

Steadily Improving Test Scores

The National Assessment of Educational Progress (NAEP) is the only consistent, longitudinal gauge of student achievement in reading and mathematics that covers the past twenty years. Results on these exams over the two decades show slow, steady, and significant increases. Students of all racial and ethnic groups are reading better today than in 1992. Student achievement in mathematics in fourth and eighth grade is dramatically better than twenty years ago. The proportion of fourth-grade students scoring below basic in mathematics dropped from 50 percent in 1990 to 18 percent in 2011. Eighth-grade students scoring below basic dropped from 48 percent to 27 percent (Ravitch, 2014).

As Diane Ravitch (2014) writes:

> NAEP data show beyond question that test scores in reading and math have improved for almost every group of students over the past two decades. . . . Students know more and can do more in these two basic skills subjects now than they could twenty or forty years ago. (p. 53)

Another indicator of improving achievement in mathematics and science is the performance of American students on the Trends in International Mathematics and Science Study (TIMSS). This quadrennial assessment is administered to a random sampling of approximately four thousand students in sixty-three countries around the world. American students have improved their scores in mathematics in both tested grades (fourth and eighth) each time the test has been administered since 1995. The United States is one of twelve countries to improve scores every year the test has been administered to fourth graders and one of only two (along with the Republic of Korea) to improve scores every test cycle for eighth graders. It is also one of only ten countries to score significantly above the TIMSS mean score on both the fourth- and eighth-grade assessments in mathematics in 2011 (Mullis, Martin, Foy, & Arora, 2012).

The performance of American students on the 2011 TIMSS science assessment is almost as impressive. Fourth graders ranked seventh in the world and eighth graders tenth. Both groups scored significantly higher than the TIMSS mean. Fourth graders did not take the assessment in 1999 but have improved their scores two of the three times the test has been administered with an overall increase from 536 in 1999 to 544 in 2011. Eighth graders have improved their scores three of the four times the test has been administered with an overall increase from 513 to 526, well above the intermediate benchmark score of 475 (Martin, Mullis, Foy, & Stanco, 2012).

Parent Satisfaction

Since 1969, the Phi Delta Kappa (PDK)/Gallup Poll has assessed the public's attitudes about public schools and the issues impacting those schools. Since 2009, when respondents were asked what grade they would give the nation's schools, 28 percent assigned a grade of D or F. In 2014, 10 percent of respondents indicated the nation's schools are failing, the highest total in the history of the poll. Only 18 percent gave the nation's schools a grade of A or B, and the percentage of respondents assigning the grade of A has never exceeded 1 percent since 2009. Americans are getting the message that the nation's schools are failing (Phi Delta Kappa, 2014).

But when PDK/Gallup asked parents with children in public schools to assess the quality of the *local* school their oldest child attends, a very different story emerges. Since 2009, three of every four parents have assigned a grade of A or B, the highest percentage of As and Bs in any five-year period of the poll's history. During that same period, slightly more than 1 percent have indicated the school is failing. Americans most familiar with their public schools love them (Phi Delta Kappa, 2014).

Student–Teacher Relations

The Organisation for Economic Co-operation and Development (OECD, 2013a) provides an annual overview of education in industrialized nations. In 2013, it asked students from those countries their perceptions of their relationship with their teachers. American teachers received high marks from their students, exceeding the OECD average in all areas and earning some of the highest ratings among all OECD countries. The percentage of students who *strongly agree* or *agree* with the following statements is presented in table 2.1.

Table 2.1: Percentage of Students Who Agree or Strongly Agree With Statements About Their Teachers

	OECD Average	United States
Students get along well with most teachers.	82 percent	83 percent
Most teachers are interested in students' well-being.	77 percent	86 percent
Most of my teachers really listen to what I have to say.	74 percent	78 percent
If I need extra help, I will receive it from my teachers.	82 percent	90 percent
Most of my teachers treat me fairly.	81 percent	90 percent

Meeting the Needs of All Students

This record of extraordinary accomplishments from the current generation of American educators comes at a time when they are educating larger numbers of students who traditionally have had little success in school: minority students, English learners, students living in poverty, and students with disabilities.

- In the fall of 2014, the number of minority students enrolled in public schools surpassed the number of non-Hispanic white students for the first time in

American history (National Center for Education Statistics, 2013).

- Between 1979 and 2003, the number of English learners in public schools grew by 124 percent at the same time the overall number of students increased by only 19 percent (Flynn & Hill, 2005). Today an estimated 4.4 million students, or nearly one in ten students enrolled in public schools, are English learners. The percentage of English learners in public schools since the passage of NCLB in 2002 has increased in all but ten states (Kena et al., 2014). In the mid-1980s, 10 percent of residents spoke a language other than English in their homes. In 2014, one in five families spoke a foreign language at home (Dinan, 2014).

- For the first time in American history, 51 percent of public school students are eligible for free and reduced lunch (Southern Education Foundation, 2015). The OECD defines poverty as less than 50 percent of the nation's median income. Using that definition, the United States is one of six OECD nations with a child poverty rate above 20 percent. It is, by far, the richest of those six nations (OECD, 2014a).

- It wasn't until 1975 that the passage of the Individuals With Disabilities Education Act established that American children with disabilities were entitled to a free and appropriate public school education. Today, the number of American students receiving special education services is 6.4 million or about 13 percent of all public school students. About 95 percent of those children ages 6–21 are enrolled in regular public schools (Kena et al., 2014).

In Tom Brokaw's (1998) account of the greatest generation, he lauds the fact that the men and women of that era were not driven by the desire for fame or recognition but by a sense of responsibility to do what was right. The same can be said of America's greatest generation of educators—the educators of today. Polls consistently show teachers are more passionate and mission driven than any other American profession (Goldstein, 2014a). In a study asking why they became a teacher, 98 percent of teachers say that teaching gave them an opportunity to make a difference in the world—one child at a time (Scholastic, 2014).

It is a good thing that our greatest generation of educators is driven by a sense of moral purpose rather than fame or recognition, because neither has been forthcoming. Public schools have certainly been the target of criticism throughout American history. Never, however, have America's educators accomplished so much for so many in the face of so many obstacles only to be subjected to unrelenting attacks and condemnation.

The Rationale for Attacking Educators

Those who contend our schools are failing despite these unprecedented accomplishments typically cite three facts to support their proposition: (1) the number of failing schools NCLB identified, (2) results from the NAEP, and (3) the poor performance of American students on international assessments, such as the Programme for International Student Assessment (PISA). Let's consider each.

> Never have America's educators accomplished so much for so many in the face of so many obstacles only to be subjected to unrelenting attacks and condemnation.

No Child Left Behind Guarantees All Schools Will Eventually Fail

The purpose of NCLB according to the Bush administration was to improve student achievement by holding states, school districts, and schools "accountable for ensuring that all students, including disadvantaged students, meet high academic standards" (White House, n.d.b). The law required states to develop a system of sanctions for schools and districts unable to make adequate yearly progress toward the ultimate goal of ensuring every student was proficient in mathematics and reading by 2014.

The law was clearly fundamentally flawed from the start. Because each state was free to establish its own standards, its own assessment, and its own definition of proficient, states that set high standards and developed rigorous assessments were penalized. For example, by 2011, 80 percent of the schools in Massachusetts were designated as failing under NCLB (Rich, 2012) even though the state's students scored among the top five countries in the world in mathematics (Mullis et al., 2012) and science (Martin et al., 2012) on the TIMSS assessment administered that same year.

Particularly perplexing was the law's provision that an entire school would be designated as failing because of the disaggregated performance of as few as thirty students in any one of the thirty-seven different subgroups of classification (for example, students with special needs, students with limited English proficiency, and so on). If even one subgroup failed to meet the proficiency standard for two consecutive years, all students in the school would be given the opportunity to transfer to a "successful school." As education policy analyst Gerald Bracey (2006) writes, a "school might be doing well by 36 of its 37 subgroups, but in federal eyes it is uniformly failing."

But perhaps the most damaging aspect of NCLB was its insistence that American schools suffer sanctions unless they did something that no nation in history had ever done or come close to doing: ensuring all its students were highly proficient. Not a single state came anywhere near achieving what the law demanded of schools (Welner & Mathis, 2015). NCLB, as designed, ensured every school in America would eventually be designated as failing and then punished schools when the inevitable occurred.

The National Assessment of Educational Progress

When the American public is bombarded with headlines like "Nation's Report Card: Only a Third of 8th Graders Can Read, Compute at Grade Level" (Hollingsworth, 2013), you can be certain the results of the latest NAEP have just been released. The NAEP, a congressionally mandated project of the U.S. Department of Education, informs the public about the academic achievement of elementary and secondary students. Assessments are administered to representative samples of nine-, thirteen-, and seventeen-year-olds every four years. Results are presented in the report the Nation's Report Card but are not provided for individual schools or students (National Center for Education Statistics, 2015).

A governing board of twenty-six members appointed by the U.S. Secretary of Education determines the standards students are to achieve, the assessments they will take, and the scores they must achieve for each category of proficiency. The board includes three teachers, two principals, and a superintendent. The other twenty members include governors, legislators, state school officials, members of state boards of education, business representatives, assessment experts, and four members representing the general public.

NAEP results are reported as percentages of students performing at the basic, proficient, and advanced levels defined as follows (National Center for Education Statistics, 2015).

- *Basic* denotes partial mastery of prerequisite knowledge and skills that are fundamental for proficient work at each grade.

- *Proficient* represents solid academic performance. Students reaching this level have demonstrated competency over challenging subject matter.

- *Advanced* represents superior performance.

The remaining students are considered *below basic*, which is left undefined.

The problem with the NAEP levels is they are impossibly high. As noted previously, American fourth- and eighth-grade students score in the top ten in the world and well above the international average on the 2011 TIMSS assessment in mathematics and science. But the Nation's Report Card that year announced that only 33 percent of fourth graders were proficient and 7 percent were advanced in mathematics. Eighth-grade scores were even worse, with 27 percent proficient and 8 percent advanced (National Center for Education Statistics, 2011). The NAEP science test was only given to eighth graders in 2011. Only 30 percent of them scored proficient and 2 percent advanced (National Center for Education Statistics, 2012a).

The National Academy of Sciences is one of several organizations that have attacked the validity of the NAEP assessments (Pellegrino, Jones, & Mitchell, 1999). It concludes that the procedures for setting achievement levels are fundamentally flawed, the appropriate validity evidence for cut scores is lacking, and the tests yield results that are not reasonable in light of other indicators of student achievement.

The National Center for Research on Evaluation, Standards, and Student Testing comes to a similar conclusion. It reports that "the achievement levels are seriously flawed—seriously enough that they cannot credibly support the conclusions to be based upon them" (Linn, Koretz, Baker, & Burstein, 1991, p. i). The report recommends that the achievement levels not be used in public reporting of national or state results.

The U.S. General Accounting Office's (1993) investigation of the NAEP reveals that the governing board considered the setting of achievement levels as "a policy function that it itself could perform with minimal technical support" (p. 5). The governing board "did not appreciate the importance of verifying the validity of its score interpretations" (U.S. General Accounting Office, 1993, p. 5). It concludes that the standard-setting approach is procedurally flawed and that the interpretations of the resulting NAEP scores are of doubtful validity.

In 2001, Congress insisted that every NAEP report include the disclaimer that NAEP achievement levels should continue to be used on a trial basis and interpreted with caution until the commissioner of education statistics determined that the achievement levels are "reasonable, valid, and informative to the public" (National Center for Education Statistics, 2012b). No commissioner has ever come to that conclusion, and the tests continue to include the disclaimer—a disclaimer that the media has routinely ignored in its reporting.

According to Diane Ravitch (2012), who served on the governing board for seven years, an *advanced* score on the NAEP indicates superb performance, the equivalent of an A+ grade. *Proficient* is the equivalent of a solid A. *Basic* represents C- or B-level performance, which, as she states, is good but not good enough. Only students who score below basic are struggling to read or perform mathematics. These are the students who demand attention, but the percentage of students scoring at this level has dropped steadily in both reading and mathematics since 1992.

As Gerald Bracey writes:

> Little wonder, then, that the National Academy of Sciences, the National Academy of Education, the Government Accounting Office and the Center for Research in Evaluation, Student Standards and Testing have all rejected the NAEP levels. They continue to exist only because there is so much political hay to be made from saying that American schools and students stink. (as cited in Indiana Public School Superintendent, 2005)

The Performance of American Students on International Assessments

Those who claim America's schools are failing routinely cite the mediocre performance of students on international assessments. Chief among those assessments is the PISA that is administered by the OECD to random samplings of fifteen-year-old students in industrialized countries every three years to measure their proficiency in reading, mathematics, and science.

On the assessment administered in 2012, the United States ranks twenty-seventh in mathematics, seventeenth in reading, and twentieth in science among the thirty-four OECD countries. Furthermore, the results demonstrate no significant changes since the test was first administered in 2000 (OECD, 2012b).

Critics present these findings as proof positive that American schools are failing, especially considering that the United States ranked fifth among OECD countries in per-pupil expenditures in 2011. They point to a nation like Finland, whose students always score among the top of OECD countries on the PISA exam while ranked sixteenth in per-pupil spending (OECD, 2011a).

The next chapter examines the differences between educational policies in Finland and the United States. At this point, however, let us put the achievements of these two countries in a larger context. Of all the nations participating in the PISA assessment, the United States has by far the largest number of students living in poverty. Finland has approximately a 3 percent poverty rate. If PISA scores just from American schools with up to 10 percent of their students living in poverty are compared to Finland's, American student achievement far exceeds Finland's. If the United States' schools with up to 25 percent of students living in poverty were considered as a nation, the United States would still rank first in the world among industrialized countries (Rebell & Wolff, 2012). But fourteen thousand elementary schools and three thousand secondary schools, or nearly 20 percent of all the schools in the United States, serve student populations with more than 75 percent of students living in poverty. These schools consistently score near the bottom of country rankings on PISA and drag down our national average (Shyamalan, 2013).

When filmmaker and author M. Night Shyamalan (2013) created a foundation to investigate the condition of American schools and how to improve them, he operated from the premise that our schools were failing. But once his researchers presented him with the evidence, he was surprised to learn that he was wrong. As he writes:

> In this case, what everyone knew just wasn't so. Despite the impression left by thousands of research studies, tens of thousands of blog posts, and millions of words in every newspaper and magazine in the country, America's schools aren't failing. (Shyamalan, 2013, p. 7)

I concur. A fair and balanced analysis of the evidence can only lead to the conclusion that American schools and the educators within them are not failing and are, in fact, achieving some of the best results in our nation's history. Unfortunately, personal and political agendas have too often trumped evidence and research when it comes to evaluating schooling in the United States.

A fair and balanced analysis of the evidence can only lead to the conclusion that American schools and the educators within them are not failing and are, in fact, achieving some of the best results in our nation's history.

It is also evident, however, that our public schools must be improved. I do not suggest that American schools are "good enough." I do not subscribe to the theory that until child poverty is eliminated in this country, our profession is incapable of raising student achievement. Educators cannot passively wait for the challenges of poverty to be resolved by others but must instead play a major role in addressing those challenges by becoming much more effective in educating children of poverty. The question is not *should* our schools be improved but *how?* The next chapter examines whether the current reform agenda is likely to bring about that improvement.

CHAPTER 3

The Firings Will Continue Until Morale Improves

There are those who contend that the attack on public schools and the educators within them represents a well-orchestrated attempt to privatize education in the United States. There is no question that a small number of very wealthy individuals and corporations has devoted tens of millions of dollars to backing candidates for governor, state legislatures, Congress, and even school boards who support their privatization agenda (Ravitch, 2014). If these individuals and corporations are successful in purchasing national, state, and local educational policy, they will provide the private sector with greater access to an enterprise with expenditures of more than $600 billion per year, with most of that money coming from public coffers. What an opportunity for entrepreneurs! For example, the eight executives of K12 Inc., the largest online, for-profit educational system in the United States, paid themselves $21 million in 2013 despite the fact that only 28 percent of their students met state standards. Eighty-six percent of the company's profits came from taxpayers, which the company describes as a "recurring revenue stream" in its annual report (Center for Media and Democracy, 2014). A significant share of its expenditures was funding 153 lobbyists in 28 states and spending $21 million in marketing in less than a year.

But for the purposes of this chapter, let us assume good intentions on the part of those who argue that the current reform agenda of expanded choice, more accountability, and tougher sanctions offers our best hope for improving public schools. I hope to examine not their motives but their assumptions and the evidence to support those assumptions.

Assumption One: Charter Schools Will Improve Other Public Schools

The rationale to support the assumption that charter schools will improve other public schools is that by freeing charter schools from the shackles of bureaucratic regulations and the time-bound traditions that encumber public schools, they will be able to serve as engines of innovations. Chester Finn, former United States assistant secretary of education under President Reagan, believes that "the single most important form of freedom for charter schools is to hire and fire employees as they like and pay them as they see fit" (Kahlenberg & Potter, 2014). With this kind of autonomy, charter schools would achieve clearly superior results. As parents in increasing numbers enrolled their children in charters to give them access to this better educational opportunity, public schools would be forced to reform or run the risk of losing all their students to charters. Competition would drive innovation and lead to better quality for consumers, in this case, parents and students.

There are now more than six thousand charter schools operating in the United States serving almost three million students, and thus, there should be ample evidence to prove their superiority. But when in 2009 the Center for Research on Education Outcomes completed one of the most comprehensive studies of charter schools ever conducted, the evidence did not support the hypothesis of charter school champions. As the center reports on its study of schools in sixteen states:

> The study reveals that a decent fraction of charter schools, 17 percent, provide superior education opportunities for their students. Nearly half of the charter schools nationwide have results that are no different from the local public school options and over a third, 37 percent, deliver learning results that are significantly worse than their students would have realized had they remained in traditional public schools. (Center for Research on Education Outcomes, 2009, p. 1)

The report goes on to state, "This study reveals in unmistakable terms that, in the aggregate, charter students are not faring as well" as students in traditional schools. "Further, tremendous variation in academic quality among charters is the norm, not the exception" (Center for Research on Education Outcomes, 2009, p. 6).

In its 2013 follow-up study of its analysis of charters in those sixteen states, the center reports that charter schools had maintained or slightly increased their impact on student learning "due in no small part to the closing of low-performing schools" (Cremata et al., 2013, p. 83). Eight percent of the original charter schools had been closed, but "had they remained open at their former levels of impact, there would have been no improvement" (Cremata et al., 2013, p. 83). The center's study expresses concerns that low-performing charter schools are not being shut quickly enough and in some cases are being allowed to replicate. As it concludes, "When the total stock of charter schools (continuing and new) is considered there is slight improvement relative to the traditional public school alternative but no absolute gains in learning" (Cremata et al., 2013, p. 83).

When the center expanded its study to twenty-seven states, it found results had improved for charters, but those results varied greatly across states. In reading, 19 percent of charter schools had worse results when compared to their local schools, 56 percent had similar results, and 25 percent had superior results. In mathematics, 31 percent had worse results, 40 percent had similar results, and 29 percent had superior results.

John Hattie (2009) has synthesized more than eight hundred meta-analyses of fifty thousand research studies of factors that impact student achievement and established an effect size or anticipated impact for each of those factors. He argues that a significantly positive effect must be greater than 0.40. He concludes that the effect size of charter schools is 0.20.

Despite the evidence that there are many charter schools failing to perform as well as traditional public schools, rarely is a charter closed due to performance. Only 3 percent of the charter schools that have opened have been shuttered for academic performance while closures for financial reasons and mismanagement have accounted for nearly four times as many closings (Consoletti, 2011). Furthermore, state oversight of charters varies widely. Seventy-five percent of schools closed for performance are located in only eight states (Resmovits, 2011). According to former president Bill Clinton, this lack of oversight violates the original bargain for charter schools: in exchange for being "unfettered," charters would either do a better job of educating students—or they would lose their charter (Resmovits, 2014).

Other concerns have been expressed about the impact of charter schools. They have resulted in increasing racial, ethnic, and economic segregation of students as a direct reflection of the school choice program (Miron, Urschel, Mathis, & Tornquist, 2010). Even beyond race, ethnicity, and income, charters increased segregation for special education and language-minority students unless they attended a charter specifically targeted to their populations (Rotberg, 2014).

Although, as public schools, charters are supposed to be free and open to all students, an investigative report by Reuters finds that across the United States, charters "aggressively screen student applicants, assessing their academic records, parental support, disciplinary history, motivation, special needs and even their citizenship, sometimes in violation of state and federal law" (Simon, 2013). Five states—Florida, Louisiana, New Hampshire, Ohio, and Texas—explicitly allow charter schools to screen applicants by academic performance. Most other states do not, yet schools have found loopholes and created barriers.

Among the obstacles to enrollment that Reuters documents are the following (Simon, 2013).

- Applications that are made available just a few hours a year
- Lengthy application forms, often printed only in English, that require student and parent essays, report cards, test scores, disciplinary records, teacher recommendations, and medical records
- Demands that students present Social Security cards and birth certificates for their applications to be considered, even though such documents cannot be required under federal law
- Mandatory family interviews
- Assessment exams
- Academic prerequisites
- Stipulations that parents must volunteer at the school a certain number of hours per year
- Requirements that applicants document any disabilities or special needs (The U.S. Department of Education considers this practice illegal on the college level but has not addressed the issue for K–12 schools.)

As the National Education Policy Center concludes, charter schools have actively shaped their student enrollments through practices that often exclude students with special needs, those with low test scores, English learners, or students in poverty (Miron, Mathis, & Welner, 2015).

I want to make it clear that I am not opposed to charter schools. Some of the most effective schools I have ever seen are charters. But with more than six thousand charter schools in operation, it should be evident that the assumption they will deliver vastly superior academic achievement for their students and thereby improve other public schools simply has not proven true.

Assumption Two: Providing Vouchers to Send Students to Other Public or Private Schools Will Improve Public Schools

The rationale to support the assumption that providing families with vouchers to use public funds to send their children to other schools is that it will energize lethargic public school educators who will risk losing their jobs if they have no students. Once again, advocates for vouchers struggle when called on to present evidence that vouchers are beneficial to either the students who receive them or the public schools they are intended to improve. After reviewing the research on vouchers, Shyamalan (2013) concludes:

> The best research to date finds relatively small achievement gains for students offered education vouchers, most of which are not statistically different from zero. Vouchers don't have the data on their side. . . . When every school in America is able to properly educate its students, then, sure: Let parents choose which one has an environment that fits their child better. But until then, encouraging parents to find, on their own, the best education for their kids guarantees only one thing, which is to reward the families with the most resources. Since that's the system that created the gap in the first place, we can depend on choice to perpetuate it. (pp. 64, 67)

The American public has consistently expressed opposition to vouchers being used to divert public tax dollars to support student enrollment in private schools. Voters have rejected referenda in twenty-seven states and continue to oppose vouchers by a wide margin—63 percent to 37 percent, according to the 2014 PDK/ Gallup Poll (Bushaw & Calderon, 2014). Unable to win voter approval for vouchers, legislatures in a number of states have created scholarship programs that have the same effect.

Florida is an interesting case in point. It was the first state to pass legislation that would allow tax dollars to be used to provide vouchers to students in "failing" public schools who could use them to enroll in private schools. Failing schools were those that received the grade of F on the Florida accountability system for two consecutive years based on student achievement on the state assessment. But students who took advantage of the vouchers could enroll in schools that never had to administer the state test.

The Florida Supreme Court ruled the law unconstitutional in 2006, and subsequent attempts to get voter approval to amend the Constitution failed (Strauss, 2012). So the legislature created the Florida Tax Credit Scholarship Program to allow individuals and corporations to donate to a program that would be used to fund private school vouchers in return for a 100 percent tax credit. As the Florida League of Women Voters reports:

> Vouchers divert money from the public school system by allowing corporations to fund the voucher program instead of paying taxes to the state. . . . These tax dollars would otherwise be available to fund the public school system. With 67,142 students receiving vouchers, that is $86,069,038 lost by public schools. Private schools receiving vouchers spend our tax money without accountability. Teachers do not have to be certified. Schools do not have to abide by curriculum standards or take state assessment tests. (Arcuri, 2015)

In summary, there is little evidence to support the premise that increasing competitive pressure on public schools through privatization improves student achievement. In analyzing the impact of this strategy around the world, the OECD (2013b) concludes, "School systems as a whole do not seem to benefit from a greater prevalence of private schools or a higher degree of competition among schools" (p. 193).

Proponents of charter schools and vouchers present them as strategies to give parents more choices when it comes to educating their children. Choice is presented as a virtue in and of itself. Americans love choice! That's why Starbucks offers more than eighty thousand different combinations of its beverages. In the eyes of advocates for charter schools and vouchers, those who oppose choice are defenders of the status quo, opposed to improving schools, and bordering on anti-American.

But is choice always a virtue? Aren't there situations in which the common good dictates limiting choice? If choice is universally good, we should be able to choose how the federal government spends our tax dollars. If a voter wants to support domestic spending but opposes military expenditures, shouldn't he or she be allowed the choice? If a resident feels he can live without the benefit of fire and police protection or has no children attending the public school, shouldn't he be able to deduct the amounts allocated to those services from his property tax? Shouldn't employers be allowed to withhold their payments to their employees' Social Security benefits if they choose not to contribute? Shouldn't drivers be allowed to ignore speed limits if they prefer to go faster?

The list can go on, but the point is simple: expanding choice is not inherently positive in a democratic society. In fact, the very concept of a social contract requires that choice be limited in areas that directly affect our collective safety, welfare, and prosperity.

Public education has been a driving force for progress through-out the history of the United States. The first public schools were called *common* schools because they served the common good. Throughout most of the 20th century, the United States was a striking example of the benefits of a highly educated citizenry. By the early 20th century, the United States had become the first country to offer every young person the opportunity to obtain a free public secondary education. Our nation also was a leader in providing access to higher education. The passage of the Morrill Act of 1862 ceded more than

Expanding choice is not inherently positive in a democratic society. In fact, the very concept of a social contract requires that choice be limited in areas that directly affect our collective safety, welfare, and prosperity.

seventeen million acres of federal government land to the states to support land grant colleges to provide training in agriculture, science, and engineering (Rippa, 1971).

The passage of the Servicemen's Readjustment Act of 1944 (commonly known as the G.I. Bill of Rights) was another initiative by the federal government to expand educational opportunities. It provided veterans with financial support to attend colleges, universities, or vocational programs. The majority of World War II veterans took advantage of the opportunity, and by 1956, more than eight million veterans had used the bill to pursue higher education or other forms of postsecondary training.

Sixty-five years after its passage, historians cite the passage of the G.I. Bill as one of the pivotal moments in American history (Altschuler & Blumin, 2009). Economist Peter Drucker (2006) agrees, describing the bill as one of the most transformational events in economic history because it signaled the shift from an industrial society to a knowledge society.

This emphasis on and commitment to education helped the United States to create the most highly educated workforce in the world by the middle of the 20th century (Paine & Schleicher, 2011). That workforce, in turn, was instrumental in making the United States the dominant economy in the world.

Public education has served our country well. It is ironic that many of those who promote the privatization of schooling through charter schools and vouchers argue that these strategies will help American students perform more like Finland's students on international tests. Finland has no private schools. None! As a result, the entire nation is vested in the success of its public schools.

Franklin Delano Roosevelt (1938) once said:

> Democracy cannot succeed unless those who express their choice are prepared to choose wisely. The real safeguard of democracy, therefore, is education. . . . Upon our educational system must largely depend the perpetuity of those institutions upon which our freedom and our security rest.

Initiatives that will ultimately weaken public education and our nation's commitment to it are certain to weaken our nation as well.

> Public education has served our country well. . . . Initiatives that will ultimately weaken public education and our nation's commitment to it are certain to weaken our nation as well.

Assumption Three: More Testing Means More Accountability

With the passage of NCLB, public schools were required to test every student in grades 3–8 on an annual basis and high school students once. The rationale behind this increased scrutiny was that it offered a way to hold schools and districts more accountable. Those who were unable to demonstrate annual yearly progress faced the prospect of losing their students to other schools. Thus, educators would be motivated to improve student learning.

The United States has invested heavily in support of this rationale. In 2012, states spent $1.7 billion on assessments with six vendors receiving 89 percent of the assessment dollars (Chingos, 2012). If, as intended, the assessments for the Common Core State Standards use more complex and more open-ended questions, the costs will go up substantially. A typical state currently spends $19.93 per student to comply with annual testing requirements. It is estimated that a battery of assessments aimed at monitoring the deeper learning of the Common Core will cost each state $55.67 per student (Rothman, 2011).

Although good assessment is an integral part of effective teaching, devoting excessive time to testing and preparing for tests reduces time that is available for instruction. Race to the Top resulted in an "explosion in the number and types of tests and assessments students must take in order to collect the data used to evaluate their teachers" (Goldstein, 2014a). Students spent between 20 and 50 hours per year taking tests and another 60 to 110 hours per year in test preparation (Nelson, 2013). Many schools in Florida devoted sixty to eighty days to standardized testing in 2014. To qualify for its Race to the Top grant, Florida school districts must now develop end-of-year assessments for every subject to help evaluate teachers. In Miami-Dade County, there are 1,600 such courses (Alvarez, 2014).

The *New York Times* reports a growing national protest by parents over the incessant testing to which their students are being subjected (Alvarez, 2014). Parents of school-age children in the United States conclude that standardized testing is not helpful by more than a two-to-one margin (Bushaw & Calderon, 2014).

Assumption Four: Intensive Supervision and Evaluation Will Lead to the Dismissal of Ineffective Teachers

As mentioned in chapter 1, the cover of *Newsweek* for March 5, 2010, presents "The Key to Saving American Education" by repeating a handwritten scrawl on a blackboard: "We must fire bad teachers" (Thomas, 2010). This mantra appears to be a driving force in state and national educational policy. As one analysis of Race to the Top regulations concludes, "Though RTTT targeted various levels of reform, the most significant emphasis was placed on improving teacher effectiveness, specifically by bolstering evaluation procedures" (Hanover Research, 2011, p. 2).

Principals are now being charged to spend more time in the classroom evaluating, ranking, and rating teachers to make decisions on compensation, retention, and dismissals. Tenure laws are under attack. Economists like Eric Hanushek and Steven Rivkin (2012) point to the research on the impact of effective versus ineffective teachers and the lifetime of economic benefits that students would enjoy if schools would remove those ineffective teachers. Even teachers themselves acknowledge that their evaluation process is perfunctory (Duffett, Farkas, Rotherham, & Silva, 2008).

Tennessee, one of the first two states to receive a Race to the Top grant, is an example of a state that has fully embraced the idea that principals must spend more time evaluating teachers to reward those who are effective and weed out those who are ineffective. The Tennessee model called for 50 percent of a teacher's evaluation to be based on principal observations, 35 percent on student growth, and 15 percent on student achievement data. Principals or evaluators must observe new teachers six times each year and licensed teachers four times each year, considering one or more of four areas: instruction, professionalism, classroom environment, and planning. These four areas are further divided into 116 subcategories. Observations are to be preceded by a preconference, in which the principal and the teacher discuss the lesson, and followed by a postconference, in which the principal shares his or her impressions of the teacher's performance. Principals must then input data on the observation using the state rubric for assessing teachers. Principals report that the process requires four to six hours for each observation (DuFour & Mattos, 2013). This intensive effort to supervise and evaluate teachers led to 98 percent of Tennessee's teachers being rated effective or better in 2012, a figure nearly identical to the results under the old system.

The effort to improve schools by supervising a faculty into better performance will only lead to higher levels of student learning if principals have the time and expertise to provide meaningful feedback to teachers. There is no evidence that these conditions exist.

The average principal oversees twenty to forty teachers, compared to an eight- to ten-employee span of control in most other professions (Goldstein, 2014a). A review of the research on the principalship identifies twenty-one distinct responsibilities principals must address in an environment where any or all of these responsibilities can be put on the back burner by crises over which the principal has little control (Marzano, Waters, & McNulty, 2005). There is growing concern that the demands on principals have grown beyond what can be expected of mere mortals. As Michael Fullan (2007) writes on the principalship:

> New expectations have been added on to the traditional ones without any consideration of whether the new role in its entirety is feasible under the current working conditions faced by principals. . . . The principalship is being placed in an impossible position. (p. 168)

Principals agree. Seventy-five percent of them report their jobs are too complex to be done well (Markow, Macia, & Lee, 2013).

Furthermore, middle and high school principals often observe teachers in content areas in which they have no background knowledge. Principals who spent their teaching careers as social studies, band, or physical education teachers are ill prepared to help a Spanish teacher improve if they cannot understand what he or she is saying to the class. They are ill equipped to enhance the pedagogy of an industrial arts teacher if they are mechanically inept

There is growing concern that the demands on principals have grown beyond what can be expected of mere mortals.

or a calculus teacher if they never took a course beyond advanced algebra. If principals are to provide effective feedback to teachers based on classroom observations, they must have expertise in both content and instruction. Unfortunately, too often they are lacking in one or the other if not both (Murphy, Hallinger, & Heck, 2013).

Because principals are routinely unable to determine the appropriateness of either the content or the level of rigor of a classroom lesson, states and districts have frequently resorted to providing them with checklists to use when observing teachers. If good teaching could be reduced to a single template, rubric, or checklist, this strategy could prove effective. However, there's no such thing as a universally effective teaching strategy; the effectiveness of any given strategy can only be determined by evidence of its effect on student learning (DuFour & Marzano, 2011). The checklist approach to providing feedback to teachers doesn't enhance the pedagogical expertise of teachers. As Marzano (2009) notes, it is "antithetical to true reflective practice . . . [and] is profoundly anti-professional" (p. 37).

One of the most comprehensive analyses of factors that improve schooling concludes "there is a robust body of empirical work that informs us that if school improvement is the goal, school leaders would be advised to spend their time and energy in areas other than teacher evaluation" (Murphy et al., 2013, p. 352). If current efforts to supervise teachers into better performance have proven ineffective (and they have), the solution is not to double down on a bad strategy and demand more classroom observations, tighter supervision, and more punitive evaluations. The effort to improve schools through tougher supervision and evaluation is doomed to fail because it asks the wrong question. The question isn't "How can I do a better job of monitoring *teaching*?" but rather "How can we collectively do a better job of monitoring *student learning*?" We will address that question in subsequent chapters.

Assumption Five: Value-Based Testing Provides a Valid Way to Reward Effective Teachers and Dismiss Ineffective Teachers

Proponents of this strategy assert that if research has established that the learning of students depends to a large extent on the quality of instruction they receive each day, establishing an objective process to reward effective teachers and dismiss ineffective ones should be a key strategy for improving schools. They also contend that value-added testing provides the means to distinguish between effective and ineffective teachers. According to the NAEP glossary of terms:

> Value added measures, or *growth measures*, are used to estimate or quantify how much of a positive (or negative) effect individual teachers have on student learning during the course of a given school year. To produce the estimates, value-added measures typically use sophisticated statistical algorithms and standardized-test results, combined with other information about students, to determine a "value-added score" for a teacher. (National Center for Education Statistics, 2015)

Rick Stiggins (2014), the founder of the Assessment Training Institute and former test development director for ACT, has written passionately and persuasively about the inappropriateness of using standardized test results for evaluating the effectiveness of teachers. The problem begins with the nature of standardized tests themselves, which, he contends, "have not been shown to be capable of differentiating between effective and ineffective teaching" (Stiggins, 2014, p. 21) for the following six reasons.

1. Time restraints for testing mean it is impossible to measure all key instructional areas students are to master, so many key targets are not tested at all. Furthermore, those areas that are tested cannot include enough items

focused on any one learning target to support a judgment about student mastery of that target.

2. Many tests sample achievement domains that span multiple grade levels. A student's performance on a standardized assessment in third grade could reflect instruction by four different grade-level teachers (K–3) rather than just one.

3. If the test is limited to assessing the knowledge and skills of a particular grade level, it imposes an artificial ceiling, because extremely capable students aren't allowed to demonstrate learning far beyond the grade-level content.

4. To maximize efficiency and minimize costs, test developers have traditionally relied on multiple-choice assessments that don't address such 21st century skills as complex reasoning, oral and written communication skills, or the ability to create complex achievement-related products. If teachers devote time to these important skills that are not addressed on the standardized test, a portion of the teacher's impact is effectively ignored.

5. The tests are closed-book, demanding recall of information, whereas in the information age, a student's ability to seek out, retrieve, and evaluate pertinent information to answer a question or solve a problem is an essential skill. Furthermore, standardized tests are typically timed and thus reward speed. The fact that a student who is a slow reader has time run out before getting to certain questions does not necessarily mean he or she doesn't know the answers.

6. The time lapse between two annual standardized tests allows for too many intervening variables to take place that are beyond the control of the teacher.

All these problems make it impossible to draw valid inferences about the effectiveness of a teacher. Stiggins (2014) concludes, "We definitely should NOT be doing this. . . . I know of no one in the measurement community who thinks this is an appropriate use of standardized test scores" (p. 2).

One of the major problems with value-added measures (VAMs) is the assumption that the single classroom teacher is solely responsible for what a student learns. This assumption is "factually wrong and may well do serious harm to the profession" (Berliner & Glass, 2014, p. 5). It flies in the face of what we know about best practice in high-performing schools where the structure and culture promote collective responsibility for each student's learning (Hargreaves & Fullan, 2012).

Imagine two teachers who teach sixth-grade language arts to students in two different middle schools with students of similar socioeconomic status. Teacher A works in a school with a safe and orderly environment, a highly effective principal, a collaborative culture in which teachers who teach the same course work jointly to analyze evidence of student learning to improve their individual and collective instruction. Furthermore, this school has a well-designed process for frequently monitoring student learning and a system of interventions that guarantees students who struggle will receive extra time and support for learning. The school climate is one in which the students themselves value academic success.

Teacher B works in a school with a chaotic environment, an ineffective principal, and no assistance from peers or mentors. There is no process for monitoring student learning and no system of interventions to support students who struggle. The students' peer culture sends the message that it is not "cool" to give one's best effort in school. As Edward Haertel (2013), professor emeritus at Stanford University, concludes, "No statistical manipulation can assure fair comparison of teachers working in very different schools with very different students, under very different conditions" (p. 24).

The biggest problem with VAMs is that there is no consensus regarding the validity of the model. The American Statistical Association's (2014) report cautions that:

- VAMs are generally based on standardized test scores and do not directly measure potential teacher contributions toward other student outcomes.

- VAMs typically measure correlation, not causation—effects, positive or negative, attributed to a teacher may actually be caused by other factors that are not captured in the model.

- VAM scores and rankings vary significantly from year to year.

- Ranking teachers by their VAM scores can have unintended consequences that reduce quality.

- There are greater opportunities for impacting achievement by focusing on systems within the school rather than on the VAM scores of individual teachers.

A review of value-added measures from the National Education Policy Center concludes, "The high volatility of teacher value-added scores indicates that they do not measure the true quality of teachers" (Adler, 2014, p. 4). One study finds that 13 percent of the teachers who were in the bottom 20 percent of value-added growth one year were in the top 20 percent the next, while 26 percent of the teachers in the top quintile dropped to the bottom 40 percent the next year (McCaffrey, Sass, & Lockwood, 2008). The margin of error for individual teachers assigned a value-added score in New York City in 2012 was fifty-three points out of one hundred for English teachers and thirty-five points out of one hundred for mathematics teachers (Goldstein, 2014a). Yet another study predicts a consistent 35 percent error rate when using results from VAMs to evaluate teachers. In other words, more than one in three teachers who are actually average in performance will be judged highly effective or ineffective, and more than one in three who are highly effective or ineffective will be overlooked (Schochet & Chiang, 2010).

The Board on Testing and Assessment (2009) of the National Research Council of the National Academy of Sciences advises, "VAM estimates of teacher effectiveness should not be used to make operational decisions because such estimates are far too unstable to be considered fair or reliable." The Educational Testing Service warns, "VAM results should not serve as the sole or principal basis for making consequential decisions about teachers. There are too many pitfalls" (Braun, 2005, p. 15). The RAND Corporation concludes the research base was insufficient to support the use of VAM for decisions about teachers or schools (McCaffrey, Lockwood, Koretz, & Hamilton, 2003).

Another practical problem with the requirement that student achievement on standardized tests must be a factor in the evaluation of teachers is that two-thirds of teachers are in nontested grades and subjects. States and districts have gone through tortuous distortions to try to address the problem. In some, an art teacher will be evaluated on the basis of how students perform in reading and writing on standardized tests. In others, kindergarten, first-, and second-grade teachers are accountable for student performance on the state test in third grade, even for students they never taught. Dana Goldstein (2014b) reports on the case of Kim Cook, a first-grade teacher in Florida who worked in a K–2 school. She earned a glowing appraisal from her principal and was voted Teacher of the Year by her colleagues but received an unsatisfactory evaluation because the third graders in another school performed poorly on the state assessment. If she receives another unsatisfactory evaluation in the following year, she can be dismissed.

It is unlikely that any profession would be comfortable with having the assessment of its members depend on such an invalid process. Perhaps that is why the American public is overwhelmingly opposed to using student performance on standardized tests to evaluate teachers (Bushaw & Calderon, 2014).

But let's examine the premise that the real problem in American education is simply that we are not firing enough teachers. To support that argument, proponents cite the infrequency in which tenured teachers are found to be unsatisfactory as proof positive that there must be a dramatic increase in the number of teachers to be axed.

One way to assess that argument is to see how teacher dismissals compare to firings in other fields and professions. While a fired computer programmer or secretary may have little difficulty in securing a new position in his or her field, tenured teachers who are dismissed for cause will have a very difficult time staying in the profession. A school district that was aware of the dismissal would almost certainly never offer a contract to a candidate who had been dismissed for incompetence or unprofessional conduct. In that sense, when a tenured teacher is fired it is more akin to a lawyer being disbarred or a doctor losing his or her license to practice medicine. Table 3.1 details the dismissal rates of teachers compared to those in the other listed positions.

Table 3.1: Dismissal Rate of Teachers Compared to Other Workers

Position	Dismissal Rate per 1,000
Teachers	21
Federal workers	2
Companies with 1,000 or more employees*	20
Disbarred attorneys	<1
Doctors losing license	3

*Note that the companies figure includes firings, resignations, and layoffs combined.
Sources: American Bar Association, 2013; Goldstein, 2014a; Wolfe, Williams, & Zaslow, 2012.

In every instance, teachers are more, not less, likely to be fired. Furthermore, in both the legal and medical fields, dismissals are far more likely to be based on findings of illegalities rather than incompetence. The assumption in these fields is that if someone has spent years preparing for the profession, has passed the board certification exams, and has met all the other requirements for entry into the profession, that person is competent. The same logic and consideration is not applied to educators.

Those claiming our schools are failing often bemoan the fact that schools don't operate more like businesses, particularly when it comes to tougher rankings and ratings and the eventual firing of employees. Yet when *Vanity Fair* magazine did an investigative piece on the decline of Microsoft, its reporters found that both former and current employees unanimously cited the initiation of the company's stacked ranking system as key to the company's downfall. According to the system, every six months, managers were required to apply a bell-shaped curve to evaluating the employees in their unit. Only a few could be identified as top performers and thus would become eligible for bonuses or promotions. Managers were required to designate some employees as unsatisfactory, and those employees received no bonus or were fired (Eichenwald, 2012).

The practice had a disastrous impact on the company's culture. Employees began to focus on competing with each other rather than cooperating. They avoided joining a team with strong members, withheld information from colleagues, and quietly sabotaged the work of others to ensure there would be members of their unit with a lower ranking.

The impact on Microsoft's bottom line was also devastating. In 2000, Microsoft was the wealthiest company in the world, with a market capitalization of $510 billion, but by June 2010, it had lost more than half of its value. In contrast, Apple, which had a value of only $4.8 billion in 2000, had become the most valuable company in the world, with a capitalized value of $541 billion.

While Microsoft's stock languished at $30 per share, Apple's stock was worth twenty times more in 2012 than it had been in 2000. A single Apple product, the iPhone, had higher sales than all Microsoft's products combined (Eichenwald, 2012).

Contrast Microsoft's ranking and rating system, which inevitably led some employees to be labeled losers each year, with W. Edwards Deming's (2000) advice on how to improve organizations. Deming, who is credited with transforming Japan's economy, argues that most of the causes of low quality belong to the system rather than the individual workers within it. So his advice to management is to "drive out fear" and "cease dependence on inspection . . . by building quality into the product in the first place" (Deming, 2000, p. 23). Although there is ample evidence that the best organizations are following the Deming path to continuous improvement, proponents of firing our way to the top continue to insist that ratcheting up fear is the best way to improve our schools.

Assumption Six: Merit Pay Will Improve Teaching and Therefore Improve Schools

Advocates for merit pay contend it is a way to reward the good teachers in a school. They assume teaching is a solo activity and compensation should go to individuals who excel. Since money is a powerful motivator, all teachers will be inspired to work harder and more effectively in an effort to qualify for the merit pay bonus.

The idea of merit pay is not new. It has been repeatedly tried and has failed for nearly a century in the United States. Organizational theorists Jeffrey Pfeffer and Robert I. Sutton (2006) describe the push for merit pay as "total nonsense." As they note:

> You don't have to read the evidence from literally decades of research to spot the problems with merit pay for schoolteachers. That evidence shows that merit-pay plans seldom last longer than five years and that merit pay consistently fails to improve student

performance. The very logic of merit pay for teachers suggests that it won't do what it is intended to do. (Pfeffer & Sutton, 2006, p. 23)

As Michael Fullan (2010) asserts emphatically, "No research exists that demonstrates that widespread benefits derive from merit pay" (p. 84). Fullan (2010) cites a seven-year study of merit pay in Portugal that finds "increased emphasis on individual teacher performance caused a significant decline in student achievement particularly in national exams" (p. 84). A three-year study by the National Center on Performance Incentives of middle school mathematics teachers in Tennessee who were offered merit bonuses of up to $15,000 finds the merit pay program had no effect on student achievement (Sawchuk, 2010). A merit pay experiment in New York City reveals student achievement actually declined during the three years of the program (Fryer, 2011).

There is ample evidence over a long period of time that merit pay does not improve the overall quality of a school. It is based on the assumption that a teacher earning $40,000 a year who is not sufficiently motivated to help students learn will suddenly spring to life if he or she has the opportunity to make $50,000 if students perform well on a standardized test. There is no evidence that teachers are withholding their best instructional strategies. I am unaware of any teacher who is thinking, "I know how to teach this concept really well, but I'm not getting paid enough to use my good instructional strategies. I'll just use my mediocre strategies instead." If someone is already doing his or her best, dangling a crunchier carrot will not improve his or her performance.

Any strategy that focuses on this individualistic approach of improving a school one teacher at a time is doomed

> There is ample evidence over a long period of time that merit pay does not improve the overall quality of a school. . . . If someone is already doing his or her best, dangling a crunchier carrot will not improve his or her performance.

to fail. Subsequent chapters will establish that the best hope for school improvement is not focusing on the individual but rather building the collective capacity of a staff through the Professional Learning Communities at Work process.

Assumption Seven: Closing Low-Performing Schools Will Improve Remaining Schools

The Race to the Top stipulation that states should close or reconstitute 5 percent of their schools each year for consistently low performance is based on the premise that students in those schools will be given access to a better education and the other schools in the state will be motivated to work harder to improve their schools. But during the first five years of NCLB, less than 5 percent of the families who could have opted to have their children leave a failing school for a different school in another part of town chose to do so (Inskeep, 2010). When Chicago closed schools for poor performance, most of the students who transferred enrolled in schools that were academically weak. Forty percent of transferees went to schools that were actually on probation, and only 6 percent went to schools scoring in the top quartile of the Iowa Test of Basic Skills (de la Torre & Gwynne, 2009).

But even if a state closes its lowest-performing schools, how does that improve the remaining schools? The assumption that educators will be more motivated to help their students succeed in order to avoid the death sentence imposed on the bottom 5 percent of schools has no basis in fact. A system designed to punish the bottom 5 percent (and there will be a bottom 5 percent every year) does not encourage the pursuit of excellence or continuous improvement. It focuses educators on the goal of avoiding the bottom, not rising to the top.

All these approaches rest on the assumption that in order to get the desired behavior from employees, organizations must come up with the right balance of punishments and rewards. While this assumption may have been valid for repetitive, low-skill tasks such as working on an assembly line, it does not hold true for knowledge workers—professionals whose work requires them to solve complex problems when there is no specific formula for arriving at the desired outcome (Pink, 2009).

A system designed to punish the bottom 5 percent (and there will be a bottom 5 percent every year) does not encourage the pursuit of excellence or continuous improvement. It focuses educators on the goal of avoiding the bottom, not rising to the top.

Teachers are clearly knowledge workers, and carrots and sticks have a negative impact on the motivation of knowledge workers (Pink, 2009). What motivates them is a sense of making progress in important work and receiving recognition for that progress (Amabile & Kramer, 2011). The key to leadership that motivates is "as simple, and as difficult, as creating the conditions for people to succeed at important work" (Amabile & Kramer, 2011, p. 25). None of these strategies to improve schools is creating the conditions that allow educators to succeed at their work.

The Proof Is in the Pudding

In the final analysis, assessing the impact of the reform movement in the United States should focus on results rather than on debating assumptions. In the next chapter, we examine the results, both here and in countries around the world, and offer recommendations regarding the kinds of policies that could benefit schools.

CHAPTER 4

Learning From High-Performing Countries

If the goal of American educational policy is to help students achieve at the highest levels in the world, it follows that we should attempt to replicate or adapt the strategies that led to such high achievement in other countries rather than continuing to embrace uniquely American reform policies that have yielded so little. McKinsey & Company, a global research group, has conducted a series of studies to determine how high-performing school systems got that way. The authors conclude that these countries recognize that "the quality of an education system cannot exceed the quality of its teachers.... The only way to improve outcomes is to improve instruction" (Barber & Mourshed, 2007, p. 13). Therefore, these countries attempt to recruit highly capable candidates to teaching, pay competitive salaries, and purposefully create favorable working conditions that support the ongoing learning of members of the profession.

The National Center on Education and the Economy concludes that three factors determine the quality of the pool of candidates from which a nation recruits its teachers (Tucker, 2014). They are:

1. The recruit's perception of the status of teachers in the country

2. Compensation offered relative to other positions requiring a college education

3. The conditions in which they will work

Singapore and Finland are consistently two of the highest-performing countries in the world on international assessments. Let's compare those countries with the United States in each of the three areas.

Singapore

Singapore limits the number of candidates for teaching positions by calculating the number of teachers it will need and opening only that many spots in its training program (Center on International Education Benchmarking, n.d.b). Candidates must graduate in the top 30 percent of their high school class and then go through a grueling application process to determine their fitness as a teacher. Only one in eight who apply are accepted.

The Singapore government provides grants that cover the entire tuition cost for their undergraduates. All candidates admitted to the teaching program are educated at the government's expense at a single university to ensure consistent instruction in curriculum and pedagogy. More than 80 percent of admitted candidates have already earned their bachelor's degree in another field. While in training for teaching, they are paid a stipend equal to 60 percent of a beginning teacher's salary. In exchange, they must commit to teach for at least three years (Center on International Education Benchmarking, n.d.b).

The Singapore government carefully monitors teachers' salaries and periodically makes adjustments in the salary structure to ensure teacher salaries are commensurate with other professions and above the average of the thirty-four nations that make up the

OECD. For the first three years of teaching, all teachers receive annual raises. After that, raises and bonuses are only available as one advances along one of three career tracks: (1) the teaching track, which allows an individual to rise to the rank of master teacher; (2) the leadership track, which grooms individuals for leadership roles in the school and larger system; and (3) the specialist track, which emphasizes research. There are thirteen levels in each track with salary increases and additional training and mentorship opportunities at each level (Center on International Education Benchmarking, n.d.b).

Teachers in Singapore are entitled to one hundred hours of professional development each year. Much of that professional development is school based, led by faculty who identify a particular problem in the school and engage the staff in action research to solve the problem. Teacher networks and professional learning communities encourage teachers to continuously share best practices (OECD, 2010b).

Opinion polls in Singapore reveal that the general public believes teachers make a greater contribution to their society than any other profession. New teachers consistently report that the status of the profession is one of the most important factors in their decision to enter teaching (Barber & Mourshed, 2007). Relatively high salaries, comprehensive training with compensation during training, and the esteem with which teachers are held in the country make teaching a very attractive career option in Singapore.

Finland

Finland also limits the number of teacher candidates admitted to training programs so that supply equals demand (Barber & Mourshed, 2007). Only students who graduate in the top 20 percent of their high school class are considered. Admission to the teacher training program occurs in two stages. The initial paper screen is based on matriculation exam scores, upper-secondary school records, and out-of-school accomplishments. Candidates who survive initial screening must take a written exam, be observed in a teaching-like activity to assess their interaction and communication skills, and be interviewed to assess the strength of their motivation to teach. They are selected, in part, on their ability to convey their belief in the core mission of public education in Finland: ensuring the learning of each student (OECD, 2010a). Only one in ten initial applicants is admitted into the teacher training program (Barber & Mourshed, 2007).

Those admitted into the teaching program can pursue their degrees at several universities, but the curriculum for teacher preparation is uniform, regardless of the school (Sahlberg, 2013). Primary-grade teachers major in education but are expected to minor in at least two of the subjects included in the primary curriculum. Those who minor in mathematics, for example, receive their training in the mathematics department rather than the education department. Secondary school teachers major in the subject area they will be teaching but devote a year to subject-specific pedagogy as well. All teachers are provided with training in diagnosing students with learning difficulties and must complete a very strong clinical component (OECD, 2010a).

Finland's teacher preparation program ensures all candidates have earned their master's degree before teaching. Candidates must write a research-based dissertation as part of their final requirements because they are expected to engage in disciplined inquiry and action research throughout their teaching career (OECD, 2010a).

The OECD (2010a) contends that the best way to assess the attractiveness of the starting salaries for teachers is to compare it to salaries for other college graduates. Using this calculation, Finnish teachers are paid well. Those at the secondary level earn 109 percent of the starting salary for other college graduates, considerably higher than the OECD average of 88 percent.

Upon taking their positions as teachers, Finland's educators are expected to invest in the success of every student. Although there are no mandatory nationwide exams other than the National Matriculation Exam that all students take at the end of upper-secondary school, there is an emphasis on using formative assessments that the teachers themselves create for early diagnosis of student difficulties and corresponding interventions. Every school has a "special teacher" assigned to it to assist in identifying and meeting the needs of struggling students. Almost a quarter of Finnish students receive extra instruction from the special teacher (Center on International Education Benchmarking, n.d.a).

Whereas many countries have approached school reform as a series of never-ending new initiatives, Finland's teachers have benefited from a very different approach. The nation's reform strategy has been driven by a shared vision or "big dream" of a more equitable society in which every student would have exactly the same opportunity to learn, regardless of family background, income, or geographic location (Partanen, 2011). Teachers have been given wide latitude to bring that vision to life. Finland's teachers enjoy tremendous professional autonomy. As the president of the Finnish Teachers Union reports, "Teachers in Finland are very independent. They can decide almost everything: how they will teach, what they will select from the basic (national) curriculum, when they will teach each particular topic" (OECD, 2010a, p. 124). There is no national mechanism for monitoring the performance of schools and no tradition of classroom supervision and evaluation by principals (OECD, 2010a). The number of hours Finland devotes to instruction each year is the fewest among OECD countries (OECD, 2014c).

According to the OECD (2010a), Finland manages:

> To make teaching the single most desirable career choice among young Finns through a combination of raising the bar for entry into the profession and granting teachers greater autonomy and control over their classrooms and working conditions than their peers enjoy elsewhere. (p. 129)

Young Finns agree. Like their counterparts in Singapore, they report that the status afforded to the teaching profession in their country was a major factor in their decision to enter the profession.

The United States

In the United States, teaching has long been considered an easy-entry occupation with a low bar and wide gate for entry. Candidates for teaching in the United States tend to be in the average-to-low range of college entrance examination scores compared to other college graduates (Ingersoll, 2007). More than 1,300 traditional institutions and a growing number of alternative certification programs provide pathways to the profession (Mehta, 2013). Programs like Teach for America operate from the assumption that any intelligent, willing person can become an effective teacher after a few weeks of training.

Upon completing the requirements to become a teacher, many Americans are hired to teach outside their field. More than a third of secondary school teachers in mathematics and English do not have a major in the subjects they are teaching. Twenty-nine percent of secondary science teachers have no degree in science. If one takes into account science teachers who are teaching outside their major (for example, a biology major assigned to teach chemistry), the figure climbs much higher. In urban settings, the percentage of educators teaching outside their majors climbs higher still (Ingersoll, 2007). No other industrialized country allows its teachers to teach in subjects for which they have not been highly trained (Tucker, 2011).

Unlike Singapore and Finland, who offer a free university program for those who qualify to be trained as teachers, students in the United States assume most of their own costs for a college education in the most expensive country in the world to attend college. Annual college costs in the United States are nearly double the OECD average (OECD, 2014c). Those who exit college with a bachelor's degree also carry an average debt of $29,000

(Carey, 2015). To repay that debt, a prospective teacher in the United States will earn 68 percent of the mean salary of other college graduates, 20 percent lower than the OECD average, and 41 percent lower than Finland's teachers (OECD 2014b). In 2012, the median income of an American teacher was $54,000, significantly less than a registered nurse ($65,000), dental hygienist ($70,000), or computer programmer ($74,000; Goldstein, 2014a).

Once they enter the profession, their jobs depend on the vagaries of a value-added measure from standardized tests that has been dismissed as invalid by a bevy of assessment experts. A poll of Finnish teachers reveals that half of them would consider quitting if Finland were to adopt a procedure to evaluate their performance on the basis of standardized tests (Sahlberg, 2013).

The constant attacks on American teachers have left them with the impression that their status has never been lower. Only 33 percent report that their opinions are valued at the district level, only 5 percent at the state level, and only 2 percent at the national level (Scholastic, 2014). Teacher job satisfaction has declined to its lowest point in twenty-five years, plummeting from 62 percent in 2008 to 39 percent in 2012 (Markow et al., 2013).

Those who perceive teaching as easy with a guarantee of lifetime employment might consider why so many people opt out of the profession. In Finland, 90 percent of those who enter teaching remain in the profession for the duration of their careers (Center on International Education Benchmarking, n.d.b). In Singapore, more than four of every five teachers who enter the profession are still in it six years later. In the United States, half of those who enter the profession are gone within six years (Tucker, 2014). The Teach for America program adds to the churn. Only 8 percent of its teachers remain in their initial placement after six years (Donaldson & Johnson, 2011). If teaching is such a cushy job, why is it only 10 percent of American parents say they would definitely encourage their own children to pursue teaching (Dolton & Marcenaro-Gutierrez, 2013)?

Assessing an Unproven Theory

Both NCLB and Race to the Top were based on theory, not evidence, because there is no educational system in the world that has used this approach to significantly raise student achievement. Essentially, the theory went like this:

We will improve our schools and raise student achievement until we accomplish our goal of being among the world leaders on international tests . . .

- If we offer enough charter schools and vouchers that educators feel competitive pressure to improve student achievement

- If we use increased supervision and test results to dismiss ineffective teachers

- If we make it easier to enter the teaching profession

- If we offer merit pay to reward effective teachers based on test scores

- If we close enough low-performing schools

In the final analysis, the impact of these assumptions must be assessed not by debating their potential merits but rather on the basis of actual results. Has the unprecedented fixation with testing, sanctions, choice, and educator dismissals achieved the objective of improving student achievement in the United States to the point that American students are comparable to the highest-performing students in the world?

A blue ribbon committee of the National Research Council studied the impact of these strategies. As *Education Week* summarizes the committee's findings, "On the whole it found the approaches implemented so far have had little or no effect on actual student learning and in some cases have run counter to their intended purposes" (Sparks, 2011, p. 1). As the committee reports, "Test-based incentive programs, as designed and implemented in the programs that have been carefully studied, have not increased student achievement enough to bring the United States close to the levels of the highest achieving countries." The committee finds that "the high school exit exam programs as currently implemented in the United States decreases the rate of high school graduation without increasing achievement" (Hout & Elliott, 2011). As Michael Hout, Sara Fruesh, and Stuart Elliot subsequently comment, "Given the immense amount of policy emphasis the incentives have received during the past three decades, the amount of improvement they have produced so far is strikingly small" (Hout, Frueh, & Elliott, 2013).

A report from the National Center on Education and the Economy is less nuanced. It states:

> The test-based accountability system now universally mandated in the United States—a system that reflects in every way the blue-collar conception of teaching as an occupation—has had ten years to prove itself. The result is very low teacher morale, plummeting applications to schools of education, the need to recruit too many of our teachers from the lowest levels of high school graduates, a testing regime that has narrowed the curriculum for millions of students to a handful of subjects and a very low level of aspiration. There is no evidence that it is contributing anything to improved student performance, much less the improved performance of the very low-income and minority students for which it was in the first instance created. (Tucker, 2014, p. 2)

The National Education Policy Center reports that the "broad consensus among researchers" is that the nation's test-based accountability system is "at best ineffective and at worst counter-productive" (Welner & Mathis, 2015, p. 7). Negative consequences associated with the strategy include the "deprofessionalizing of teachers and teaching"; abandoning a tradition of learning that encompassed the arts, social studies, and science;

> Our national policy has served to denigrate and alienate the very people who are most critical to improving achievement of our students: the educators who serve them.

and inattention to the skills most needed and valued in the 21st century, such as problem solving, critical thinking, reasoning, and working effectively with others to establish and achieve goals (Welner & Mathis, 2015, p. 4).

Our national policy has served to denigrate and alienate the very people who are most critical to improving achievement of our students: the educators who serve them. A 2013 report on teacher status around the world issued an ominous warning for those who continue on this path.

> If teachers aren't respected in society, children won't listen to them in class, parents won't reinforce the messages that are coming from school and the most talented graduates will continue to disregard teaching as a profession. Over time, this declining respect for teachers will weaken teaching, weaken learning, damage the learning opportunities for millions and ultimately weaken societies around the world. (Dolton & Marcenaro-Gutierrez, 2013, p. 4)

The record-setting levels of student achievement generated by the current generation of American educators have occurred *despite* rather than because of NCLB and Race to the Top. Student achievement was rising faster prior to the passage of NCLB than it has in the aftermath of that legislation. Consider the following.

- The rate of progress on NAEP at grades 4 and 8 was generally faster in the decade before NCLB took effect than since. That is a consistent trend both overall and for individual demographic groups, including black students, English learners (ELs), and students with special needs.

- Score gaps in 2012 were no narrower and often were wider than they were in 1998 and 1990.

- Score gains slowed after NCLB for ELs, while score gaps increased between ELs and non-ELs.

- In three of four grades and tests, scores for students with disabilities flattened or declined, while gaps with whites remained unchanged or widened.

- Scores for high school students have stagnated. NAEP scores were highest for blacks, and gaps the narrowest, in 1988. Hispanic student scores and gaps have stagnated since NCLB (FairTest, 2015).

- The dramatic increase in the number of students taking AP exams began well before NCLB. The percentage of increase in both the number of students taking exams and the number of exams written was actually higher in the decade before NCLB went into effect than since its passage (College Board, 2013).

Furthermore, the stated goal of the current reform policies is to make American students among the highest scoring in the world on international assessments such as PISA. After more than a decade of implementation, when the impact of those policies is assessed against that goal, they can only be described as failing to come anywhere near their intended objective.

International research indicates that the highest-performing countries owe their success to approaches that are the antithesis of the American approach. They select teachers from among their most talented graduates; train them extensively, often at public expense; create collaborative structures and time to support building shared

The record-setting levels of student achievement generated by the current generation of American educators have occurred *despite* rather than because of NCLB and Race to the Top. . . . International research indicates that the highest-performing countries owe their success to approaches that are the antithesis of the American approach.

knowledge and ongoing learning; and, very importantly, honor the profession. They nurture the human capital that represents the most vital asset of any school system because they recognize that "successful and sustainable improvement can therefore never be done *to or even for* teachers. It can only ever be achieved *by and with* them" (Hargreaves & Fullan, 2012, p. 45). It is time for the United States to acknowledge its theory of reform has failed to make America one of the highest-performing nations in terms of educational achievement and to embrace policies that have been shown to work in many places around the world.

> It is time for the United States to acknowledge its theory of reform has failed to make America one of the highest-performing nations in terms of educational achievement and to embrace policies that have been shown to work in many places around the world.

More Effective Policies

It is true that the small size of Singapore and Finland allows them to be more nimble and cohesive in their educational reform efforts than what might be possible in the United States. Comparing them to the United States is like comparing the agility of a kayak to a battleship. It is also true that the enormous difference in the rate of poverty in the United States compared to these two nations makes comparing educational achievement difficult. But there are consistent lessons about effective school-reform policies in countries around the world that we would be foolish to continue to ignore.

Change the Scope, Frequency, and Purpose of Testing

As mentioned earlier, standardized testing in the United States is a $1.7 billion industry that has narrowed the curriculum and led to a significant loss of instructional time in American schools. High-performing nations reject the American idea of testing every child every year starting in third grade and instead use testing two or three times during the entire K–12 experience.

The few tests they do administer, however, call on students to demonstrate critical thinking, creativity of expression, rhetoric, persuasive writing, and the ability to apply their learning to real-world applications. In Singapore, even the mathematics test administered in fourth grade is comprised of only 20 percent multiple-choice questions. Fifty percent of the questions require long responses in which students must explain how they arrived at a solution. In Finland, the Matriculation Mathematics Examination administered to high school students requires students to respond to only ten of the fifteen questions that are presented in the three-hour exam. The questions are lengthy, multistep problems, and students must explain their work and justify their responses (Driskell, 2015).

Two other trends in the assessment practices of high-performing countries are of note. First, students are assessed not only in mathematics and language but also in subject areas throughout the curriculum. Second, examples of highly rated responses are made available to students, teachers, parents, and the general public so that everyone understands the standards students are called on to achieve (Driskell, 2015).

If the United States adopted this approach, it could move away from its multiple-choice approach to testing only language arts and mathematics and instead focus on higher-order thinking skills and the ability to apply those skills across disciplines that are assessed on the PISA exams. These tests are more expensive to create and score, but the increased costs would be offset by the fact that they would be given to students only in fourth, eighth, and tenth grade rather than each year. The tenth-grade assessment would focus on college and career readiness, giving students time to address deficiencies that the assessment might help to reveal. States could also assess random samplings of students in other grades to monitor trends in student achievement. We would abandon our current practice of over-testing students on multiple-choice tests and then complaining when they experience difficulty on the PISA exam, which presents an entirely different assessment challenge.

Very importantly, we would abandon what the director of Finland's Centre for International Mobility and Cooperation describes as America's "toxic use of school accountability" (Sahlberg, 2013). Scores would not be used in the evaluation of individual teachers but would be a vehicle for identifying struggling schools. States would then be called on to send experts into the school to help assess problems and identify possible remedies. States would be responsible for supporting the school and helping to build the capacity of the staff to address and overcome its challenges. The focus would be on capacity building and creating internal systems of accountability rather than increasingly punitive sanctions from external sources.

> The focus would be on capacity building and creating internal systems of accountability rather than increasingly punitive sanctions from external sources.

This strategy has been used effectively in the Canadian province of Ontario, which has consistently scored twenty or more points above the OECD average on all three of the areas assessed by the PISA exam. If an elementary school in Ontario is unable to help at least 75 percent of its students meet the provincial standard on its assessments, it becomes part of the Ontario Focused Intervention Partnership (OFIP, n.d.). Rather than resorting to sanctions, the program takes a capacity-building approach, operating under the assumption that the educators in the school must be the force for change, and the Ministry of Education must help build their collective capacity to overcome their challenges.

OFIP provides support for onsite professional learning in the form of offering advice, sharing research into effective practices, creating structures to encourage collaborative inquiry into problems of practice, gathering and analyzing data to identify student learning needs, monitoring progress, building networking opportunities with other schools of similar demographics that have been successful in overcoming their challenges, and funding a $15,000 stipend to provide the staff with release time for planning, monitoring, reflecting, and integrating what is being learned in classroom practice. A provincial capacity-building team provides ongoing consulting services directly to the school.

Schools in this program must complete a needs assessment, develop an action plan, engage the faculty in a school-based professional learning community, and participate in formal and informal learning opportunities. When the program began in 2003–2004, 780 elementary schools were identified as in need of assistance. By 2014, the number had shrunk to 63 even though the prerequisite standard of achievement required of schools had been raised. Furthermore, the rate of improvement for OFIP schools has exceeded provincial averages throughout the program's history (OFIP, n.d.).

Pay the College Costs of Students Who Graduate in the Top Quarter of Their Class Who Agree to Teach for Five Years

It is unlikely that we will attract the top high school graduates to teaching if they have to assume a $29,000 debt for a position that pays 68 percent of the average salary of college graduates in America. To make teaching more attractive to those students, the United States should invest in their education, as is common practice in high-performing countries. As a nation, we are eager to assume the college costs for students with athletic ability and students seeking to develop military leadership at our service academies. If education is a national priority, we should be willing to do the same for exceptional students who want to enter the teaching profession.

Of course, as many former students know, even a college professor with a deep knowledge of a subject can still be a terrible teacher, so candidates for these scholarships should be required

As a nation, we are eager to assume the college costs for students with athletic ability and students seeking to develop military leadership at our service academies. If education is a national priority, we should be willing to do the same for exceptional students who want to enter the teaching profession.

to complete an intensive interview process to assess their potential as a teacher before qualifying and continue to be assessed as their education continues.

It is important to present an explicit caveat at this point. While there are policies that can be adopted to attract top high school students to teaching as a long-term strategy to improve the status of the profession, *it is far more important to focus on building the collective capacity of those already in the profession.* Students do not receive their education in the long term—they need more effective schools and more effective educators today, and thus, the policy priority should be enhancing conditions for adult learning in our schools. This issue is addressed in later chapters.

Establish Career Ladders With Increasing Responsibilities and Compensation for Teachers

Raising the bar for admission to the profession will accomplish nothing unless the way in which teachers are compensated also changes dramatically. One of the inherent challenges in the teaching profession is that it is not designed to foster a sense of advancement or recognition. As currently practiced in the United States, the responsibilities of a master teacher with twenty years of experience are identical to those of a first-year teacher making the transition into the profession.

Most school districts structure their teacher compensation scale to encourage continuing education and experience. Often referred to as *step and column*, teachers receive higher salaries for earning continuing-education credits, postgraduate degrees, and years of service. The underlying premise behind this practice is that greater content knowledge and teaching experience will improve teacher effectiveness. In reality, these practices produce only minimal gains in student achievement. Postgraduate degrees have an effect size of 0.09, significantly below the 0.40 threshold Hattie (2009) recommends for confirming a practice has a positive impact on student achievement. Likewise, studies that have correlated years of experience and teacher effectiveness have found that beginning teachers are less effective during their first two years in the classroom, show improvement until about the fifth year, and then level off in terms of effectiveness (Rice, 2010). While there are benefits to promoting continuing education and rewarding teacher experience, it is unlikely these strategies alone will significantly improve core instruction. In later chapters, I make the case for the ongoing, job-embedded professional development that does lead to continuous improvement of practice.

The National Center on Education and the Economy calls for the states to address the need for teachers to have an opportunity for career advancement while remaining in the classroom (Tucker, 2014). It proposes that every state require districts to establish a multistep career ladder that would enable teachers to advance through a series of stages with increases in compensation and responsibility as they do so. Advancement would be based not on years in the classroom but on expertise and a willingness to assume greater responsibilities within the school or district. Teachers at the top of the ladder would be responsible for assuming leadership roles in improving the school and mentoring new teachers. They might have a voice in determining which teachers should be offered tenure. They could be assigned to a troubled school to help overcome its problems. As mentioned earlier, Singapore has used this strategy to great effect. High-performing nations have tapped into the expertise of their educators as a powerful force for continuous improvement. So should the United States.

> High-performing nations have tapped into the expertise of their educators as a powerful force for continuous improvement. So should the United States.

Establish Clear Standards Regarding What Teachers Should Know and Be Able to Do

In 1995, the Holmes Group, a coalition of deans of American graduate schools, issued a report titled *Tomorrow's Schools of Education*. The report criticizes shoddy teacher education programs characterized by a lack of quality control, enormous gaps between education schools and the world of practice, instruction in outmoded conceptions of teaching and learning, the needless division between theory and practice, and the poor field placement of students. It called for revolutionizing teacher preparation and offered recommendations for a curriculum that would include child development, subject matter content, pedagogy, technology, classroom management, inquiry-based action research, and collaborative skills. The group cautions that its recommendations require classrooms and schools to be "thoughtfully organized as communities of learning" (Holmes Group, 1990, p. vii).

More than a decade later, the former president of Teachers College, Columbia University issued a report criticizing teacher education programs for a curriculum in disarray, disconnected faculty, low admission standards, insufficient quality control, huge disparities in instructional quality, and providing students with inadequate preparation. As he summarizes the situation, "At the moment, teacher education is the Dodge City of the education world . . . unruly and disordered" (Levine, 2006, p. 109).

One of the most recent attempts to influence the quality of teacher preparation programs was a National Council on Teacher Quality report that tries to shame institutions of higher learning by assigning grades to each university's programs. It concludes that teacher preparation programs are "an industry of mediocrity churning out first-year teachers with classroom-management skills and content knowledge inadequate to thrive in classrooms with ever-increasing ethnic and socioeconomic student diversity" (Greenberg, McKee, & Walsh, 2013b, p. 3). It decries the fact that only a quarter of the programs limited admissions to students who had graduated in the top half of their class and that only 7 percent of the programs provided their students with uniformly strong experiences.

The authors of the report discovered that one of the most "serious and profound problems with teacher preparation" is the manner in which the professors in these programs define their mission (Greenberg et al., 2013b, p. 6). According to the report, professors felt the purpose of their programs was not to train students in specific skills like classroom management, assessment, or instructional strategies, but rather it was to instill a "professional mindset" (Greenberg, McKee, & Walsh, 2013a, p. 6).

The report goes on to offer seventeen different specific standards that all teacher preparation programs should be required to address. It also calls for universities to provide evidence that their students are acquiring the intended knowledge and skills and that they establish a process to monitor the impact of their graduates on student learning. The Obama administration agrees and has proposed tying federal student aid for higher education to how well colleges fare on access, affordability, and student success in 2018 (White House, n.d.a).

Until there is widespread agreement on what a beginning teacher must know and be able to do, teacher preparation programs will continue to be in disarray. The National Governor's Association Center for Best Practices and the Council of Chief State School Officers (NGA & CCSSO) were able to coordinate their efforts to create the Common Core State Standards to clarify what students should be able to know and do at different levels of the K–12 system. Although the Common Core has become caught up in political debates of late, the fact that forty-five states reached initial agreement on this issue was a major accomplishment. A similar effort needs to occur in higher education, with a corresponding commitment to creating rigorous assessments to help determine whether teacher candidates have acquired the intended knowledge and skills.

The need for this initiative is even more pronounced given the number of new teachers entering the profession. The combined effect of increasing student enrollments and retiring teachers from the baby boom generation means that novice teachers make up a greater share of the teacher workforce than ever. In 1988, the mode or most common level of experience for teachers was fifteen years; in 2013, the most common level of experience was one year. Research consistently shows that students taught by first-year teachers lose ground academically compared to those taught by experienced teachers (Greenberg, McKee, & Walsh, 2013a). It is time to tame the Dodge City of education.

Provide Universal Early Childhood Education

The achievement gap in American education begins prior to the day students enroll in school. Therefore, one way to close the gap would be to provide early childhood education that could narrow the discrepancy between socioeconomic groups as children enter school. But as a nation with one of the highest child poverty rates among OECD countries, America lags far behind the others in early childhood enrollment. On average, 70 percent of three-year-olds are enrolled in early childhood education in OECD countries compared to 38 percent in the United States. For four-year-olds, the percentages are 84 percent and 66 percent respectively. America ranks thirty-third out of thirty-eight countries for both age groups (OECD, 2014c). Furthermore, the economically disadvantaged students who would benefit most from preschool are far less likely to attend than their more affluent peers (Samuels, 2015).

Analysis of the performance of high school students on both TIMSS and PISA assessments reveals the benefits of preschool education. The 13 percent of students who had not attended preschool scored fifty points lower on the TIMSS mathematics assessment than those who had. PISA results reveal that in nearly all participating countries and economies, students who attend preprimary school tend to perform better at the age of fifteen than students who do not attend, even after accounting for students' socioeconomic status (Mullis et al., 2012). The OECD (2013a) concludes that preschool programs can help close the achievement gap and recommends that governments adopt policies that ensure that disadvantaged students and families have access to high-quality, local preprimary education. It also recommends that governments subsidize preprimary education to ease the financial burdens on families.

Two meta-analyses of the research on high-quality preschool education come to similar conclusions regarding the exceptional benefits of those programs. Students who participated had a post-program impact of 0.35 standard deviation, or about half of the achievement gap between black and white students (President's Council of Economic Advisers, 2014). Students in all socioeconomic groups benefited, but the children living in or near poverty experienced the greatest benefits (Yoshikawa et al., 2013). Hattie's (2009) synthesis of the research suggests an even stronger effect size of early childhood education of 0.45.

Both studies conclude that there are tremendous cost benefits to be gained from high-quality preschool programs. Those benefits include increases in parental earnings and employment, reduced spending for special education and grade retention, and greater educational attainment and earnings. Hirokazu Yoshikawa and colleagues (2013) conclude that every dollar spent on preschool education yields a return of $7. The President's Council of Economic Advisers (2014) estimates the return to be at $8.40.

Although the academic gains in student achievement from preschool programs seem to diminish over time, children who attend preschool go on to show positive effects on important adolescent and young adult outcomes, such as high school graduation, reduced teen pregnancy, years of education completed, earnings, and reduced crime (Yoshikawa et al., 2013). Both studies support the following conclusion:

> Recent meta-analyses drawing together the evidence across decades of evaluation research now permit us to say with confidence that preschool programs can have a substantial impact on early learning and development. Positive effects on children's development are found for language, literacy and early math skills; for social and emotional outcomes; and in children's health. (Yoshikawa et al., 2013, p. 14)

It is probably too much to hope that the United States could develop a comprehensive program to reduce child poverty that could earn bipartisan support. But a poll on the question of government spending to support the preschool education of four-year-olds living in poverty shows Americans support the idea by more than a two-to-one margin (*Education Next*, 2014). Certainly, as a nation and as individual states, we should be able to agree that one of the most cost-effective ways to address the poverty problem is providing early childhood programs characterized by intensive, developmentally focused curricula with integrated professional development and careful monitoring of children's progress (Yoshikawa et al., 2013).

Support Career and Technical Education as a Pathway to the Middle Class

Chapter 6 presents the dramatic, even life-threatening consequences for students unable to succeed in America's K–12 educational system. Here, I want to stress that, according to a report from the Center on Education and the Workforce (CEW), those who navigate the system and graduate from high school unprepared for postsecondary learning face serious challenges as well. High school graduates have a difficult time in the 21st century American economy. One in four was unemployed in 2012, and between 2002 and 2012, wages for those with only a high school diploma fell 12 percent to just $19,400—below the poverty threshold for a family of four (Carnevale, Jayasundera, & Hanson, 2012).

There are, however, twenty-nine million "middle jobs" in the American economy, or one in every five jobs, that pay between $35,000 and $90,000 and offer opportunities for career advancement. These careers require education and training beyond high school but less than a bachelor's degree (Carnevale et al., 2012). The five pathways to these jobs are associate degrees, postsecondary certificates, employer-based training, industry-based certification, and apprenticeships.

The challenge facing the United States is that the percentage of high school students pursuing the career and technical education (CTE) programs that align with these pathways has been declining for decades. The United States now lags behind other advanced economies in CTE training. For example, whereas 25 percent of Canadian students pursue postsecondary education that leads to sub-baccalaureate attainment, only 10 percent of American students take that path, ranking our nation sixteenth in the world. Apprenticeship programs illustrate the discrepancy. Only three of one thousand jobs in civilian employment in the United States are held by apprentices compared to forty-three in Switzerland, forty in Germany, and thirty-nine in Australia—countries where apprenticeship is a major element of the transition from school to work (Carnevale et al., 2012).

The CEW proposes a two-part strategy for making well-paying middle jobs more accessible to American students. It starts with federal and state governments investing more heavily in CTE programs of study that align secondary and postsecondary curricula, allow for dual enrollment, reduce duplication and remediation, and create opportunities for students to earn money while they are learning (Carnevale et al., 2012).

The second part of the CEW strategy calls on the federal government to establish a Learning and Earnings Exchange that links high school and postsecondary transcript information with employer wage records. School counselors and students would have up-to-date access to career opportunities and the potential earnings of those careers. It would also illustrate the financial consequences of dropping out of school and the limited availability of jobs for those who end their education with a high school diploma. Students would then be in a better position to make informed choices about what to study, schools would be better positioned to provide relevant curriculum, and employers would have more success in finding the skilled workers they need.

Postsecondary education and training are no longer one of several pathways to the middle- and upper-income classes but increasingly represent the only pathway. Postsecondary education and training are not, however, synonymous with earning a bachelor's degree. The federal and state governments could and should do a better job of helping young men and women use career and technical education to access well-paying jobs in the American economy.

Stipulate That Teachers Are Provided With Time for Collaboration

Teachers in the United States devote approximately 1,051 hours to classroom instruction each year compared to OECD averages of 792 hours for elementary schools and 658 hours for secondary schools (OECD, 2012a). The number of hours in the workday of the two groups is similar, but teachers in OECD countries devote significantly less time to actual classroom instruction with students and far more time to working collaboratively with their peers on instructional issues because collaborative time is part of their routine schedule. Teachers in the highest-performing countries devote fifteen to twenty hours per week to preparing and analyzing lessons, developing assessments, gathering evidence of student learning, analyzing that evidence to inform their practice, and meeting with and intervening with students individually and in small groups (Tucker, 2014). For example, an American teacher who took a position in Finland found that the biggest adjustment he had to make was that he taught ten fewer hours each week than he had in the United States and that he spent more time working with other educators than working alone (Walker, 2013).

The lack of time for educators to work with colleagues is a distinctly American problem. In the United States, teachers are deemed to be working only when they are standing in front of a class delivering instruction. There is virtually no time for teachers to confer with colleagues regarding all the other tasks of teaching—preparing, planning lessons, developing curriculum, creating assessments, reflecting on evidence of student learning, providing additional help for struggling students, or engaging in action research. We continue to cling to the idea that teachers "work" (that is, teach) 176 days each year and they "learn" on the four days set aside for professional development on the school calendar. We have yet to establish a cultural norm in which working and learning are interwoven, ensuring educators are continuing to grow and learn as part of their routine work practice.

The National Center on Education and the Economy recommends that states require districts to ensure that at least a quarter of the time a teacher is expected to be at work should be devoted to collaborating with his or her colleagues (Tucker, 2014). Delaware took the lead in this area. In its Race to the Top application, it stipulated that all core subject teachers would be provided with at least ninety minutes each week to work as members of collaborative teams. This time would be considered sacred and was not to be preempted for any other purpose. Teacher teams would use the time to gather and examine achievement data of their students and use the data to inform, adjust, and improve instruction. Any teacher who refused to participate or was disruptive to the collaborative process would be reprimanded by the administration. The state would provide data coaches to every school for two years to assist them in building their internal capacity to continue creating a collaborative culture focused on evidence of student learning (U.S. Department of Education, 2010).

At the end of the first full year of implementation, every grade level and every subgroup experienced improvement, and the percentage of students scoring as advanced proficient increased in both subject areas (DuFour & Fullan, 2013). Within two years, the percentage of students in the state scoring proficient in reading increased from 61 percent to 72 percent and from 62 percent to 70 percent in mathematics. Educators attributed the gains to the statewide implementation of PLCs. By the end of the 2013 school year, 82 percent of the teachers in the state reported that their collaborative team had a transparent, collaborative culture, and 95 percent said they were comfortable discussing classroom data on their students with their peers (Delaware Department of Education, 2013).

But Delaware also provides a cautionary tale for those interested in school reform. The state funded its effort to support schools and districts with the money it received in its Race to the Top grant. When the grant stopped after three years, many districts abandoned the initiative (Mitchell & Neubauer, personal communication, 2015). Building a collaborative culture must ultimately become an ongoing priority that can be addressed within local budgets. Viewing it as an add-on tied directly to external funding increases the likelihood that when the funding runs dry, the initiative will lose momentum.

The good news is that educators in the United States are hungry for more time to work with their colleagues. *The MetLife Survey of the American Teacher* finds a "remarkable consensus among teachers and principals on the importance of collaboration and its potential for having a major impact on improving student learning" (Markow & Pieters, 2010, p. 14).

Part II will establish that while providing time for educators to collaborate is a necessary condition for improving schools, it is not sufficient. How they use that time will determine whether or not it impacts student and adult learning in a positive way.

Later in the book, you will find specific recommendations for high-leverage strategies to help collaboration yield the best results.

Support Schools as They Make the Transition to Professional Learning Communities

If a school can only be as good as the quality of the educators within it, it is imperative that government policies support conditions that lead to the ongoing learning and continuous improvement of teachers and principals. The McKinsey & Company investigation of the world's highest-performing educational systems has the following three conclusions.

1. To get the most out of the talent of any faculty, it is critical that systems support the development of that talent.

2. The most powerful avenue for developing educator talent is high-quality collaborative, job-embedded professional development.

3. The best process for providing this professional development is the professional learning community process in which:

> Teachers work together to research, try, and share best practices, analyze and constantly aim for high, internationally benchmarked standards, analyze student data and plan instruction, map and articulate curriculum, and observe and coach each other. PLCs are an indication of a broader trend towards professional development that is increasingly collaborative, data-driven, and peer-facilitated, all with a focus on classroom practice. (Barber & Mourshed, 2009, p. 32)

Researchers from around the world have confirmed the power of the PLC process. It has been endorsed by virtually all the professional organizations for educators in the United

The PLC process creates internal accountability that is more powerful and effective than current efforts to hold schools accountable.

States. It is consistent with recommendations for best practice from organizational theorists outside of education. Each of its various elements is grounded in a solid research base. (See www .allthingsplc.info/files/uploads /advocates.pdf for the list of PLC advocates and what they are saying about PLCs.) The PLC process creates internal accountability that is more powerful and effective than current efforts to hold schools accountable. So rather than continuing to pursue the discredited policy of privatization, sanctions, and punishment, state and national leaders should focus on helping educators build their collective capacity to engage in a proven process that offers our best hope for sustained and substantive school improvement. Part II elaborates on the conditions that support the PLC process.

The Educators We Deserve?

The fact that contemporary American educators have accomplished so much despite the reforms thrust upon them since 2003 is quite remarkable. They are told that their schools are failing and that they are the cause of the failure despite record levels of achievement. They are being held accountable for achieving a level of student performance that has never been attained anywhere in the world in a system that was originally designed to sort and select students based on perceptions of their ability and future occupations. They teach a higher percentage of students living in poverty than any industrialized nation and can anticipate that one of every five students they are teaching does not speak English at home. They are often assigned to teach in subject areas outside their expertise. They have gone into crushing debt to assume a position that pays them 68 percent of what their college-graduate peers are earning. They have watched as governments have approved pathways to teaching that require almost no training—a not-so-subtle suggestion that anyone can teach. As the National Center on Education and the Economy concludes:

> The whole system was treating its school teachers as if the work they did required little knowledge or skills—was in fact semi-skilled work—and the most important thing was to make sure that an adult was in front of the students, at the lowest possible cost to the public, regardless of the skills that adult brought to the job. (Tucker, 2014, p. 9)

Marc Tucker (2014) is exactly right that, as a nation, *"We do not have the teachers we deserve; we have better teachers than we deserve"* (p. 9, emphasis added).

CHAPTER 5

A Word About Teacher Unions

As discussed in chapter 1, many of the critics of public education point to teacher unions as the main problem with public schools. They allege that the primary goals of the National Education Association (NEA) and the American Federation of Teachers (AFT) are making life easier for teachers and opposing what needs to be done to improve student achievement. The key to improving schools, therefore, is to strip unions of their power (Moe, 2011).

The validity of this hypothesis should be relatively easy to establish because there are examples of both states and countries that have teacher unions and those that do not. If the hypothesis is correct, states and nations unencumbered by teacher unions should consistently outperform those with unions. However, the opposite is true.

A study in the *Harvard Educational Review* reports that the presence of teacher unions has a significant and *positive* relationship with student performance on both the SAT and ACT exams—the two most common college entrance exams in the United States (Carini, Powell, & Steelman, 2000). An analysis of student performance on the National Assessment of Educational Progress shows that only one nonunion state (Virginia, ranked at sixteenth) had an average score above the median while seven of the ten nonunion states scored in the bottom fifteen in the nation. Conversely, nine of the ten states with the highest rankings were states with strong teacher unions (Strauss, 2010). One of those states, Massachusetts, benchmarks the achievement of its eighth-grade students with other nations on the TIMSS exams in science and mathematics. It came in second in the world in science and sixth in mathematics (Martin et al., 2012).

The Organisation for Economic Co-operation and Development assesses the allegation that teacher unions are the major obstacle to higher student achievement in the United States. It concludes:

> The fact is that many of the countries with the strongest student performance also have the strongest teachers' unions, beginning with Japan and Finland. There seems to be no relationship between the presence of unions, including and especially teachers' unions, and student performance. But there may be a relationship between the degree to which the work of teaching has been professionalised and student performance. Indeed, the higher a country is on the world's education league tables, the more likely that country is working constructively with its unions and treating its teachers as trusted professional partners. (OECD, 2010b, p. 238)

The province of Ontario is an excellent example of a high-performing system that has benefited from a partnership between a government and its teacher unions. The conservative government in place at the turn of the 21st century had instituted a provincial curriculum and assessment system and strict accountability measures. In doing so, it had gone to war with its teacher unions, cutting funding, slashing professional development days in half, and airing television advertisements demonizing teachers. The unions responded with strikes and lockouts, and student achievement remained flat (Tucker, 2012).

When Premier Dalton McGuinty took office in 2003, he concluded that gaining the trust and cooperation of teachers was vital to improving Ontario's schools. So he included the province's four teacher unions in developing Ontario's school reform agenda and listened to what they had to say. The ability of the different parties to find common ground resulted in a four-year collective bargaining agreement that led to a sustained focus on improving Ontario's schools and exceptional student performance on international examinations. The partnership continued throughout the agreement with quarterly meetings between the system's leaders, teacher unions, superintendents' organizations, and principals' association to discuss the ongoing reform (OECD, 2010a).

So two facts should be evident. First, the presence of teacher unions does not inevitably lead to lower student achievement. Second, unions can play an important role in reforming schools in ways that benefit student learning. The OECD (2011b) report on what the United States can learn from strong-performing countries warns that our nation is unlikely to reach the levels of their performance unless it "leverages more effective union-management relations at local and state levels" (p. 239).

It is also evident, however, that teacher unions in the United States are at a crossroads. Although nearly three of every four Americans reported in 2011 that they had "trust and confidence in the men and women who are teaching children in the public schools," nearly half expressed the belief that unions had hurt the quality of public school education (Bushaw & Lopez, 2011, p. 11). Three years later, a different poll revealed that the majority of respondents with an opinion felt that unions had a negative rather than positive impact on schools (*Education Next*, 2014). The largest teacher union, the National Education Association, lost 230,000 members, or 7 percent of its membership, between

2009 and 2013. States are eliminating or curtailing collective bargaining. The Democratic Party, the one-time unquestioning ally of teacher unions, has begun to challenge union policies. The Editorial Board (2014) of the *New York Times* criticizes the "stupidity" of several union-backed laws. The *Vergara v. California* decision that declared several of California's teacher protection laws unconstitutional has called many traditional union positions into question (Editorial Board, 2014).

So leaders of the NEA and AFT, along with state and local affiliates, must decide if they are going to hunker down and continue to cling to positions that are increasingly under attack as harmful to students or if they will become a force for the kinds of reforms that consistently have been shown to have a positive impact on student learning. They must decide whether they will work to change some of their "anachronistic policies" or face the likelihood that the changes will be foisted on them (Editorial Board, 2014). Suggestions regarding some of those changes follow.

Teacher Tenure

The origins of teacher tenure in the United States are not found in collective bargaining but in the reformers of the Progressive Era who recognized that teacher positions were being used as political patronage and that dismissals based on gender, marital status, pregnancy, religion, ethnicity, race, sexual orientation, or political ideology were commonplace (Goldstein, 2014a). Tenure laws were passed to end this capricious approach to the hiring and firing of teachers by requiring districts to show just cause for firing a teacher who had qualified for tenure.

Opponents of tenure argue that it is tantamount to guaranteeing a person a job for life. Defenders of tenure (including unions) rightly point out that tenure offers no such guarantee but merely an assurance of due process before dismissal. Public attitudes toward tenure depend a great deal on how the issue is framed. When asked if they supported a lifetime contract for teachers who had been teaching for two or three years, 73 percent of respondents said no. When asked if they agreed that a teacher who had been teaching for two or three years should receive a formal legal review before he or she could be terminated, 66 percent said yes (Bushaw & McNee, 2009).

The problem that has arisen is that the due process for dismissal of a tenured teacher has become so time-consuming, complex, and expensive that it is no longer viewed as a viable option for removing an ineffective teacher. The judge in the *Vergara* case was struck by the fact that defense witnesses attempting to justify tenure often provided testimony that convinced him it should be abolished. For example, there was agreement in the court that dismissing a tenured teacher in California could take from two to ten years and cost from $50,000 to $450,000. Defense witnesses also agreed that 1 to 3 percent (or between 2,750 and 8,250) of California's teachers were "grossly ineffective" (Treu, 2014, p. 8). Another defense witness acknowledged that dismissals were "extremely rare" because "administrators believe it to be 'impossible' to dismiss a tenured teacher under the current system" (Treu, 2014, p. 11). While the judge agreed that tenured teachers should be entitled to due process, they were not entitled to "*uber* due process" that was so complex, time-consuming, and expensive that it did not offer a realistic alternative for dismissing grossly ineffective teachers.

Union leaders at all levels should no longer engage in the disingenuous argument that tenured teachers can be readily dismissed if administrators would simply do their job. Unions have helped create the system that makes it almost impossible for them to do their jobs. When the superintendent of Los Angeles Unified School District says he has 350 tenured teachers who have received multiple unsatisfactory evaluations that should be dismissed but can't be because of their existing protections (Treu, 2014), the entire profession suffers. When readers of the *Huffington Post* (2012) learn New York City will be paying a staggering $22 million in a single year to hundreds of teachers who are "doing absolutely nothing" because they have been removed from the classroom but can't be dismissed, the entire profession suffers.

Perhaps union leaders should listen to their members. When 92 percent of teachers assert tenure should not protect ineffective teachers (Scholastic, 2012) but the majority of teachers acknowledge it is too difficult to remove an ineffective teacher, unions should take notice. When nearly half of teachers admit there is a colleague in their own building who should not be in the classroom (*USA Today*, 2008) or when teachers say they would assign a grade of F to 5 percent of the teachers in their school (*Education Next*, 2014), union leaders at all levels should view this as a wake-up call for change rather than a reason to redouble their defenses of a system that is not in the best interests of students, teachers, or the professions they represent.

For starters, unions should take the lead in advocating for lengthening the time necessary to qualify for tenure. A survey of more than ten thousand teachers reveals that, on average, respondents feel a teacher should not be eligible for tenure until he or she has been teaching for 5.4 years rather than the two or three years of experience required in many states (Goldstein, 2014b).

Most importantly, union leaders at all levels should be presenting concrete proposals for accelerating due process. For example, TNTP (2014), formerly known as The New Teacher Project, proposes to reduce the hearing to one day and the appeal process to ninety days. Unions should either get behind proposals like these or develop concrete proposals designed to accomplish the same objective: simplifying the tortuous process to dismiss a tenured teacher.

Last In, First Out

Most states do not mandate that seniority be the deciding factor or even the predominant factor when it comes to decisions about teacher layoffs due to budget cuts, program dissolution, declining enrollments, or school closings. The issue is, however, likely to arise in local collective bargaining. In its study of one hundred large districts, the National Council on Teacher Quality (2010) finds in all but twenty-five of those districts, seniority determines whether a teacher stays or goes. In only sixteen of the districts is performance given greater weight than seniority. So, generally speaking, when it comes to teachers, the rule is last hired, first fired, or last in, first out (LIFO).

LIFO was the law of the land in California, that is, until it was ruled unconstitutional in the *Vergara* case. As Judge Treu explains in his ruling, he could find no compelling rationale for a law that required a gifted junior teacher who was benefiting students to be removed while a grossly ineffective teacher who was consistently harming them retained a position. As he writes:

> The State Defendants'/Intervenors' position requires them to defend the proposition that the state has a compelling interest in the *de facto* separation of students from competent teachers and a like interest in the *de facto* retention of incompetent ones. The logic of this position is unfathomable and therefore constitutionally unsupportable. (Treu, 2014, p. 14)

Another example of logic-defying LIFO is the industrial arts teacher with twenty years of experience teaching auto mechanics. He also, however, completed a minor in history as an undergraduate and thus is certified to teach that subject. Should his industrial arts program be abolished, he can claim the position of a less-senior teacher with a master's degree in history and a long record of superlative evaluations. This does not make sense to the general public and gives the impression the union is more interested in rewarding the person who has a longer history of paying dues than in ensuring a quality instructor in the classroom.

Since state law trumps local policy, any state could pass a law stipulating how districts must address the layoff question. For example, the policy could establish the following three elements (National Council on Teacher Quality, 2010).

1. Nontenured teachers would be dismissed first. Performance should be a factor in the decision as to which nontenured teacher would be laid off and which would be retained.

2. Use performance, seniority, and credentials—with performance receiving the greatest weight—in decisions regarding the layoff of tenured teachers.

3. Allow a teacher's exceptional performance and/or filling a particular need to exempt him or her from being laid off.

These examples are not intended to serve as a model policy but as merely an example of how the issue might be addressed in a way that demonstrates student needs are a major factor in these decisions. Union leaders could improve on the example and work with their state legislatures to demonstrate that seniority should not be the sole factor to be considered in layoffs.

Support Alternative Ways to Compensate Teachers

As mentioned in chapter 3, there is no basis in research to support merit pay as a way to improve our schools. On the other hand, there is no compelling reason that schools should suspend the laws of supply and demand in their salary structures. It makes little sense that a district should be required to pay a physics teacher the same starting salary as an elementary school teacher or a physical education teacher when it cannot find physics teachers but receives ten applications for every elementary opening and fifty for each physical education position. Local unions have a legitimate interest in bargaining a minimum starting salary for their members, but districts should be free to compensate teachers at higher levels to help fill a need.

Career ladders are another area that should warrant the attention of union leaders. Career ladders have been tried and abandoned in the past in the United States, typically because of cutbacks in spending. But the opportunity to advance along a career ladder is common practice in nations with the highest-performing school systems.

As mentioned earlier, teaching in this country is unique in that it offers little opportunity for a sense of advancement or recognition. In most professions, people have an opportunity to pursue expanded responsibility with corresponding increases in compensation. A bookkeeper in a large firm can strive for the position of accountant, then certified public accountant, then manager for one of the firm's major clients, then junior partner, and finally be embraced as a full partner. This is the way most professions operate. The teaching profession could too if unions worked with districts and states to establish career ladders for their members to navigate if they so desired.

Support Conditions for Professional Learning Communities

Both the National Education Association and the American Federation of Teachers have issued statements supporting the idea that schools should be organized into PLCs. Both organizations have put forth ideas and agendas for improving schools that are congruent with the PLC process. I have repeatedly witnessed, however, local collective bargaining processes in which union representatives threw up roadblocks to implementing the PLC process in their district.

For example, in some instances, union representatives have demanded extra compensation if teachers were to be expected to work together during their contractual day. Rather than seeing collaboration and collective responsibility as organic to school improvement, they insist they are add-ons, and therefore, teachers must be paid extra to do what best practice dictates they should already be doing.

There have been instances of union representatives resisting any effort to provide time for teachers to collaborate that does not require shutting down the schools and leaving issues such as child care, transportation, and supervision of children up to parents to resolve. They insist that these are problems that administrators must solve and are not the responsibility of the union. Some local unions continue to cling to the position that any effort to bring teachers together must not infringe on the individual teacher's assumed right to plan and prepare in isolation. They remain unmoved by the fact that there is virtually no evidence to suggest that individual planning and reflection have a positive impact on student learning and there is an abundance of evidence that teachers who engage in collaborative planning and reflection improve student learning. Collaboration represents a change in working conditions, and they must defend the status quo.

Furthermore, it is not uncommon for local unions to defend contract language that requires a super-majority of its members to approve revisions to current work conditions, such as creating weekly teacher collaboration time or an intervention period during the school day. Our Founding Fathers decided a simple majority was sufficient to pass most federal laws and approval of three-fourths of the states could revise the Constitution. It is tragically comical to think that it is easier to amend our nation's most sacred document than to revise the bell schedule of the local high school in some districts. Such policies allow a small minority of educators to trump the will of the majority, regardless of the professional merits of the change proposal. In reality, these policies are designed to defend the status quo by making change extremely difficult to enact.

In some districts, the local union has insisted that teachers must be free to use any collaborative time the district provides in any way they see fit. Once again, it is abundantly clear that unless educators focus on the right work, providing them with time to collaborate will not benefit either student or adult learning. In a truly *professional* learning community, union leaders and district leaders would build shared knowledge, or would learn together, about the nature of the right work and mutually pledge to support it. They would not allow sharing war stories; commiserating with each other; or swapping personal preferences on instruction, materials, or assessments to pass for professional collaboration.

Those who vilify teacher unions must remember, however, that unions have not received anything in either compensation or working conditions that legislatures and boards of education did not willingly give them. Local boards of education share fully in the culpability for failure to use the collective bargaining process in ways that enhance the teaching profession and the learning of students. Over the course of time, they have agreed to contract language that has constrained the district's ability to "select staff, promote staff, deploy staff, discipline staff, train staff, and let staff go when they were not doing the job" (Tucker, 2012).

> In a truly *professional* learning community, union leaders and district leaders would build shared knowledge, or would learn together, about the nature of the right work and mutually pledge to support it. . . . I remain convinced that teacher unions have been a positive force for progress in the United States and can be again.

So again, unions must decide, and soon, whether or not they want to play a leadership role in advancing meaningful reforms in this country. Assuming a role of leadership means they must be willing to relinquish some earlier victories and change long-standing positions. Their challenge is exacerbated by the fact that the National Education Association and American Federation of

Teachers have little control over the collective bargaining that occurs in the thousands of local school districts throughout the United States. Unlike Ontario, where negotiations can determine the direction of education for the entire province, each local teachers union in the United States has enormous discretion regarding its priorities and positions. Nevertheless, I remain convinced that teacher unions have been a positive force for progress in the United States and can be again. To be that positive force, however, they must do more than oppose America's current ill-advised and ineffective reform strategy. They must be willing to embrace a leadership role in articulating, advocating, and, most importantly, *acting on* a new agenda that is based on research that is proven to best serve students and educators alike.

CHAPTER 6

Laying the Foundation of a Professional Learning Community

In the first part of this book, I attempted to establish the following.

- American educators are under attack because of the allegation our schools are "failing" when, in fact, students are achieving at the highest levels in the history of the United States.

- The federal and state policies that dominate the school reform agenda in the United States are ill conceived, are based on faulty assumptions, and have no record of improving student achievement anywhere in the world.

- The predominant strategy to improve schooling in high-performing nations is to develop the capacity of educators by embracing and implementing the principles of the Professional Learning Communities at Work process.

- There are a number of reforms that the federal government, state governments, local school boards, and teacher unions could adopt that would have a positive impact on both student and adult learners in our schools.

In this second part of the book, I present the following truths.

- While our current generation of teachers is getting the best results in the history of our nation, these results are not good enough. A student's success in the K–12 system is an essential prerequisite for access to opportunities in the global economy.

- To achieve the goal of high levels of learning for all students, we must drastically reculture and restructure how schools have traditionally functioned.

- There has never been greater worldwide consensus on how to improve student achievement. The key to improving schools is developing the capacity of educators to function as members of high-performing teams in schools and districts that embrace the PLC process. This ongoing process requires educators to:

  > Work collaboratively in recurring cycles of collective inquiry and action research to achieve better results for the students they serve. Professional learning communities operate under the assumption that the key to improved learning for students is continuous, job-embedded learning for the educators. (DuFour, DuFour, Eaker, & Many, 2010, p. 11)

- Our profession has a better understanding than ever of the specific elements of the PLC process and what must be done to put those elements in place.

- Although the prevalent educational reform strategies in the United States are not aligned with the PLC process, educators in the United States have not been forbidden to bring the process to life in their schools and districts.

- In many schools and districts in which educators claim to be operating as PLCs, they have avoided the real work necessary to implement the process because they assign a higher priority to preserving their traditional structure and culture.

- When professionals become aware that there are better ways to meet the needs of those seeking their services, they have an obligation to apply the new practices. The great majority of American educators know better. It is time for them to do better. They must acknowledge that it is within their sphere of influence to create conditions that lead to higher levels of student and adult learning, and they must accept responsibility for doing so.

The use of the word *truths* to describe these points is deliberate. I could have opted to soften the statement by calling them *beliefs, hypotheses, assumptions,* or *assertions.* I am convinced, however, that the evidence to support each statement is so apparent and compelling that there is no need to hedge or equivocate. The remaining chapters directly challenge educators to fully implement the PLC process and provide specific steps and strategies for doing so.

> While our current generation of teachers is getting the best results in the history of our nation, these results are not good enough.

Laying the Foundation of the PLC Process

When educators visit one of the many schools that serve as a model of the PLC process (see "See the Evidence" on AllThingsPLC [www.allthingsplc.info/evidence] for examples), they are typically interested in learning what the educators in that school are doing to solve logistical problems. They pose such questions as:

- "How did you organize teachers into teams?"
- "How do you provide time for teachers to collaborate?"
- "What is your daily schedule, and how does it provide time for intervention or enrichment?"
- "Who selects the team leader?"
- "How are team leaders compensated?"
- "What happens if a teacher elects to opt out of the collaborative team process?"
- "What happens if students miss a deadline for turning in their work?"

These are certainly excellent questions that are worthy of consideration. But my first bit of advice to those about to implement the PLC process is to focus less on what educators in high-performing PLCs *do* and more on how the members of the organization *think*—the mindset of those educators. The assumptions, beliefs, expectations, and commitments of people in any organization shape the culture of that organization. The primary challenge in the PLC process is changing, and not merely tweaking, the existing culture. The best way to address that challenge is to engage the staff in building consensus regarding the four essential pillars of the PLC foundation—(1) shared mission, (2) vision, (3) collective commitments, and (4) goals—and then using that foundation to drive the daily work of the organization.

> The assumptions, beliefs, expectations, and commitments of people in any organization shape the culture of that organization. The primary challenge in the PLC process is changing, and not merely tweaking, the existing culture.

Each of the four pillars asks a different question of the educators within the organization (see figure 6.1). When teachers

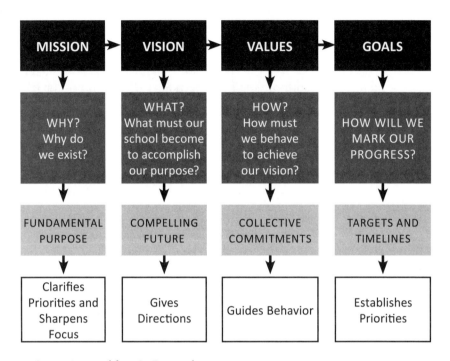

Source: Reprinted from DuFour et al., 2010, p. 31.

Figure 6.1: The foundation of a professional learning community.

and administrators have worked together to consider these questions and reached consensus on how to respond, the likelihood increases that all subsequent work will have the benefit of firm underpinnings. If staff members have not collectively considered each question, have done so only superficially, or are unable to establish common ground regarding their positions on the questions, any and all future efforts to improve will stand on shaky ground (DuFour et al., 2010).

Mission: Why Do We Exist?

In working with educators from around the world since the late 1990s, I have found that almost all educators work in organizations that have articulated a mission statement. These statements are intended to clarify the fundamental purpose and priorities of the organization for its members and the families they serve. Mission statements answer the question, *Why do we exist?* Most mission statements, whether they come from a school in New York, Alabama, Ontario, or Singapore, sound very similar to one another. In fact, they sound so familiar that in workshops, I ask educators to join me in choral response at certain points as I recite my version of the universal mission statement:

> It is the mission of our school to help each and every child realize his or her full potential and become a responsible and productive citizen and a lifelong learner who is able to use technology effectively and who appreciates the multicultural society in which we live as we prepare for the global challenges of the 21st century.

appreciate our indiv + strengths differences

This example resonates with most educators, and the choral response activity generates chuckles around the room. Please don't misunderstand. I am not making light of the sentiments reflected in the universal mission statement, as they do capture what the fundamental purpose of schools should be: ensuring high levels of learning for *all*. My point is this: most schools and districts have world-class mission statements. The task at hand for educators embarking on the PLC journey may not require writing a new mission statement but rather examining and aligning every practice, policy, and procedure to this fundamental purpose of the organization.

To make this point in a different way, I ask the same educators who just engaged in choral recitation to imagine that schools are now subjected to "truth in advertising" laws. What if every school had to post a mission statement that described the actual practices happening in the building? The results might sound like the following:

> **Candid mission statement 1:** It is our mission to help students learn *if* they are conscientious, responsible, attentive, developmentally ready, fluent in English, and come from homes with concerned parents who take an interest in their education.

Candid mission statement 2: Our mission is to create a school with an unrelenting focus on learning; *failure is not an option*. But, ultimately, it will be the responsibility of the student and his or her parents to take advantage of the opportunities for learning.

Candid mission statement 3: Our mission is to take credit for the accomplishments of our highest achieving students and to assign blame for low performance to others.

Candid mission statement 4: It is our mission to ensure the comfort and convenience of the adults in our organization. In order to promote this mission, we place a higher value on individual autonomy than we do in ensuring that all students learn. We will avoid any change or conversation that might create anxiety or discomfort or infringe on individual autonomy. (DuFour, DuFour, & Eaker, 2008, pp. 114–115)

If mission statements and practices are to align, educators have two choices. They can rewrite their mission statements to reflect their actual practices and traditional mindsets. Conversely, they can begin the difficult work of examining everything the adults do through the lens of a genuine commitment to ensuring high levels of learning for all students.

In the end, creating a learning-focused culture requires an organization to answer this question: Are we here to ensure students are *taught*, or are we here to ensure that our students *learn*? In too many schools, educators cling to the belief that it is their job to provide their students with the *opportunity* to learn but the ultimate responsibility for success or failure in

In the end, creating a learning-focused culture requires an organization to answer this question: Are we here to ensure students are *taught*, or are we here to ensure that our students *learn*?

school falls on each student and his or her parents. This teaching-focused approach is best captured by the common school mantra "It is the teacher's job to teach and the student's job to learn." Some educators have vehemently defended this belief, arguing that it is unfair to hold educators accountable for student success. But if educators believe that they have fulfilled their responsibility simply by presenting a lesson, it will be impossible for all students to learn at high levels. This approach is akin to a patient going for medical treatment and being told by the doctor, "I will try once to provide effective treatment for your ailment, but if my initial actions prove ineffective, I absolve myself of all responsibility—it is your job to come up with a better solution."

A learning-focused culture understands that the school was not built so that teachers have a place to teach—it was built so that the children of the community have a place to learn. These cultures acknowledge that when professionals with college degrees in specific subjects, and credentials in the pedagogies of instruction, provide initial teaching that is ineffective for some students, it is unrealistic to expect parents to be the solution. Instead, they accept responsibility to ensure that every student succeeds.

Why should we commit to learning for all? Part I of this book attempted to establish that current American educators have helped students reach unprecedented levels of achievement; however, it also stressed the need for dramatic improvement because the implications for students who are unsuccessful in school have never been more dire. The following section illustrates that point and establishes why it is so important that educators are committed to high levels of learning for all students.

We Must Prepare Students for Their Future, Not Our Past

- In 1973, only 28 percent of jobs required postsecondary education; by 2020, 65 percent of jobs will require postsecondary education.

- In 1970, 74 percent of the middle class was comprised of high school graduates and dropouts; in 2007, only 23 percent of the middle class was comprised of high school graduates, and only 8 percent were dropouts.

- Between 1970 and 2007, the percentage of middle-class Americans with college degrees increased from 26 percent to 69 percent.

- Between 1970 and 2007, the percentage of upper-class workers with postsecondary education and training increased from 44 percent to 81 percent. (Carnevale, Smith, & Strohl, 2010, 2013)

Those Who Have Not Learned How to Learn Will Be Left Behind

- By 2018, nine out of ten workers with a high school education or less will be limited to three occupation clusters—food and personal services, sales and office support, or blue-collar jobs—that either pay low wages or are in decline.

- In the next five years, sixty million Americans are at risk of being locked out of the middle class, toiling in low-wage jobs that require a high school education or less as employer demand for workers with postsecondary degrees and training continues to surge.

- In the 20th century, illiterates were those who could not read. In the 21st century, illiterates will be those who have not learned how to learn and continue their learning beyond the K–12 system. (Carnevale et al., 2010)

We Must Preserve the American Dream as the Land of Opportunity and Social Mobility

- A child born in the bottom 20 percent of family incomes is ten times more likely to stay there than a child in the top 20 percent is of falling to the bottom 20 percent (Greenstone, Looney, Patashnik, & Yu, 2013).

- A child born in the top 20 percent of family incomes is five times more likely to stay there than a child in the lower 20 percent is to rise to the top 20 percent (Greenstone et al., 2013).

- More than 80 percent of children in the top 20 percent of family incomes earn a bachelor's degree (Greenstone et al., 2013); a child born to a high school dropout has a one in seventeen chance of earning a bachelor's degree (Edsall, 2012).

- Education is the most powerful tool for helping students of poverty rise (Bendor, Bordoff, & Furman, 2007).

We Are Falling Behind the Rest of the World

- The United States dropped from first in the world in percentage of high school graduates to twenty-second out of twenty-seven advanced economies (Broad Foundation, n.d.).

- The United States dropped from first in the world in the percentage of young (twenty-five- to thirty-four-year-old) workers with college degrees to second in 1995 and to fourteenth in 2012 (Gurria, 2011).

- For the first time in American history, we have a higher percentage of fifty-five- to sixty-five-year-olds with college degrees than twenty-five- to thirty-five-year-olds (College Board, 2008).

Our Current System Isn't Working

- Potential dropouts can be predicted as early as first grade and identified with accuracy by third grade (American Psychological Association, 2012; Sparks, 2013).

- More than one-third of students entering college require remedial courses (Strong American Schools, 2008).

- Thirty-four percent of students who enter college drop out within the first year (ACT, 2013).

- Only 36 percent of students who enter a four-year public college earn a bachelor's degree within five years (ACT, 2013).

- Only 29 percent of those who pursue a two-year degree earn it within three years (ACT, 2013).

There Are Serious Implications for Those Who Fail

- Students who drop out of school are three times more likely to be unemployed (Breslow, 2012).

- These students are more likely to live in poverty (earn an annual salary of $20,241 or less; Breslow, 2012).

- High school dropouts in the United States earn thirty-five cents for every dollar a college graduate earns and sixty cents for every dollar a high school graduate earns. The United States has one of the largest income discrepancies between college graduates and high school dropouts of all major economies in the world (OECD, 2014b).

- Female dropouts will live an average of ten and a half fewer years than females who graduate from college. Male dropouts will live an average of thirteen fewer years than males who graduate from college. The gap for both sexes is widening (Tavernise, 2012).

- High school dropouts are sixty-three times more likely to be incarcerated (Breslow, 2012).

- On average, each high school dropout costs taxpayers $292,000 over his or her lifetime (Breslow, 2012).

Educators in PLCs embrace the mission of learning for all because they understand that if students don't learn, the stakes are too high, and the lifelong implications are too dire.

Educators in PLCs embrace the mission of learning for all because they understand that if students don't learn, the stakes are too high, and the lifelong implications are too dire. Therefore, they work to bring their mission to life by aligning what they *do* with what they say is their mission. Without a sincere commitment to help all students learn, it will be difficult for any district or school to bring the PLC process to life.

Vision: What Must We Become?

The vision pillar asks, "*What must we become in order to accomplish our fundamental purpose?*" In pursuing this question, educators collectively attempt to create a compelling, attractive, aspirational future that describes what they hope their organization will become in order to help all students learn.

When I survey educators in workshops and institutes and ask, "How many of you have a mission statement for your school or district?" virtually everyone stands up. When asked, "How many of you have a written shared vision statement for your organization—one that is known and owned by all the various stakeholders?"—far fewer answer in the affirmative. Many of those who do acknowledge that although there may be a vision document somewhere in a binder in their school or district, it was created by an individual or small group to satisfy a requirement and plays no role in driving school improvement.

The power of a vision statement will depend less on its eloquence and more on the degree to which stakeholders throughout the school or district share it and align their collective actions with it. The first step in establishing a meaningful vision statement is building shared knowledge among those stakeholders regarding both the current reality of the organization and the research base on effective schooling practices. The next step is engaging them in a dialogue about their hopes and dreams for their school or district. As Jim Kouzes and Barry Posner (2006) advise:

> The power of a vision statement will depend less on its eloquence and more on the degree to which stakeholders throughout the school or district share it and align their collective actions with it.

> If you're going to stir the souls of your constituents, if you are going to lift them to a higher level of performance, then this is what you need to know: It's not the leader's vision, it's the people's vision that matters most. (p. 113)

A vision statement that emerges on a poster from a board retreat is unlikely to impact the daily practices of an educator's life. A shared vision, however, can serve as a powerful catalyst for change.

A vision statement does not give explicit directions for proceeding on the school improvement journey, but it does provide a general sense of direction and shared priorities that benefits everyone in the organization. The journey can "begin with the end in mind" (Covey, 1990, p. 89). Very importantly, a shared vision serves as a filter for assessing both the current reality in the school and proposals for programs or procedures to improve upon that reality. The answer to the question, Does this align with and advance our vision? becomes a key criterion for making decisions.

According to a Japanese proverb, "Action without vision is a nightmare," but "Vision without action is just a daydream." Both observations are correct. Most educators are familiar with action without vision, as they have been caught up in the busywork of an endless parade of disconnected, fragmented new initiatives when their schools lurch from one direction to another. On the other hand, a vision that does not result in action is useless.

Creating a vision is a critical step in an improvement process, but it is never sufficient.

Addressing the first two pillars, mission and vision, is essential work but only represents half of the shared foundation of a PLC; there's more work to be done. When educators articulate the mission of their school, they can wax philosophic. When they describe the school they hope to create, they focus on the future, saying, in effect, "Someday we hope our school will be like this." But the third pillar of the foundation turns philosophy and aspirations into action because it addresses how each member of the organization can immediately contribute to moving the school or district in the right direction.

Collective Commitments (Values): How Must We Behave?

The third pillar of the foundation, the values pillar, clarifies the collective commitments members of each stakeholder group in the organization make to one another. The values pillar does not ask, "Why do we exist?" or "What do we hope to become?" Rather, it asks, *"How must we behave to create the organization we have described in our shared vision so we can better achieve our fundamental purpose?"* In addressing this question, educators shift from thinking about the future of their school to making commitments to act in certain ways—starting today.

> Collective commitments guide the individual work of each member of the staff and clearly describe how each person can contribute to the improvement initiative.

Collective commitments guide the individual work of each member of the staff and clearly describe how each person can contribute to the improvement initiative. When members of an organization understand the purpose of their organization, know where it is headed, and then pledge to act in certain ways to move it in the right direction, they don't need prescriptive rules and regulations to guide their daily work. Policy manuals and directives are replaced by commitments and covenants. As a result, members of the organization enjoy greater autonomy and creativity than their more rigidly supervised counterparts.

Most educators understand the importance of collective commitments and faithfully apply them—in their own classrooms. Teachers know that student learning begins with and is built upon a safe and orderly classroom. Unless students feel respected and procedures are clearly defined to ensure class time is used effectively, high levels of learning are impossible. Because creating these conditions is so important, teachers don't assume that all students will know and demonstrate positive academic and social behaviors but instead will clearly define, teach, and reinforce these expectations with their students.

These conditions are no different for adult learning in a PLC. Successful collaboration requires a learning environment in which individuals feel respected and procedures are developed to ensure that meeting time is used efficiently and effectively. These three collective commitments include:

1. Procedural meeting expectations, such as meeting attendance, punctuality, preparedness, division of labor, and the follow-through of team decisions

2. Behavioral expectations, including how the team will address disagreements between team members

3. Protocols to successfully address when team norms are violated

Without these expectations, adult collaboration can quickly digress into what a classroom looks like without clear student expectations: chaos.

Leaders benefit from clearly defined commitments as well. When leaders in traditional hierarchical structures address an employee's inappropriate behavior and demand change, their rationale tends to be "You are violating our policies" or "Because I am the boss, and I said so." If, however, the members of the organization have specified collective commitments, leaders operate with the full weight of the moral authority of the group behind them. Inappropriate behavior is recognized as a violation of collective commitments, and the leader moves from the role of "boss" to the promoter and protector of what the members have declared as important or sacred.

In his study of Adlai E. Stevenson High School in Lincoln-shire, Illinois, Thomas Sergiovanni (2005) stresses the important role that collective commitments have played in making the school a national model of the ongoing power of the PLC process. As he writes:

> The commitments of each of the constituent groups represents promises, and public promises at that. Teachers for example are telling students, administrators, and everyone else what they intend to do to implement the school's vision. Since promises made must be promises kept, Stevenson is not only developing an accountability system that is public, but a covenant of obligations that unites its various groups as a community of responsibility. (Sergiovanni, 2005, p. 60)

Finally, when educators achieve agreement about what they are prepared to start doing and then *implement* those agreements, they begin closing the gap between what we know schools should do and what schools have traditionally done—between the vision and their current reality. Those who "do" develop deeper knowledge, greater self-efficacy, and a stronger sense of ownership in results than those who only talk about what should be done (Pfeffer & Sutton, 2000). Attention to clarifying collective commitments is one of the most important and, regrettably, least utilized strategies in implementing and sustaining the PLC process. Very few of the educators who attend PLC workshops and institutes indicate that they have addressed this third pillar, but they all agree they should.

Schools that do address the commitments pillar will not benefit from the process if staff members are unwilling to hold each other accountable when the commitments are violated. As every teacher knows, the only classroom rules that matter are the ones that are actually enforced. Students quickly realize when rules are stated but not expected. Adult behavior is no different. In the absence of staff collective commitments and the willingness to hold each other accountable, schools often struggle with building a collaborative culture because of personal conflict and adult drama. Student learning suffers because adults are unable to establish a truly professional relationship.

Goals: How Will We Mark Our Progress?

The fourth pillar of the PLC foundation calls upon educators to clarify the goals they hope to achieve as they implement their improvement strategies. The goals pillar asks, *"How will we know if we are making progress toward our shared vision?"* Addressing this question allows educators to identify targets, timelines, and results—evidence that their new behaviors are making a positive difference for the students they serve.

The PLC process is grounded in the following three big ideas (DuFour et al., 2010).

1. We accept **learning** as the fundamental purpose of our school and therefore are willing to examine all practices in light of their impact on learning.

2. We are committed to working together to achieve our collective purpose. We cultivate a **collaborative culture** through the development of high-performing teams.

3. We assess our effectiveness on the basis of **results** rather than intentions. Individuals, teams, and schools seek relevant data and information and use that information to promote continuous improvement.

Effective goals are essential components of those big ideas. A focus on learning rather than teaching requires evidence that content has not only been taught but learned. Goals provide a means of tracking that evidence. Furthermore, goals are absolutely essential to the collaborative team process. In the absence of a common goal, there can be no true team. Effective goals generate joint effort and help collaborative teams clarify how their work can contribute to organizational improvement initiatives. Finally, well-written goals demand evidence of results rather than activity. The next chapter will offer examples of results-oriented goals.

> In the absence of a common goal, there can be no true team.

A results-oriented culture is attentive to finding a balance between the attainable goals that teams feel they can achieve in the short term and stretch goals—goals so ambitious they could not possibly be achieved unless practices within the organization change significantly. In a school with a 70 percent graduation rate and a 30 percent failure rate, stretch goals such as "Within the next five years, 100 percent of our students will graduate on time" or "Our school will have a 0 percent failure rate" will not be accomplished in the short term. They instead serve as targets that beckon. Reaching the target will require incremental progress. More importantly, continuing the same practices and policies that have resulted in high failure and dropout rates will make it impossible to reach the goals. Stretch goals ultimately require all members of an organization to change the way they work and the way they *think* in order to achieve significantly better results.

It is equally important, however, that in addition to stretch goals, educators establish short-term goals and identify the steps they will take to achieve them. Achievable short-term goals are vital to creating a sense of positive momentum and contributing to the confidence and self-efficacy of a staff. Confidence is merely "positive expectations for favorable outcomes" (Kanter, 2004, p. 7). When people expect to be successful, they are more likely to put forth the effort to ensure it. Establishing clear, results-oriented short-term goals and purposefully and publicly celebrating progress toward the achievement of those goals are powerful motivational strategies, strategies that appeal to intrinsic motivation rather than carrots and sticks (Amabile & Kramer, 2011; Pink, 2009).

Thus, goals play a key role in motivating people to honor their commitments so a school can move closer to fulfilling its fundamental purpose of learning for *all*. Once again, educational researchers and organizational theorists provide abundant evidence on the importance of measurable goals as a key element in improvement. Most educators would acknowledge that goal setting is not a new idea; however, in traditional schools and districts, goals often take the form of projects and tasks to be completed by educators. In the PLC process, goals must be results oriented: "If we achieve our goal, more students will learn at higher levels."

> When people expect to be successful, they are more likely to put forth the effort to ensure it.

How Long Does It Take to Build a Shared Foundation?

When I first began the principalship at Adlai E. Stevenson High School in Lincolnshire, Illinois, in 1983, I worked closely with union leaders and department chairs to help everyone in the organization build shared knowledge about both the school's current reality and best practices regarding school improvement. Through collaborative study and dialogue in small-group sessions conducted over the first few weeks of the school year, the faculty of that comprehensive high school addressed the four essential pillars and was able to achieve consensus on each. The board of education adopted the mission, vision, and collective commitments as board policy, the first policy in its voluminous policy manual. Members of the board pledged that they would use that policy as the primary factor in making decisions. A copy of the mission and vision, as well as the different collective commitments that had been established by the board, administration, faculty, and support staff, was sent to every resident. All this was accomplished within the first nine weeks of the school year, and the school improvement journey was well underway.

The board also adopted three long-term stretch goals.

1. We will eliminate student failure.

2. We will dramatically increase the percentage of students who succeed in the most rigorous curriculum in every department.

3. We will increase the school's mean score on the ACT exam from 21.9 to 26.0.

The original vision and collective commitment statements created in 1983 have been slightly modified four times in the intervening years. The mission and goals have remained constant. The foundation has served as the core of the orientation program for all new staff and students each year. In 2015, more than thirty years later, despite dramatic changes in student enrollment (from 1,600 students to 4,500), the retirement of the faculty who built Stevenson's foundation, and multiple changes in every leadership position within the district, educators and students at Stevenson continue to be guided by a clear purpose, a deep understanding of the ideal school they are trying to create, the collective commitments necessary to move the school in the right direction, and the targets that help them mark their progress. To access the current shared mission, vision, collective commitments, and goals that drive their daily work, visit Stevenson's webpage (www.d125.org).

A similar process can be used to establish a shared foundation for an entire district rather than a single school. For an example of a district's shared foundation and a description of the process used to build it, visit School District 54's mission and goals page (http://sd54.org/board/mission).

Not Just Words on a Piece of Paper

Educators reading this chapter may be inclined to dismiss its message. After all, their school probably has a mission statement, they have a vague sense of what they want their school to become, and they write school improvement goals every year. So they might conclude that this chapter offers nothing new: "We've been there, done that."

It is evident, however, that in many schools, the steps outlined in this chapter are perfunctory exercises that have little impact on the day-to-day practices of the educators within them. When I asked one principal if his school was guided by a shared vision, the principal was unable to articulate that vision. He was able, however, after considerable searching, to retrieve a document that had been written, filed, and forgotten several years earlier. It was comical to hear him ask his secretary if she knew where his vision was.

In another example, I met with each of a school district's school improvement teams to review their plans for raising student achievement. The plans were voluminous, addressing ninety-five different areas for potential improvement that were based on four or five broad goals. But, when the teams were asked how many of them could list those four or five improvement goals for their school, not a single member could do so. The fact is, schools don't have goals; people do (or don't). If a faculty is unaware of the school's goals, there are no goals.

A shared foundation can serve as a powerful catalyst for school improvement. It is devoid of power, however, if educators view addressing the foundation as merely a task to complete before they return to business as usual.

> Schools don't have goals; people do (or don't). If a faculty is unaware of the school's goals, there are no goals.

When a strong foundation is truly guiding the members of a PLC, they don't view it as a document to be put on a shelf or sent to the central office and forgotten. They use it constantly to examine every existing and proposed process, program, and procedure and collectively ask:

- "Is this consistent with our purpose?"
- "Will it help us become the school we envision?"
- "Are we prepared to commit to doing this?"
- "Will it help us to achieve our goals?"

The shared foundation becomes the lens through which educators examine their own current reality and ask, "Are we engaging in practices and processes that are preventing our students from learning at high levels?" When a misalignment between practice and shared foundation is discovered, educators build shared knowledge—learn together—about better or best practice. As new practices are identified through this collective inquiry, members of the PLC engage in action research—learning by doing—in order to achieve better results for the students they serve. Over time, this cycle of examining traditional practice; learning better ways; implementing the newly learned concepts, skills, strategies, and processes; and very importantly, evaluating the changes on the basis of student results ultimately leads to a new culture and thus a new mindset about teaching and learning.

The process of creating the foundation of a PLC is yet another area within the sphere of influence of educators where they can do something well and have a profound impact on shaping the culture of their school, or they can go through the motions while continuing to embrace the status quo. Going through the motions leads to a misalignment between stated priorities and actual behavior. People throughout the organization receive mixed messages that undermine credibility and generate cynicism. When a state proclaims the importance of having highly qualified educators in every classroom but persists in making it easier for virtually anyone to teach without formal training, it sends the message that teaching is not a true profession. When a district calls on educators to work together and take collective responsibility for student learning but then offers merit pay bonuses for individual teachers whose students perform well on standardized tests, educators realize that the system rewards individualism rather than collaborative efforts. When a principal asserts a school is committed to a collaborative culture and helping all students learn but then fails to provide time for teachers to collaborate or for struggling students to receive additional time and support for learning, the claim is recognized as rhetoric rather than reality. When teachers agree to work in collaborative teams to better serve their students but individual teachers continue to teach what they want when they want, assess however they want, and apply their own criteria to evaluating the quality of student work, it is clear that individual autonomy is the greater priority.

But if building the foundation is done well, a natural outcome is the creation of a collaborative culture and collective responsibility for student learning, the topic of the next chapter.

[Handwritten annotations:] Vision should drive individual goals for recert — how will it impact student learning

Our Commitment — We commit to the students of Brits that we will

CHAPTER 7

The Imperative of a Collaborative Culture

In every decade since the 1970s, researchers have concluded that one of the major obstacles to substantive school improvement in the United States is the long-standing tradition of teacher isolation. Since 1971, psychologist Seymour Sarason (1996) has reported that because teachers rarely have contact with one another, they "are psychologically alone even though they are in a densely populated setting" and that they adapt to being alone by creating a culture of *individuals* concerned about himself or herself rather than a culture of *group* concerned with the pursuit of the profession's best practices (p. 133). In his 1975 book, Dan Lortie describes how the isolation of classroom teachers prevents them from developing and sharing knowledge of their craft.

The 1980s brought John Goodlad's (1984) analysis of the work of teachers and his conclusion that teacher autonomy and isolation cause them to make decisions on curriculum, assessment, and instruction without the benefit of input from colleagues. Susan Rosenholtz (1986) notes two distinctly different school cultures: one in which collaboration, continuous improvement, and shared learning were the norm and the other in which autonomy and privatization left the question of quality teaching up to individual teachers to pursue according to their very different perspectives of quality.

In the 1990s came Judith Warren Little's (1990) critique of school cultures titled *The Persistence of Privacy*, Ann Lieberman's (1995) finding that the most powerful impediment to school improvement is teacher isolation, and the National Commission on Teaching and America's Future (1996), which concludes that the norm of teachers working in isolation prevents the collaboration and shared learning essential to improving student achievement.

The turn of the century brought Richard Elmore's (2004) critiques of the *pathologies* of American schooling that leave "all matters of practice as matters of idiosyncratic taste and preference . . . in which isolation is the norm" (p. 87). Judith Warren Little and her colleagues (Little, Gearhart, Curry, & Kafka, 2003) re-emerged with the lament that the culture of isolation, privacy, noninterference, and the unwillingness of teachers to work together to examine evidence of student learning continues to prevent teachers from getting around to the hard work of improving instruction. Yet another study concludes, "The most persistent norm that stands in the way of 21st century learning is isolated teaching in stand-alone classrooms" (Fulton, Yoon, & Lee, 2005, p. 1).

In 2012, a study of high-performing systems finds that the tendency of American teachers to close their classroom doors and work in isolation makes peer learning impossible (Stewart, 2012). Two other studies comparing the United States to systems around the world finds that American teachers cling to the traditional view of working in a closed classroom in isolation from colleagues (OECD, 2013c) and that such isolation "is the enemy of consistent improvement" (Mehta, 2013).

Elmore (2003) is merely repeating more than thirty years of consistent findings when he writes:

> The design of work in schools is fundamentally incompatible with the practice of improvement. Teachers

spend most of their time working in isolation from each other in self-contained classrooms. . . . The problem with this design is that it provides almost no opportunity for teachers to engage in continuous and sustained learning about their practice in the setting in which they actually work. . . . This disconnect between the requirements of learning to teach well and the structure of teachers' work life is fatal to any sustained process of instructional improvement. (p. 127)

This isolation has not been foisted on educators; they have readily embraced it.

John Goodlad (1984) finds that teachers prefer working in isolation because it allows them to conduct teaching in a cloak of privacy and autonomy, which, in turn, creates a powerful force for maintaining the status quo. Roland Barth (1991) laments that "God didn't create self-contained classrooms, fifty minute periods, and subjects taught in isolation. *We* did—because we find working alone safer and more preferable to working together" (p. 128).

> This isolation has not been foisted on educators; they have readily embraced it.

Little has changed in the decades since these observations. Since 2010, I have asked tens of thousands of educators to complete this sentence if they had ever said it or heard it said in their school: "I wish they would just give me my room, give me my kids, and . . ." Each time, the audience answers with an enthusiastic "Leave me alone!"

Our profession will not benefit from yet another study calling attention to the need to overcome teacher isolation in order to achieve substantive school improvement. Nor will it benefit from further additions to the already overwhelming research base, from both inside and outside of education, on the importance of and benefits derived from a culture and climate that foster collaboration and collective responsibility. When the National Education Association, the American Federation of Teachers, the National

Board of Professional Teaching Standards, the National Commission on Teaching and America's Future, the National Council of Teachers of Mathematics, the National Council of Teachers of English, the National Science Teachers Association, the National Association of Secondary School Principals, the National Association of Elementary School Principals, the National Middle School Association, Learning Forward, and the North Central Association on Accreditation and School Improvement urge their members to work collaboratively to bring the PLC process to life in their schools, there is little reason to believe another endorsement from yet another professional organization will somehow create the tipping point for concerted action.*

It is impossible to justify the enormous gap between what is generally recognized as best practice in our field and the actual conditions that continue to exist in too many schools. The members of our profession have not been forbidden to close that gap; we simply have chosen not to do so. Until teachers and administrators acknowledge their responsibility for perpetuating isolation and commit to creating a new culture of schooling, little is likely to change.

> It is impossible to justify the enormous gap between what is generally recognized as best practice in our field and the actual conditions that continue to exist in too many schools. The members of our profession have not been forbidden to close that gap; we simply have chosen not to do so.

Laying the Groundwork for a Powerful Collaborative Culture

Chapter 6 emphasized the importance of building the PLC process on a solid foundation of shared mission, vision, collective commitments, and goals. If that foundation reflects what we

For examples of research and endorsements, see "Finding Common Ground in Education Reform, Professional Learning Community Advocates—A Presentation of the Research" on www.allthingsplc.info (www.allthingsplc.info/files/uploads/advocates.pdf).

know to be best practice, it will call for creating a collaborative culture and for commitments on the part of teachers and administrators alike to commit and contribute to such a culture. Three keys to moving forward will be assigning people to meaningful teams (rather than groups), providing time for educators to work together, and ensuring there is clarity regarding the right work.

Assigning People to Meaningful Teams

The fundamental structure of a school or district embracing the PLC process will be the collaborative team of educators rather than isolated classrooms or schools. The key term here is *team*. By *team*, I do not mean loosely connected groups that assemble for traditional grade-level, department, faculty, or parent-conference meetings. A team, by definition, operates differently from a group. Members of a team work *interdependently* to achieve *common goals* for which members are *mutually accountable*. Absent these three key elements, a group may be congenial or collegial, but its members are not a team. Groups don't become teams simply because that is what someone labels them. The act of meeting together does not define a team. Committees or task forces can serve useful purposes in a school or district, but they are not teams either.

Since the fundamental purpose of a PLC is to ensure high levels of learning for students, the goals that team members establish should specifically call for evidence of improved learning for the students they serve (Timperley & Alton-Lee, 2008). These goals are results oriented rather than activity oriented. "We will implement the Common Core State Standards for our grade level" could serve as a commitment made by a team or a strategy members will use to improve student achievement, but it is not a goal. The focus of that statement is what teachers will do. There is no reference to how it will impact student learning.

> Members of a team work *interdependently* to achieve *common goals* for which members are *mutually accountable.*

The SMART goals acronym can help teams establish appropriate goals. A SMART goal is (O'Neill & Conzemius, 2006):

Strategic and specific—The team's goal aligns with the goals of the school or district.

Measurable—The goal includes quantifiable terms.

Attainable—The team believes the goal is achievable.

Results oriented—The goal requires evidence of improved student learning.

Time bound—The goal will be accomplished within a specific period of time.

The following are examples of appropriate SMART goals for teams.

- Last year, 73 percent of our students met the proficiency standard on the state assessment. This year, 80 percent of our students will meet that standard.

- Last year, 75 students scored 3 or higher on the AP exam in United States history. This year, 85 students will score 3 or higher on that exam.

- Last year, when we gave this unit assessment, 78 percent of our students were able to establish a central claim. This year, 83 percent of our students will demonstrate that proficiency on the assessment.

- Last year, 89 percent of our students reached level 3 on our 5-point rubric for this art project. This year, 94 percent of our students will reach level 3 on the project.

A team of principals might establish the following SMART goal: "Last year, 15 of our 27 schools achieved the district benchmark of 90 percent student proficiency in both reading and mathematics. This year, we will work together to get at least 20 schools to reach that benchmark."

Note that the team may elect a state indicator, national indicator, local indicator, or combinations thereof. The goal may be for an entire year, a semester, or a unit. But in every instance, the team is committed to using past student achievement as a benchmark for improved student learning.

Goals that adhere to the SMART acronym should be established *by* teams rather than *for* teams. Teams that set their own goals are much more committed to achieving them than when someone else establishes the goal for the team (Pink,

> Goals that adhere to the SMART acronym should be established *by* teams rather than *for* teams.

2009). It is imperative, however, that every team establishes one or more goals because, by definition, the absence of a goal precludes members from functioning as a team. Furthermore, without goals that are immediately applicable to student learning, "teams will drift toward superficial discussions and truncated efforts" (Gallimore, Ermeling, Saunders, & Goldenberg, 2009, p. 548).

At the school level, the most powerful team structure is typically the grade-level team in elementary schools and course-specific or subject-area teams in secondary schools. These structures readily align with shared responsibility for student learning. Teams based on common content are much better suited to the process of clarifying essential outcomes, gathering evidence of student learning, assessing the effectiveness of varied instructional strategies, engaging in action research, and learning from one another (Forum for Education and Democracy, 2008; Fulton & Britton, 2011; Little & Bartlett, 2010; Stigler & Hiebert, 2009). Other structures such as interdisciplinary teams, vertical teams, or districtwide teams can also be effective, provided that team members share essential learning outcomes and their focus is on a collective effort to improve student achievement.

With a SMART goal in place, teams should clarify the commitments they are prepared to make to one another regarding how they will work to accomplish their goal. Common commitments represent the essence of a team (Katzenbach & Smith, 2006). These commitments are best stated as specific behaviors rather than beliefs. "We believe in sharing the workload" is not a commitment. "I will be a fully participating member of the team" is. Each member of the team should participate in clarifying the commitments and should agree to honor them. Additionally, the team should determine how members will address violations of their team norms. Once the norms are in place, teams should reference them at the beginning and end of each meeting until they become fully internalized (Goleman, Boyatzis, & McKee, 2004).

Commitment building is central to the interaction of the collaborative team process. The best teams recognize that "at its core, team accountability is about the promises we make to ourselves and others, promises that underpin two critical aspects of teams: commitment and trust" (Katzenbach & Smith, 2006).

Teams that are clear on their goals and the commitments they make to achieve them are much more effective and find participation far more rewarding than groups that are inattentive to these two crucial elements of high-performing teams (Goleman et al., 2004; Lencioni, 2005). Conversely, inattention to establishing goals and clarifying expectations is one of the most frequent causes of team failure (Blanchard, 2007).

Providing Time for Collaboration

When I asked educators at the turn of the 21st century if they were provided with time to meet with their colleagues on a regular basis during the contractual day, very few answered in the affirmative. By 2015, the great majority indicate that they do have structured time to collaborate. This time has been provided in a number of creative ways. The reproducible from *Learning by Doing, Second Edition* (DuFour et al., 2010) provides a brief overview of ways schools and districts are addressing the challenge of time. (See figure 7.1, pages 129–130.)

Common Preparation Time

Build the master schedule to provide daily common preparation periods for teachers of the same course or department. Each team should then designate one day each week to engage in collaborative, rather than individual, planning.

Parallel Scheduling

Schedule common preparation time by assigning the specialists to provide lessons to students across an entire grade level at the same time each day. The team should designate one day each week for collaborative planning. Some schools build back-to-back specials classes into the master schedule on each team's designated collaborative day, thus creating an extended block of time for the team to meet. Specials teachers must also be given time to collaborate.

Adjusted Start and End Time

Gain collaborative time by starting the workday early or extending the workday one day each week. In exchange for adding time to one end of the workday, teachers get the time back on the other end of that day. For example, on Tuesdays, the entire staff of Adlai Stevenson High School in Lincolnshire, Illinois, begins its workday at 7:30 a.m. rather than the normal 7:45 a.m. start time. From 7:30 to 8:30 a.m., the entire faculty engages in collaborative team meetings. Classes, which usually begin at 8:05 a.m., are delayed until 8:30 a.m. Students who can arrange for their own transportation arrive to school then. Buses run their regular routes so that no parent is inconvenienced and students are delivered to the school at 7:40 a.m. Upon their arrival they are supervised by administrative and noninstructional staff in a variety of optional activities (such as breakfast, library and computer research, open gym, study halls, and tutorials) until classes begin. To make up for the twenty-five minutes of lost instructional time, five minutes is trimmed from five of the eight fifty-minute class periods. The school day ends at the usual time (3:25 in the afternoon), and again buses run on their regular schedules. Because they began work fifteen minutes early (7:30 rather than 7:45), Stevenson teachers are free to leave fifteen minutes earlier than the normal conclusion of their workday (3:30 rather than 3:45). By making these minor adjustments to the schedule one day each week, the entire faculty is guaranteed an hour of collaborative planning without extending their workday or workweek by a single minute.

Source: DuFour et al., 2010, pp. 125–127.

Figure 7.1: How schools are addressing the challenge of time.

Continued →

Shared Classes

Combine students across two different grade levels or courses into one class for instruction. While one teacher or team instructs the students, the other team engages in collaborative work. The teams alternate instructing and collaborating to provide equity in learning time for students and teams. Some schools coordinate shared classes so older students adopt younger students and serve as literacy buddies, tutors, and mentors during shared classes.

Group Activities, Events, and Testing

Teams of teachers coordinate activities that require supervision of students rather than instructional expertise, such as watching an instructional DVD or video, conducting resource lessons, reading aloud, attending assemblies, or testing. Nonteaching staff members supervise students while teachers engage in team collaboration.

Banked Time

Over a designated period of days, extend the instructional minutes beyond the required school day. After you have banked the desired number of minutes, end the instructional day early to allow for faculty collaboration and student enrichment. For example, in a middle school, the traditional instructional day ends at 3:00 p.m., students board buses at 3:20, and the teachers' contractual day ends at 3:30. The faculty may decide to extend the instructional day until 3:10. By teaching an extra ten minutes for nine days in a row, they "bank" ninety minutes. On the tenth day, instruction stops at 1:30, and the entire faculty has collaborative team time for two hours. The students remain on campus and are engaged in clubs, enrichment activities, assemblies, and so on, sponsored by a variety of parent and community partners and cosupervised by the school's nonteaching staff.

In-Service and Faculty Meeting Time

Schedule extended time for teams to work together on staff development days and during faculty meeting time. Rather than requiring staff to attend a traditional whole-staff in-service session or sit in a faculty meeting while directives and calendar items are read aloud, shift the focus and use of these days and meetings so members of teams have extended time to learn with and from each other.

As mentioned in chapter 4, American educators spend more time in direct instruction and less time collaborating with their colleagues than educators in most countries. This continues to be true even with the steps that have been taken in recent years to provide time for collaboration.

Providing adequate time for professional collaboration will require a re-examination of long-standing assumptions both by policymakers and educators. Policymakers must recognize that developing curriculum, planning lessons, creating assessments, analyzing evidence of student learning to inform professional practice, and engaging in action research are vital to the teaching and learning process and are best addressed when teachers work together rather than in isolation.

Educators must consider abandoning unexamined practices and positions that have been exempt from questioning. They are correct to value individual teacher preparation time, but it should not be viewed as a fundamental right on par with life, liberty, and the pursuit of happiness. There is no evidence that reflective preparation and teaching by an isolated teacher have a positive impact on student learning; however, there is abundant evidence that reflective teaching is powerful when it is collective and based on evidence of student learning (Hattie, 2009). Yet there are educators who insist they must have five hours of personal planning time each week while they resist devoting even one hour to collaborative work. The only rationale for this position is "This is how we have always done it." Tradition and the status quo trump evidence of best practice.

> Providing adequate time for professional collaboration will require a re-examination of long-standing assumptions both by policymakers and educators.

Something that is even more sacred to educators than preparation time is the imperative of small class sizes. Everyone—teachers, administrators, parents, and sometimes even policymakers—is in favor of small class size. I recognize that I may be branded a heretic for the following statement, nevertheless: *there is little evidence to suggest that, beyond the primary grades, smaller class size has a positive impact on student achievement.*

In 1996, California launched a program to dramatically reduce class size in elementary schools from an average of twenty-nine to twenty students. After six years and $7 billion in expenditures, three things were evident: (1) the program was very popular with parents and teachers, (2) instructional practices had not changed, (3) and there was little to no impact on student achievement (Bohrnstedt & Stecher, 2002).

The California findings are not unique. An analysis of 112 studies that look at the impact of class size on student achievement finds only nine that indicate a positive relationship, and even then, the effect was not substantial (Barber & Mourshed, 2007). Hattie's (2009) synthesis of research on class size led to his conclusion that "merely reducing the number of students in front of teachers appears to change little—in teaching and in outcomes" (p. 88). Attempting to improve student learning by reducing class size is one of the most expensive and least productive strategies a state or district might pursue, and yet it remains a top priority for educators (Hanushek & Rivkin, 2006; Shyamalan, 2013; Tucker, 2014).

In light of these findings, one way to increase the amount of time for teachers to collaborate at the secondary level would be to increase class sizes. For example, assume a high school English teacher is responsible for 120 students. The teacher could be assigned to teach five fifty-minute classes each day with twenty-four students each or four classes with thirty students. The larger class size would provide the teacher with an additional 250 minutes each week that could be devoted to collaborative work with colleagues or small-group work with students. This is standard practice in countries like Japan, where the ratio of students to teachers is similar to the United States but the classes are considerably larger so that teachers have more time to work with colleagues.

With literally thousands of schools in the United States now providing time for teachers to collaborate on a regular

basis during their contractual day, it is
becoming more difficult for school
administrators to assert they are unable
to find time for teachers to collaborate.
No one "finds" time for collaboration;
we must *make* time for collaboration. It
is disingenuous for any district or school to claim that collaboration is a priority and then fail to provide adequate time for
educators to engage in collaboration. What has become abundantly clear, however, is that merely providing time for educators
to collaborate will not improve student achievement unless they
devote their attention and energy to the right work.

> No one "finds" time
> for collaboration;
> we must *make* time
> for collaboration.

Avoiding the Real Work of Collaborative Teams

Members of a profession are obligated to seek out and apply
the best practices in their field to meet the needs of those they
serve. In light of the preponderance of evidence supporting collaborative structures and culture and the absence of evidence
demonstrating the benefits of teacher isolation, the collaborative
team should be the fundamental structure of every school. Yet
there are schools and districts that ignore readily available common knowledge and continue with a traditional structure that
results in teacher isolation. They assign a greater priority to preserving the status quo than they do to supporting student and
adult learning.

There are also schools and districts that look for ways to provide the illusion of collaboration while avoiding the real work of
a collaborative team. They make participation on a collaborative
team optional because individual comfort and happiness trump
best practice.

They accept the idea that it is impossible for a teacher to collaborate if no one in the building teaches what he or she teaches.
It is evident that proximity does not ensure collaboration. Two
teachers can be in classrooms that are side by side yet work in

total isolation. It is equally evident that with today's technology, distance does not negate the possibility of collaboration with someone outside the building. Nevertheless, singleton teachers are allowed to opt out of the process or, perhaps worse, are assigned to the "leftover" team in which the principal tells an art teacher, music teacher, physical education teacher, and industrial arts teacher to "go collaborate."

There are schools and districts that assign people to groups rather than teams. Members meet on a regular basis, but the essential elements of teamwork—interdependence, common goals, and mutual accountability—are nonexistent. Groups are often created on the basis of personal interests rather than shared responsibility. There may be groups for student discipline, parent involvement, faculty morale, and so on—topics worthy of consideration but inattentive to the focus on student and adult learning that drives the work of a collaborative team in a PLC.

The most common shortcut of the collaborative team process is assigning educators to grade-level or course-specific teams and allowing "collaboration lite" to substitute for the real work of high-performing teams. Members settle for coordination instead of true collaboration. If team meetings focus on who will make copies of handouts for the upcoming unit, planning field trips, commiserating about students, sharing war stories, or discussing personal preferences for teaching a particular concept, there is no reason to anticipate that students will learn at higher levels.

A study of districts that implemented the PLC process for a minimum of three years attempted to ascertain why some districts experienced dramatic gains in student achievement while in others achievement remained flat. The study reveals that both high- and low-yield districts provide time for teachers to collaborate. The difference in achievement in those districts was a function of what occurred during the team meetings. High-yield districts put processes in place to ensure that teams are focused on the right work.

Achieving Clarity Regarding the Right Work

Educators can sincerely believe that ensuring all students learn at high levels is their fundamental mission, but genuine conviction and a sense of moral purpose do not ensure that they are clear on how to proceed. A major obstacle to successful implementation of the PLC process is the lack of clarity regarding what that process entails. Over and over, I see schools and districts that claim to be professional learning communities that do none of the things that PLCs actually do.

A survey by the Boston Consulting Group (2014) on teacher perceptions of effective professional development illustrates the point. According to the survey, teachers prefer professional development that is relevant to their context, helps them plan and improve their instruction, is teacher driven, includes hands-on strategies applicable to their classrooms, is highly interactive, is sustained over time, and recognizes that teachers are professionals with valuable insights. These are the exact conditions that effective collaborative teams create in high-performing PLCs. In fact, the 7 percent of the teachers in the survey who saw themselves as members of strong collaborative cultures report significant benefits in their day-to-day work in key areas, such as planning lessons, developing teaching skills and content, and aligning curriculum and expectations. They report "dramatically higher satisfaction with day-to-day work" and their "perceived effectiveness" (Boston Consulting Group, 2014, p. 8). Educators who actually engage in the right work in their collaborative teams find it exceptionally valuable.

But when the consulting group asked teachers to assess the professional development in their own districts, they gave their lowest marks to what they called professional learning communities. Teachers report that in their district, working in a team is just "another meeting," a place to "share their frustrations," or "a social hour" (Boston Consulting Group, 2014, p. 7). If these are accurate characterizations of their meetings with colleagues, they are correct that these meetings are a waste of their time. They are completely wrong, however, to suggest that what they are doing has anything to do with the PLC process.

Both the Job Outlook 2012 and Job Outlook 2015 surveys of employers found that what they value most in a prospective employee is "the ability to work in a team structure" (National Association of Colleges and Employers, 2011, 2014). This ability was rated 4.6 on a 5.0 scale, with 4 being very important and 5 representing extremely important.

Albert Einstein once said that "example isn't another way to teach, it's the only way to teach." How tragic it will be if educators, the members of the institution established to prepare students for their future, are unable to model the very behavior deemed most important to the success of those students.

Improving schooling will require significant changes in the behavior of educators—teachers and administrators alike. When it comes to making those changes, ambiguity is the enemy. Lofty goals and nebulous aspirations ("We must become more collaborative") must be translated into concrete tasks and behaviors because "the hardest part of change—the paralyzing part—is precisely in the details" (Heath & Heath, 2010, p. 53). Subsequent chapters address the details of the right work of collaborative teams in PLCs.

CHAPTER 8

Providing Students With Access to a Guaranteed and Viable Curriculum

It is not unusual for educators in a district or school to assert that the core mission of their organization is to ensure that all students will learn. But until they collectively address the fundamental question, "Learn what?" such an assertion will remain empty rhetoric rather than a commitment to student success.

Both common sense and a solid research base support the importance of educator clarity regarding the specific knowledge, skills, and dispositions all students should acquire as a result of their schooling. Terms may vary.

- A guaranteed and viable curriculum (Marzano, 2003)
- Learning standards that are most essential (Reeves, 2002)
- Essential curricular goals (Lezotte, n.d.)
- A compact list of learning expectations (Saphier, 2005)
- Enduring understandings (Tomlinson & McTighe, 2006)
- Learning intentions (Hattie, 2012)

What is consistent is the notion that if all students are to acquire the intended outcomes—of their schooling, their grade level, their subject, and each unit of instruction—educators must be crystal clear on and committed to teaching those outcomes.

What is also evident is the growing consensus that the curriculum needed to provide all students with the knowledge, skills, and dispositions required for the 21st century will be far more rigorous and challenging than either teachers or students are accustomed. The National Governors Association Center for Best Practices and Council of Chief State School Officers (2008) call for Common Core State Standards in mathematics and language arts to be benchmarked against the highest-performing nations in the world. Educators must now ensure that *every* student who graduates from high school is ready for college or a career and is equipped with the following abilities (Conley, 2007; EdLeader21, n.d.; Hewlett Foundation, 2012; Partnership for 21st Century Schools, 2009; Pellegrino & Hilton, 2012).

What does that look like in 2nd grade? maked chart

- Critical-thinking skills and problem-solving skills
- Creativity and innovation
- Effective communication through clear and convincing written and oral expression
- Collaboration skills
- Inferential reasoning
- Analytical-thinking skills
- Self-directed learning (in other words, having learned how to learn)
- Transference of learning to new situations
- Evaluation of sources for importance and credibility
- Openness to and utilization of critical feedback

An analysis of the comparative rigor of traditional state tests and the assessments being prepared by the two consortia charged with creating the assessments for the Common Core State Standards (CCSS) illustrate the challenge educators are facing. Norman Webb has modified Benjamin Bloom's taxonomy to classify depth of knowledge (DOK) criteria into the following four levels, with levels 3 and 4 representing deeper learning (Herman & Linn, 2013).

- **DOK 1:** Basic comprehension
- **DOK 2:** Application of concepts or procedures involving some mental processing
- **DOK 3:** Applications requiring abstract thinking, reasoning, or more complex inferences
- **DOK 4:** Extended analysis or investigation that requires synthesis and analysis across multiple contexts and nonroutine applications

Table 8.1 (pages 139–140) illustrates the new focus on higher-order skills.

Table 8.1: Projected Increase in Rigor Using Webb's Depth of Knowledge Criteria

State Assessments	Consortia Assessment Specifications
No students were assessed with items at DOK 3 or 4 in mathematics.	All students will be assessed with items at DOK 3 and 4.
None of the items was at DOK 3 or 4 levels in mathematics.	Seventy percent of items in mathematics will be assessed at DOK 3 and 4 levels.
Sixteen percent of students were assessed at DOK 3 or 4 in language arts.	All students will be assessed at DOK 3 and 4 in language arts.

Continued →

State Assessments	Consortia Assessment Specifications
Fourteen percent of selected response items in reading were at DOK 3, none at DOK 4. Forty-nine percent of items were at DOK 3, and 11 percent were at DOK 4 on open-ended reading.	Sixty-eight percent of items in reading will be assessed at DOK 3 and 4.

The consortia assessments reflect a "dramatic upward shift in intellectual rigor and toward deeper learning" (Herman & Linn, 2013, p. 17). Now all students in tested grades using consortia tests will be held accountable for a level of performance that few if any students were required to demonstrate in their former state assessments.

Creating the 21st Century Curriculum

The question arises as to who should create the curriculum to help students and teachers meet this tremendous challenge. In most countries, this issue is a no-brainer. Because quality education is considered a national imperative, the national government provides the curriculum guidelines for educators to follow.

The peculiar nature of education in the United States makes the issue of curriculum development much more complex. Education has been left to the purview of each of the fifty states, and NCLB revealed enormous differences in the rigor of standards and assessments from state to state (Toppo, 2007; West, 2005).

In 2009, the National Governors Association Center for Best Practices and Council of Chief State School Officers attempted to establish a more coordinated national focus on essential outcomes by launching the CCSS initiative in mathematics and language arts. The Obama administration endorsed the effort and required states to join a consortium to establish standards and assessments as a prerequisite for access to Race to the Top funds.

By September 2009, fifty-one states and territories had initially agreed to endorse the CCSS. Soon, however, the initiative became caught up in a political debate about the overreach of the federal government into a states' rights issue (even though it had been launched by the states). By the summer of 2014, the number of states endorsing the Common Core had shrunk to forty-three (Common Core State Initiative, n.d.). The situation is likely to deteriorate even further. The *Washington Post* reports that new Republican majorities in state legislatures across the country are preparing fresh legislative assaults against their states' participation in the initiative (Wilson, 2014). The most ambitious attempt to reach consensus on what American students should know and be able to do is clearly under attack.

But whether a state embraces the CCSS or rejects them, the question of curriculum development remains relevant. The CCSS present the intended outcomes for different grade levels but have left the question of curriculum up to the states to address. The states, in turn, have typically left curriculum development up to each of the more than eighteen thousand school districts in the United States to resolve (National Center for Education Statistics, 2014b). But even at the district level, it is unlikely that students have access to a guaranteed and viable curriculum. The following observation from E. D. Hirsch (1996) remains true today:

> We know, of course, that there exists no national curriculum, but we assume, quite reasonably, that agreement has been reached locally regarding what shall be taught to children at each grade level—if not within the whole district, then certainly within an individual school . . . the idea that there exists a coherent plan for teaching content within the local district, or even within the individual school, is a gravely misleading myth. (p. 26)

So the question remains, Who should create the curriculum to provide students with 21st century skills? The National Center on Education and the Economy calls on each state to establish the curriculum that provides those skills (Tucker, 2014), but states are unlikely to move into the curriculum development business in the near future. Thus, districts are confronted with the immediate issue of how to establish a curriculum to help students acquire the intended outcomes. Should the central office take the lead in this endeavor, or should it be left to teachers to create the curriculum?

District Approaches to Curriculum Development

In previous books on the PLC process, my colleagues and I emphasize that the process requires a culture that is simultaneously loose and tight. Some aspects of the culture are loose; that is, people throughout the organization are empowered to make important decisions and to be creative and innovative. Other aspects of the culture are tight—they are nondiscretionary, and everyone in the organization is expected to honor them. The section that follows (adapted from *Cultures Built to Last* [DuFour & Fullan, 2013]) considers both a too-tight and a too-loose approach to curriculum development at the district level.

District A: The Too-Tight District

The leaders of District A view the challenge of the CCSS in much the same way they have approached other initiatives: by asking, "How can we best implement this new program?" They look to experts to determine both the one right way to translate the standards into grade-level curriculum and how to implement the curriculum in classrooms. The experts may be internal, but they are more likely to come from outside the organization. They draft a new district curriculum to align with the CCSS and a pacing guide to establish precisely which skills and concepts will be taught and when. They may develop scripted lessons that teachers are expected to present with fidelity. They adopt a new textbook series to support the new curriculum. The district leadership presents the curriculum documents, pacing guides, and new textbooks to teachers with little explanation beyond the pronouncement the materials represent the new curriculum for all students.

The main vehicle for holding teachers accountable for delivering the prescribed curriculum is the district's formal supervision and evaluation process or district benchmark assessments. Principals are expected to conduct frequent walk-through observations of classroom teaching to ensure that the appropriate content is being taught at the correct time in the stipulated way.

District leaders exclude teachers from decisions about implementing the new standards. They may explain that removing teachers from the dialogue about curriculum standards and the process to bring those standards to life in the classroom is their attempt to be sensitive to the needs of overworked teachers by doing the work for them. But when district leaders remove teachers and principals from the dialogue and the decision-making process, they remove them from the learning that is one of the most significant by-products of the process.

District B: The Too-Loose District

The central office leaders of District B provide teachers with CCSS documents for their course or grade level and leave the issue of curriculum development and implementation to each teacher to resolve. The district pretends that because teachers are operating from the same documents, they are providing students with a guaranteed curriculum. They ignore the fact that teachers may or may not read the documents, may interpret them differently, may assign very different priorities to different standards, may vary tremendously in the amount of time they devote to different standards, and may or may not have the skills to teach the standards. There is no process to monitor whether or not individual teachers address the content and no process to assess whether or not students are acquiring the intended outcomes.

As a result of this too-loose approach, each student's access to and experience with the curriculum does not depend on the state in which he or she resides, the district in which his or her school is located, or even the school he or she attends. The most significant variables impacting a student's success in acquiring the knowledge and skills of the CCSS in the too-loose district will be the degree to which the individual teacher to whom he or she has been assigned addresses the new standards and the skill with which that instructor teaches the curriculum.

The following assertions serve as guidelines for creating a curriculum that is truly guaranteed and viable.

Both District Leadership and Teachers Have an Important Role in Developing a Guaranteed Curriculum

The question, Should the central office *or* the teachers take the lead in creating a guaranteed curriculum? creates a false dichotomy. The best districts will reject this "Tyranny of Or" and will instead embrace the "Genius of And" (Collins & Porras, 2004). They will include representative teachers in the creation of the curriculum; however, they will also recognize they must engage every affected teacher in the process of studying the curriculum. They will provide teachers with a starting point, a recommended curriculum that has been developed with the help of their colleagues. That curriculum will serve not as commandments carved in stone but as a catalyst for the study of and dialogue about the curriculum by all teachers. Suggestions as to how districts might approach this appear later in the chapter.

There Is No Such Thing as a Single District Curriculum

In every school and in every district, there are three levels of curriculum at work each day. The first is the *intended* curriculum. This is what someone else has said students should learn. It might be the national committee on Common Core State Standards, the central office, a committee of teachers, or a textbook publisher who articulates the intended curriculum.

The second level of curriculum at work in every school is the *implemented* curriculum. This is the content that is taught when the classroom door is closed and each teacher makes decisions about what to emphasize and what to skip.

The third level of curriculum is the *attained* curriculum, or what students actually learn. The challenge for schools, of course, is to determine how to have the most powerful impact on the attained curriculum—what students actually learn. An important part of the answer to that challenge is to ensure that the implemented curriculum—what gets taught when the door is closed—is *guaranteed and viable*. The fact that it is *guaranteed* means specific content is certain to be taught in specific courses and at specific grade levels, regardless of the teacher to whom a student is assigned. The fact that it is *viable* indicates that there is enough instructional time available to actually teach the content identified as guaranteed. A curriculum cannot be guaranteed unless it is also viable (DuFour & Marzano, 2011).

The Best Way to Ensure an Implemented Curriculum Is Guaranteed and Viable Is to Engage Teachers in the Process of Creating It

The committee that created the CCSS cannot guarantee that those standards will be taught in a single classroom. Neither can a state board of education, state superintendent, district superintendent, or principal. When it comes to establishing a guaranteed and viable curriculum, the guarantee that matters most is the one that comes from the people who are actually called to implement it—the teachers. Therefore, collaborative teams of teachers responsible for teaching the same subject or grade level should be engaged in a collaborative process to:

> The challenge for schools, of course, is to determine how to have the most powerful impact on the attained curriculum—what students actually learn.

- Study the intended standards together

- Agree on priorities within the standards

- Clarify how the standards translate into student knowledge, skills, and dispositions

- Establish what proficient work looks like

- Develop general pacing guidelines for delivering the curriculum

- Most importantly, commit to one another that they will, in fact, teach the agreed-on curriculum, unit by unit

Until Team Members Have Agreed on and Can Consistently Apply the Criteria They Will Use in Judging the Quality of Student Work, It Is Impossible for Them to Provide Students With a Guaranteed and Viable Curriculum

Consider the following statements from the CCSS for two different grade levels (NGA & CCSSO, 2010).

> Grade 8: "Write narratives to develop real or imagined experiences or events using effective technique, relevant descriptive details, and well-structured event sequences." (p. 43)

> Grade 12: "Write narratives to develop real or imagined experiences or events using effective technique, well-chosen details, and well-structured event sequences." (p. 46)

While eighth graders are to use relevant descriptive details, twelfth graders must use well-chosen details. Other than that less-than-informative distinction, the wording for the two grade levels is identical. Yet certainly, there should be different expectations regarding the writing of two groups of students years apart in their education. Every team must grapple with the question, What does proficient work look like for our students? Furthermore, once they have established their criteria for assessing the quality of student work, they must practice applying the criteria to samples of student work until they are confident they are providing students with consistent feedback. They should also be able to provide students and parents with clear illustrations of the different levels of quality work to help them understand the benchmark students are expected to achieve.

Creating a Viable Curriculum Will Require Educators Both to Assign Priority to Certain Standards and to Elect Not to Teach Other Standards

The fact that the American K–12 curriculum is overloaded, the proverbial mile long and half inch deep, is so well established that it has become a cliché. Mid-continent Research for Education and Learning (McREL) identifies 256 standards and nearly 4,000 benchmarks that states and national organizations had identified as essential. In estimating the time required to teach all that content, McREL concludes that the K–12 system would need to be converted to K–21 (Marzano, Kendall, & Gaddy, 1999). Although the number of standards may have declined since this study, American teachers continue to be asked to cover more topics than any other teachers in the world (National Science Board, 2004) at the same time that researchers find that trying to cover too many topics per grade has a decidedly negative impact on student learning (Schmidt & Houang, 2007). An NGA and CCSSO (2008) study criticizes state curriculum as little more than "a laundry list of topics resulting in too much repetition across grades" and a curriculum in which "you teach everything everywhere because then somehow somebody will learn something" (p. 24).

The CCSS seek to address this issue by reducing the number of standards, but the problem remains. Consider the following fourth-grade English language arts standard from the CCSS (NGA & CCSSO, 2010, p. 28). A student will:

> Demonstrate command of the conventions of standard English grammar and usage when writing or speaking:

   a. Use relative pronouns (*who, whose, whom, which, that*) and relative adverbs (*where, when, why*).

   b. Form and use the progressive (e.g., *I was walking; I am walking; I will be walking*) verb forms.

   c. Use modal auxiliaries (e.g., *can, may must*) to convey various conditions.

   d. Order adjectives within sentences according to conventional patterns (e.g., *a small red bag* rather than *a red small bag*).

   e. Form and use prepositional phrases.

   f. Produce complete sentences, recognizing and correcting inappropriate fragments and run-ons.

   g. Correctly use frequently confused words (e.g., *to, too, two; there, their*).

This single standard includes multiple elements to be taught and assessed. It is one of forty fourth-grade standards in language arts alone. As DuFour and Marzano (2011) conclude, "When one considers the fact that a busy fourth-grade teacher has only thirty-six weeks and 180 days in the school year, the task of teaching forty-three standards appears daunting if not impossible" (p. 93). The likelihood of success is diminished even further when the teacher is also asked to ensure student proficiency in all the grade-level standards for mathematics, social studies, science, the arts, and physical education.

High-performing countries have moved in the opposite direction, concentrating on reducing the content of their curriculum so that students can cover fewer concepts in greater depth. A study of those countries concludes, "World-class content standards cover a smaller number of topics in greater depth at every grade level, enabling teachers to spend more time on each topic so that all students learn it well before they advance to more difficult content" (NGA & CCSSO, 2008, p. 24). Since 1990, the national core curriculum in Finland has become much less detailed and prescriptive, serving more as a framework that provides teachers with considerable latitude in determining content and pedagogy (OECD, 2010a). In 2006, Singapore, whose curriculum already covered significantly fewer topics than American schools, launched the Teach Less, Learn More reform initiative to cut its curriculum content even further. The initiative encouraged school-based curriculum reform to "provide teachers with more scope for innovation in their teaching and to reduce the curriculum load on our students. . . . [and provide] our students with the time . . . to take part in learning activities that will help them to think more critically and creatively" (Singapore Ministry of Education, 2010). The Singapore Ministry of Education (2010) reports that one of the most significant lessons to emerge from the initiative is that "structured time has to be formally set aside in the time table in order to support teachers in their efforts to collaborate and plan together."

> High-performing countries have moved in the opposite direction, concentrating on reducing the content of their curriculum so that students can cover fewer concepts in greater depth.

How to Establish a Guaranteed and Viable Curriculum

Ultimately, the problem of too much content and too little time forces teachers either to rush through content, focusing on coverage rather than learning, or to exercise judgment regarding which standards are the most significant and essential. Traditionally, individual teachers have addressed this choice in isolation. In a PLC, this issue is not left to each teacher to resolve individually. Instead, collaborative teams of teachers who teach the content work together to *build shared knowledge* regarding essential curriculum. They do what people do in learning communities: they learn together. They sit down together to analyze and discuss the standards they are being asked to teach.

The insights of Douglas Reeves (2002) are particularly help-ful in guiding this work. He offers a three-part test for teams to consider as they assess the significance of a particular standard.

1. **Does it have endurance?** Do we really expect our stu-dents to retain the knowledge and skills over time, as opposed to merely learning it for a test?

2. **Does it have leverage?** Will proficiency in this standard help the student in other areas of the curriculum and other academic disciplines?

3. **Does it develop student readiness for the next level of learning?** Is it essential for success in the next unit, course, or grade level?

Mark

A fourth question that is inferred from this list and should be addressed is, "What content do we currently teach that we can eliminate from the curriculum because, although it may be nice to know, it is not essential?"

In smaller districts, arrangements can be made to have every teacher of a grade level or course engage in a process with his or her colleagues in other schools to create a guaranteed and viable curriculum. The district should set aside two or three days at the start of the school year for teachers to meet in these grade-level or course-specific teams to clarify the most essential learnings for their students. The teams could proceed as follows.

1. All members are provided with a copy of the following for the team's grade level or course.

    a. The Common Core State Standards or standards unique to their state

    b. The district curriculum guide

    c. A "wish list" of skills from the grade level or course above theirs that articulates the three or four key skills entering students should have to succeed at that level

2. After discussing their findings, each team posts three pieces of butcher paper on the wall with the headings "Keep," "Drop," and "Create."

3. Each member is then given three different colored sticky notes—yellow for Keep, pink for Drop, and green for Create—and asked to assess the significance of each standard.

4. The team considers each standard, and each member is asked to place it in one of the three categories.

5. When the team has completed its task, it presents its findings to the teachers in the grade levels above and below its own to seek feedback and look for redundancy.

6. The team establishes a pacing calendar that stipulates the sequencing of the content and the amount of time that will be devoted to each unit. Note that this pacing calendar will not be prescriptive, as in, "We must all be on page 20 on Tuesday." It will indicate the skills and concepts to be taught in a particular unit and the length of the unit. Day-to-day decisions about instruction are left to the judgment of each teacher.

Tom Many, the former superintendent of Kildeer Countryside School District 96, used a similar process to great effect in a suburban Chicago district serving 3,100 students from preK through eighth grade in its seven schools. Teachers were able to build consensus on the guaranteed curriculum for their course, identify topics that could be dropped, and find gaps between what they agreed was essential and what they were actually teaching in their classrooms. The result was a clearly defined set of outcomes for each grade level in all curricular areas. Teachers became clearer, more consistent, and more confident in their ability to provide students with a guaranteed and viable curriculum. Furthermore, they were committed to the curriculum because they had played a major role in shaping it. District 96 continues to be

Look up

one of the highest-performing elementary districts in Illinois. (To see District 96's standards for each grade level, visit the Curriculum and Instruction page of its website: www.kcsd96 .org/curriculum/curriculum-frameworks.cfm.)

In larger districts, it will not be feasible to bring all the teachers of a grade level or course to a single location to engage in this work, and so the individual school becomes the setting for curriculum development. Collaborative teams within the school would follow the same process. They would, however, add some steps to the process. Once the team members had agreed on the most essential standards for their course or grade level, they would post their findings to an electronic bulletin board for review from similar teams in the district. The district might establish some guidelines to assist with the review. For example, if the majority of teams declare a standard essential but an individual team did not, that team must include it.

After the preceding steps have been taken across a district to identify the critical curriculum that all students must be taught, site-level teacher teams must dig deeper. Unit by unit, teacher teams must identify the absolutely essential learning targets that all students must learn for success in the next unit, grade, or course. When a team of teachers agrees on these essential learning targets, the teachers are doing more than placing a higher priority on them—they are making promises that they will work together to ensure that every student will learn them. This list of "promises" does not represent all that will be taught in each unit, term, or year, but it represents the minimum that all students must master to learn at high levels.

With this clarity about what students are to learn, teachers are prepared to tackle the next challenge of ensuring high levels of learning for all students: determining how they will gather evidence of each student's proficiency. The next chapter will address this challenge, but it is important to understand that it is impossible to have an effective assessment process unless educators understand what they are trying to assess. Equally important, creating a guaranteed and viable curriculum is not an event but a never-ending process. Each year, teacher teams should review and revise these essential outcomes. This will allow new teachers to participate in the learning and ownership of the curriculum, as well as allow teams to review their curriculum and make adjustments based on the needs of their students.

When educators are asked to create a guaranteed and viable curriculum, many explain that they can't for the following three reasons.

1. We are required to cover it all.

2. All the curriculum is essential.

3. It is all on the state test.

> Creating a guaranteed and viable curriculum is not an event but a never-ending process.

When asked if they currently are able to cover the entire required curriculum, and give each standard equal time and weight in their teaching, educators universally answer, "No." In reality, the process of interpreting, prioritizing, and eliminating standards is being done every day by individual teachers in the privacy of their classroom. If this process can be done individually in private, there is no reason why it cannot be done collectively.

Moving Toward What Works

If the key to the quality of any school is truly the quality of the educators within it, and if an essential element of good instruction is clarity regarding what students must learn, schools and students benefit when educators engage in a process that builds their knowledge of and commitment to teaching the essential curriculum. The too-tight district suggests that teachers simply do what they are told rather than think. But this approach does not result in the commitment that is essential to a truly guaranteed curriculum. As Stephen Covey (1990) warns, "Without involvement there is no commitment. Mark it down, asterisk it, circle it, underline it. *No involvement, no commitment*" (p. 143). Furthermore, in failing to engage teachers in analysis of and dialogue about the curriculum, the too-tight district does nothing to build their capacity to deliver it effectively. It is time to end this approach to providing students with a guaranteed curriculum.

Educators should also acknowledge the hypocrisy of distributing documents—CCSS, state standards, district curriculum guides—and pretending those documents result in a guaranteed curriculum. We must demand more of ourselves than creating the illusion of providing students with equal access to the most essential outcomes and take the necessary steps to create the internal accountability that promotes it.

> We must demand more of ourselves than creating the illusion of providing students with equal access to the most essential outcomes and take the necessary steps to create the internal accountability that promotes it.

We must also avoid what Carol Ann Tomlinson and Jay McTighe (2006) refer to as the *twin sins* of teaching. At the elementary level, the sin is the reluctance of educators to abandon their favorite kid-friendly projects that are not linked to any essential outcome. We must ask how spending class time to build models of missions, frontier forts, or colonial Williamsburg contributes to our students acquiring the most essential skills. We must abandon the even more ridiculous practice of grading those projects when we know that some dads build better forts than other dads. Kids may love dinosaurs, but they don't need to learn about them in every grade. The fact that a teacher took lots of pictures while visiting a foreign country over the summer should not automatically result in a new unit for students in the fall.

At the secondary level, we must avoid the sin of a perverse compulsion to cover the content. The goal should be more than racing through the textbook (which, by the way, contains more topics and pages than the textbooks of almost every country in the world). A focus on coverage is a focus on teaching rather than a focus on learning. It should be little comfort to be able to say at the end of the year, "Well, I taught it," if it is evident that students didn't learn it.

The initiatives to establish the CCSS, state standards, or district curriculum guides will all be for naught unless teachers are convinced of the value of the outcomes and are committed to ensuring their students acquire them. As the OECD (2009) concludes, "Involving teachers themselves and drawing on their expertise when developing . . . initiatives is a first step toward ensuring their commitment to them as well as being essential to tapping into their knowledge and experience" (pp. 16–17). It should be evident that a collaborative team of teachers who have agreed they will teach a particular skill or concept in an upcoming unit, and then work together to create a common assessment to gather evidence as to whether or not each student has met the agreed-on proficiency standard, is far more likely to provide students with access to a guaranteed curriculum than teachers who are merely provided documents and told to go teach.

> A focus on coverage is a focus on teaching rather than a focus on learning.

District leaders should create a process to ensure every teacher is engaged in the essential work of clarifying what students must know and be able to do. If they do not, however, principals should take the initiative to provide teachers with the time and support to establish a guaranteed and viable curriculum within their own school. If principals fail to take the lead, teachers should lead them and insist that they be given an opportunity to engage in this important work. It is time to stop passing the buck and waiting for someone else to act responsibly. We know what the right work looks like. We have not been forbidden to engage in the right work. It is time to roll up our sleeves and do it.

CHAPTER 9

Assessment to Inform and Improve Professional Practice

A genuine commitment to helping all students learn at high levels requires a systematic process to monitor each student's learning on an ongoing basis and then use evidence of student learning to:

- Provide students with relevant, actionable information about the progression of their learning towards clearly defined standards and targets

- Respond to the individual needs of students in a coordinated way

- Inform and improve the individual and collective practices of professionals within the school

This assessment process is *formative,* which the OECD defines as "frequent, interactive assessments of students' progress and understanding to identify learning needs and adjust teaching appropriately" (Looney, 2005, p. 21). Some authors refer to formative assessment as assessment *for* learning (Black, Harrison, Lee, Marshall, & Wiliam, 2004; Fullan, 2005; Stiggins, 2007).

John Hattie (2012) prefers to use the term assessment *as* learning. Regardless of the nomenclature, the big idea behind formative assessment is that evidence of student learning is used "to adjust instruction to better meet student needs" (Wiliam, 2011, p. 43). Formative assessment is not a specific test; it is a process that uses multiple indicators of student learning. It is not something to be purchased; it is a skill that educators must master. It is not something that occurs at the end of instruction; it is an integral part of good instruction. It is not designed to result in a final score or grade; it is a process to inform students, better meet their needs, and improve professional practice (Orland & Anderson, 2013).

Determining if an assessment is formative or summative is not based on the format of the test, the scope of the material being assessed, or when the assessment is administered during a given unit of study. Instead, the critical determining factor is how the results are used. If students and teachers use the information to confirm areas of student proficiency, identify where specific improvement is needed, and most importantly, provide students with support and additional opportunities to demonstrate mastery of the material, then the assessment is formative.

In fact, in some cases, an assessment can be both summative and formative. For example, an end-of-unit assessment might be given to determine if students have mastered specific essential standards. For students who demonstrate mastery, the assessment is summative. But for students who do not meet the required proficiency, the assessment becomes formative. The information will indicate to both the teacher and specific students that additional time and support are needed to help those students develop proficiency.

This is *not* how assessment has traditionally been viewed or used in the United States, which has relied far too heavily on summative assessments, or assessments *of* learning. Whereas the formative assessment process asks, "Is each student *learning* the intended knowledge and skills?" summative assessments ask, "Has the student *learned* the content by the deadline?" A summative assessment is intended to result in a dichotomous answer—pass or fail, proficient or not proficient—or to produce a grade of A, B, C, D, or F.

The standardized tests that have been used to hold American schools accountable are an example of summative assessments. The focus is on differentiating the number of students who demonstrate or fail to demonstrate proficiency on the day of the test. The tests address too many skills and fail to provide teachers with specific information on the difficulties students are experiencing. Furthermore, the results are often unavailable until weeks or months after students have taken the tests, frequently after the school year has ended. As a result, they are of little value at the instructional level (Stiggins, 2014).

> Whereas the formative assessment process asks, "Is each student *learning* the intended knowledge and skills?" summative assessments ask, "Has the student *learned* the content by the deadline?"

What is even worse, however, is that the assessment process of most schools continues to be driven by summative assumptions. Teachers typically present a unit of instruction, administer a test, assign a grade to each student, and move on to the next unit. Even if large numbers of students are unable to demonstrate proficiency, educators are far more prone to attribute the problem to a lack of student effort and motivation than any weakness in their instruction (Markow & Pieters, 2010). This is particularly troubling in light of the very compelling research on the power of formative assessment to improve student learning. As W. James Popham (2013) writes:

> Ample research evidence is now at hand to indicate emphatically that when the formative-assessment process is used, students learn better—lots better. This should come as no surprise, for the essence of formative assessment is surely commonsensical. Formative assessment is simply a planned process wherein teachers, or their students, use assessment-elicited evidence of student learning to decide whether to make changes

in what they're currently doing. . . . It's really not surprising that formative assessment works so well. What is surprising is how few U.S. teachers use the process.

The nearly exclusive use of summative assessments in American schools should not be surprising. Once again, the original purpose of our traditional system of K–12 education was to prepare only a small percentage of students to transition to postsecondary education. Subsequently, the goal of assessment was to rank individual students' progress in comparison to others', create a bell-shaped curve of results, and then use those results to determine which students would be promoted.

Summative assessments are not without merit. There are times during the school term and from year to year when it is important to formally and specifically determine what students have learned. The problem is the huge imbalance between formative and summative assessment at most schools, with most students receiving an almost exclusive diet of summative assessments used to rank each student's progress, with virtually no formative opportunities for students to learn from their mistakes, receive additional instruction, and then try again until they succeed.

Ongoing Formative Assessment in the Classroom

One critical element of an effective formative assessment process is the ongoing, almost minute-by-minute checks for understanding effective teachers use during daily instruction. The best teachers have a variety of strategies to solicit feedback on student understanding while they are teaching. Some of these strategies include the following.

Effective Questioning

Effective questioning requires the teacher to be in control of who will respond and when. If a teacher allows students to shout out the answer as soon as a question has been asked, the quickest and loudest students will respond. All other students recognize there is no need for them to engage in consideration of the question. The same is true if the teacher does not allow callouts but only selects volunteers to respond. Again, passive students can opt out of the question-answer process. If the teacher calls on a student before asking the question ("Bob, how did the Lend-Lease Act of 1941 signal a shift in America's noninterventionist policies?"), everyone other than Bob can relax. If the teacher asks the question prior to calling on a student, the entire class must consider the question.

Questions should cause students to think, but even the best questions will have little impact on student learning if students don't consider the question. So effective teachers will carefully plan questions that match the depth of learning required of students, present the question, provide adequate wait time for all students to consider it, and then randomly select a student to respond. Even then, the process should continue to encourage students to consider their classmate's answer rather than make them feel they can disengage. The effective teacher will typically redirect the student's response to other students, ask them to restate their classmate's answer, and ask them if they agree, disagree, or can add something to the original response.

Passive students can always respond to a question with a simple "I don't know." Effective teachers, however, will not let them off the hook so easily. They will instruct the student to think about the question, listen to how others respond, and then explain which answer he or she liked best and why. Students can also use game-show strategies, such as "phone a friend" or "ask the audience," prior to answering (Wiliam, 2011). The important message to get across to students is that they cannot opt out of participating in the classroom dialogue.

Strategies to Check for Student Understanding

Perhaps the least effective question a teacher can ask is, "Are there any questions?" Too often, this query results in silence, and the teacher moves on with the lesson. Effective teachers will create a variety of strategies to check for student understanding. They will ask students to write an answer to a question in their notes or solve a problem as the teacher walks around the room looking to see if there are common misconceptions among students. These teachers will create ways for students to signal their level of understanding, such as green light ("I've got it, and I can explain it to others"), yellow light ("I think I have it"), or red light ("I'm confused and need help"). They will use whiteboards, clickers, iPads, and smartphones to poll students to get instantaneous responses to a question. They will use exit slips that call on students to demonstrate their understanding of a key concept as they leave the room so teachers can examine responses and make decisions about where to go next in their instruction.

> Effective teachers will create a variety of strategies to check for student understanding.

High-Quality Questions

Both of these strategies depend on the ability of teachers to create high-quality questions that engage students and provide insights into their thinking. But an analysis of teacher questioning reveals that more than 90 percent of the questions merely rehearse things students already know or deal with classroom management rather than lead to new learning (Wiliam, 2011).

So how might teachers learn to create high-quality questions? Assessment experts are virtually unanimous in recommending that the best forum for this learning is the collaborative team process (Black et al., 2004; Popham, 2008; Reeves, 2007). Once a team has agreed on the essential learnings of a unit, members should immediately turn their attention to how they will assess the learning through both their ongoing minute-by-minute checks for understanding in the classroom and the more formal team-developed common formative assessments that will be used during or at the conclusion of the unit. Questions integrated into instruction that align with the essential learning and provide insights into student thinking are vital to the teaching and learning process. By working together in their collaborative teams, teachers can create a library of good questions and help one another become more effective in generating and using this important instructional tool. In fact, Dylan Wiliam (2011) contends, "Sharing high-quality questions may be the most significant thing we can do to improve the quality of student learning" (p. 104).

Team-Developed Common Formative Assessment

In urging educators to take advantage of the power of formative assessments, I must sheepishly admit that I relied almost exclusively on summative assessments during my teaching career. The very fact that I was giving a test signaled to my students that "This unit is over." They received a grade, and we moved on, regardless of whether or not a particular student demonstrated proficiency. As a result, I left lots of students behind.

Today our profession knows better. The power of formative assessment to improve student learning is one of the most well-documented research findings in the field of education (Black et al., 2004). To realize that power, however, educators must approach assessment with a very different mindset than the one that has prevailed over the decades.

> Educators must approach assessment with a very different mindset than the one that has prevailed over the decades.

Consider a team of four seventh-grade language arts teachers who have agreed to address three essential outcomes in the unit they are about to teach. The team wants students to be able to (1) determine the central idea of two different texts that provide conflicting information on the same subject, (2) identify similarities and differences in the texts, and (3) distinguish between facts and opinions in the texts. The team members also establish the amount of time they will devote to the unit, high-level questions they can use during instruction, and the common formative assessment they will administer to their students at the conclusion of the unit. Each member of the team teaches the unit to the best of his or her ability, and at its conclusion, the team administers the common assessment to its students.

The team has the results of the assessment within twenty-four hours of administering it. Members then review the results of the assessment as presented in figure 9.1 (pages 165–166) and apply their data analysis protocol (figure 9.2, page 167).

Which Students Need Additional Time and Support to Achieve at or Above Proficiency on an Essential Skill?

The team first turns its attention to the students who were unable to demonstrate proficiency. The results reveal that only 9 of their 130 students struggled to identify the central idea of the reading passages and only 4 had difficulty answering questions dealing with similarities and differences. Forty students, however, where unable to distinguish facts from opinions in the texts. The team agrees that the nine students will be assigned to intervention targeting how to identify the main idea of a reading passage during the block of time set aside to give students additional time and support. This time is provided as part of the schedule and does not require the students to miss any new direct instructions.

The students report to intervention, where the teacher understands they need additional support with the specific skill of identifying the main idea of a reading passage. After four days of this focused support, the teacher indicates that seven of the students are ready to demonstrate they are now proficient. The team administers form B of their assessment, and all seven students score at the proficient level. The two remaining students in intervention continue to receive support until they can demonstrate mastery of this essential skill. This systematic intervention will be discussed in much more detail in the next chapter.

Essential Reading Skills: Common Assessment Results (Target Score 3/4)

Student	Main Idea: Passage 1					Main Idea: Passage 2					Similarities and Differences					Fact Versus Opinion				
	Class 1	Class 2	Class 3	Class 4	Totals	Class 1	Class 2	Class 3	Class 4	Totals	Class 1	Class 2	Class 3	Class 4	Totals	Class 1	Class 2	Class 3	Class 4	Totals
1	4	3	4	4		3	3	3	4		3	3	3	4		4	2	3	3	
2	3	4	3	4		3	4	3	3		3	4	3	4		3	4	2	3	
3	4	4	3	4		4	3	3	3		4	3	4	3		2	3	3	2	
4	1	3	4	3		1	3	3	4		2	3	4	4		1	2	3	3	
5	4	3	3	4		3	4	4	4		3	3	3	3		3	3	2	3	
6	2	4	3	3		1	3	4	3		3	3	3	3		3	3	2	2	
7	4	3	4	3		3	4	3	3		3	4	4	3		4	3	4	3	
8	3	3	3	3		2	3	3	3		3	3	3	3		2	3	3	2	
9	3	3	4	3		2	3	3	4		4	3	3	3		3	3	3	3	
10	4	4	3	4		3	3	4	3		4	3	4	4		4	3	3	3	
11	3	3	3	3		3	4	3	3		3	4	4	4		3	3	2	3	
12	3	3	4	3		3	3	3	3		3	4	3	3		4	4	2	2	
13	4	4	3	3		2	4	3	4		3	4	4	3		4	3	3	2	
14	3	4	3	3		3	3	4	3		3	4	4	4		2	4	3	2	
15	3	3	4	3		3	3	4	3		3	4	4	3		2	4	3	3	
16	4	3	3	3		4	3	3	3		4	4	4	4		4	3	2	2	
17	3	3	3	3		2	3	4	3		3	3	3	3		3	4	3	2	
18	3	3	3	4		3	2	3	3		3	3	3	4		3	2	2	4	
19	4	3	4	4		3	3	3	4		3	2	3	4		4	2	2	4	
20	4	3	4	3		4	4	3	4		3	4	3	4		4	3	3	3	
21	3	4	3	3		3	4	3	3		3	4	4	2		2	4	3	1	

Figure 9.1: Sample assessment results.

Visit go.solution-tree.com/PLCbooks for a reproducible version of this figure.

Continued →

Essential Reading Skills: Common Assessment Results (Target Score 3/4)

Student	Main Idea: Passage 1					Main Idea: Passage 2					Similarities and Differences					Fact Versus Opinion				
	Class 1	Class 2	Class 3	Class 4	Totals	Class 1	Class 2	Class 3	Class 4	Totals	Class 1	Class 2	Class 3	Class 4	Totals	Class 1	Class 2	Class 3	Class 4	Totals
22	3	4	3	3		3	3	4	4		3	4	4	4		2	4	3	3	
23	4	3	3	4		4	3	2	4		4	3	3	4		4	2	2	4	
24	3	3	4	3		3	3	4	4		3	3	3	3		3	2	3	3	
25	2	4	3	4		1	4	4	4		3	4	3	4		1	3	2	4	
26	4	3	4	4		4	4	3	3		4	4	4	3		3	3	3	3	
27	4	3	4	4		4	3	4	4		4	4	3	4		3	3	4	3	
28	3	4	3	3		4	4	3	4		4	4	2	3		3	4	2	3	
29	3	4	4	3		3	4	3	4		4	4	4	4		3	4	3	3	
30	3	3	4	4		3	4	3	3		3	3	3	3		1	2	3	2	
31	4	3	4	4		3	3	4	4		3	4	3	4		3	3	3	3	
32	3	4	3	4		4	4	3	4		3	4	4	4		2	4	2	4	
33		4	3				3	3				4	4				3	3		
Total 1s	1	0	0	0		3	0	0	0		0	0	0	0		3	0	0	1	
Total 2s	2	0	0	0		4	1	1	0		1	1	1	1		9	8	10	9	
Total 3s	16	20	19	18		17	19	20	16		22	14	18	15		13	14	21	17	
Total 4s	13	13	14	14		8	13	12	16		9	18	14	16		7	11	2	5	
Percent Proficient	91%	100%	100%	100%		78%	97%	97%	100%		97%	97%	97%	97%		63%	76%	70%	69%	

Data Analysis Protocol

Team: _____ Teacher:_____ Date:_____

This analysis is based on our team's common assessment of the following essential learnings.

1. Which of our students need additional time and support to achieve at or above proficiency on an essential learning?

_____
_____
_____
_____
_____

2. What is our plan to enrich and extend the learning for students who are highly proficient?

_____
_____
_____
_____
_____

3. What is an area where my students struggled?

_____
_____
_____
_____
_____

4. What strategies were used by my teammates whose students performed well?

_____
_____
_____
_____
_____

5. In what area did our team's students struggle? What do we believe is the cause of the struggle? What is our plan for improving the results?

_____
_____
_____
_____
_____
_____
_____
_____
_____

Figure 9.2: Data analysis protocol.
Visit **go.solution-tree.com/PLCbooks** *for a reproducible version of this figure.*

What Is Our Plan to Enrich and Extend Learning for Students Who Are Highly Proficient?

The team's analysis also reveals that ten students were highly proficient on each of the skills on the common assessment. One member accepts responsibility for finding more challenging reading material for these students. She discovers that the *New York Times* has created a lesson on distinguishing fact from opinion using high-interest op-ed pieces from the newspaper, and the team agrees this source will be an excellent way to challenge highly proficient students.

What Is an Area Where My Students Struggled but One or More of My Teammates Had Students Achieve at High Levels?

Next, the team turns its attention to identifying strengths and weaknesses of individual members in teaching these skills. The analysis reveals that seven of the nine students who struggled to identify the main idea were in one teacher's classroom, and so the team members offer ideas, materials, and lesson plans to assist their colleague. The teacher will also observe the strategies his colleagues use during intervention to bring the seven students to proficiency.

In What Area Have Our Students Struggled, What Is the Cause, and What Is Our Plan for Improving Results?

Finally, the team acknowledges that no one achieved stellar results on helping students differentiate between facts and opinions on the two reading passages. Students were able to identify facts with reasonable accuracy but were prone to cite opinions as facts. Only 69 percent were able to demonstrate proficiency on that skill. Members recognize there are too many students to assign to intervention and that they must reteach the skill in the next unit. They also recognize, however, that they need some help in developing more effective strategies. One member agrees to contact the district's director of language arts to see if she can offer ideas for professional development or helpful materials. Another agrees to search for a video of an effective lesson on the topic on the Teaching Channel and LearnZillion and to bring the videos to the next team meeting for analysis. A third member will do an Internet search on strategies and materials for teaching fact versus opinion, and the fourth will solicit help from other language arts teachers in the school.

When the team prepares to teach this same unit next year, the team members begin with their protocol for team analysis prior to teaching a unit (see figure 9.3, pages 170–171). They review the results from their common assessment in the previous year. They are reminded that students struggled with distinguishing between fact and opinion and review some of the strategies they used to address that deficiency last year. Members set a SMART goal to help at least 80 percent of their students demonstrate proficiency on their *initial* common formative assessment.

The point to stress is that if the learning is essential, the team should be committed to helping *all* students acquire the intended outcome. The team may not feel that going from 69 percent proficient to 100 percent proficient is attainable in initial instruction. So an interim step of 80 percent is permissible with the understanding that students who are not initially proficient when the assessment is administered will be provided with the time and support to ensure their success in acquiring the intended knowledge and skill.

The Power of Team-Developed Common Formative Assessment

In the scenario described in the previous section, the collaborative team of teachers used assessment for much more than assigning grades. *Evidence of student learning* was used to better meet the intervention and enrichment needs of individual students, to identify individual teachers who could benefit from the support of their team, and to reveal areas where the entire team needed ideas for strengthening its instructional practice.

Protocol for Team Analysis Prior to Teaching a Unit

I. Review of prior common assessment for this unit:

a. Based on analysis of the results from common assessments from last year, we have identified the following area or areas in which students in general struggled.

_____

_____

_____

_____

_____

_____

b. We believe a primary cause of their struggle with this content was the following.

_____

_____

_____

_____

_____

c. We have identified the following action plan for improving student achievement that we will implement as we teach this new unit.

_____

_____

_____

_____

_____

d. We have established the following SMART goal for this unit to improve on last year's results.

_____

_____

_____

_____

_____

For example:

Last year, 70% of our students met or exceeded our proficiency target on the following essential skill/standard on our team's CFA administered at the end of the unit.

Figure 9.3: Protocol for team analysis prior to teaching a unit.

SMART goal: At least 80% of this year's students will meet or exceed our proficiency target on our team's CFA administered at the end of the unit.

II. Identifying prerequisite skills/vocabulary for this unit:

   a. We have concluded that students need the following skills/vocabulary to be successful.

In this unit: definitions and examples of facts verses opinions.

_____

_____

_____

_____

   b. Our plan for gathering evidence about student proficiency in prerequisite skills/vocabulary and addressing the needs of those who lack those skills is as follows:

      1. Provide readings to see if students can differentiate between facts and opinions.

      2. Have students discuss their answers in class and ask other students to agree or disagree with the responses.

      3. Ask students to make statements reflecting facts.

      4. Ask students to create statements reflecting opinions.

III. The administration could help us achieve our goal in this area by:

We don't require administrative help for this beyond our standard collaborative team time.

The power of this process is well established in research. Michael Fullan (2011b), who studies schooling in countries throughout the world, reports that in every case of significant school improvement, there are "common assessment frameworks linked to individualized instructional practice. . . . Progress and problems were also transparent . . . with corresponding discussions of how to improve results" (p. 45). Ron Gallimore and his colleagues (2009) find that until collaborative teams of teachers began using results from common assessments to identify problems in student learning and engaging in sustained action research to address those problems, they were unable to improve student achievement. Allan Odden and Sarah Archibald (2009) find that schools able to double student achievement use common formative assessments for each unit "to provide detailed and concrete information on what students know and do not know with respect to discrete curriculum units" (p. 68). This process meant "instruction was something out in the open, as it was the subject of public and professional conversations and the focus of ongoing professional development" (Odden & Archibald, 2009, p. 79). Schools that are highly effective in helping students in poverty achieve remarkable success help collaborative teams of teachers build common formative assessments and use the data both to intervene for students who need extra time and support and to inform instructional practice by discussing why a particular teacher is having success in teaching a concept and others are not (Chenoweth, 2009). A longitudinal study by the University of Chicago notes that common formative assessments create the feedback loop to teachers that is essential to continuous improvement. As the study concludes, "Absent shared evidence of student learning associated with common pedagogical practices, there is little basis for collective exploration of the cause-and-effect linkages at the core of improving teaching and learning" (Bryk, Sebring, Allensworth, Luppescu, & Easton, 2010).

Despite the widespread agreement on the power of common formative assessment to improve student and adult learning, the process is not yet the norm in American schools, nor will it become the norm until it becomes part of the organizational routine (Timperley, 2009). Teachers must be provided with time, professional development, and ongoing support to develop high-quality assessments, particularly in light of the very different and more rigorous assessments that are emerging from the Common Core State Standards. They must have technology to ensure they receive the results promptly and time to collectively consider the evidence of student learning.

> Teachers must be provided with time, professional development, and ongoing support to develop high-quality assessments.

The use of protocols for examining student achievement data and student work can also make a significant contribution to building a team's capacity to examine evidence of student learning. Protocols are intended both to help teams focus the conversation as members examine the results of common assessments and to provide a safe environment for the conversation. Effective protocols will ensure all voices are heard on the critical issue at hand, help members look closely at evidence of student learning, examine success as well as failure, and help participants to become skillful in facilitating dialogue on the right work (McDonald, Mohr, Dichter, & McDonald, 2007).

But the major challenge to implementing the common formative assessment process in the way described here is not structural but cultural. The process must be guided by a learning orientation rather than a blame orientation. The goal is to improve professional practice continuously, not to seek out and destroy a teacher who may be struggling to teach essential concepts and skills. In other words, school and district leaders cannot use the same punitive strategies and mindsets that have driven state and national reform efforts.

Hattie (2009) reminds leaders that the key to effective professional dialogue based on evidence of student learning will be their ability "to create school, staffroom, and classroom environments where error is welcomed as a learning opportunity, where discarding incorrect knowledge and understandings is welcomed, and where participants can feel safe to learn, re-learn, and explore knowledge and understanding" (p. 239). Fullan (2011a) calls on leaders to suspend judgment and approach poor results as a problem of capacity building:

> The process must be guided by a learning orientation rather than a blame orientation. The goal is to improve professional practice continuously, not to seek out and destroy a teacher who may be struggling to teach essential concepts and skills.

"What can we do to build the capacity of this teacher or school to be more effective in what needs to be done?"

One way to undermine the effectiveness of this collaborative process is to use it to rank, rate, and assess teachers or principals. If four of the most effective teachers in the world each teach a concept to the best of their ability to similar students under similar conditions and create and administer a common assessment, one of them will rank fourth in terms of the results. If four of the most inept teachers in a horribly ineffective school create a common assessment and administer it to their students, one would have the best of the horrible results. The same analogy applies to ranking principals within a district on the basis of student achievement on a state assessment. The issue is not how teachers or principals rank but rather how each teacher, each team, and each principal uses the results to get better. If teachers and principals are demonstrating a commitment to seeking and implementing more effective practices, leaders should focus on supporting their efforts to become more effective. In this way, a school or district uses evidence of student learning to align with the underlying assumption of the continuous improvement philosophy: using *ourselves as benchmarks* and then working to improve on our previous performance.

> The issue is not how teachers or principals rank but rather how each teacher, each team, and each principal uses the results to get better.

There may be a few educators who simply refuse to engage in any process that may call upon them to change their practices. They are not given a free pass. Chapter 11 addresses how to deal with this problem.

The Benefits of Team-Developed Common Formative Assessments

The benefits that accrue to educators from the process described in this chapter are so self-evident that it should be standard practice in every school. Among the benefits are the following.

Support for a Guaranteed and Viable Curriculum

Common formative assessments are essential for monitoring whether the intended guaranteed curriculum is being implemented by each member of the team. Everyone on the team knows that there will be checks, unit by unit, to determine if the curriculum is being taught and, more importantly, learned.

Better Assessments

Common formative assessments that members of a collaborative team create represent "the best practice in assessment" (Reeves, 2004, p. 71) and the "gold standard in educational accountability" (Reeves, 2004, p. 114). When members of a team work together to consider how they will approach assessing the skills and knowledge of their students, when every item or performance task is vetted by the entire team before it becomes part of the assessment, there is a much greater likelihood that the end result is a quality assessment compared to assessments that isolated teachers create.

Greater Equity for Students

When what a student learns, how the student is assessed, and the rigor of the assessment are left to the discretion of each teacher, the variance from classroom to classroom makes a mockery of a school's promise to provide students with equal access to educational opportunity. Common assessments help to provide a degree of consistency in teacher expectations that is essential to treating students fairly.

Diminished Likelihood Educators Will Blame Poor Performance on the Quality of the Test

When students struggle on tests created by others—the textbook, the district, the state—it is not uncommon for educators to attribute their struggles to the poor quality of the test. That likelihood is diminished when the teachers themselves create an assessment that they agree is a valid way to gather evidence of student learning. As a result, they are more prone to consider variability across classes as a function of instruction than a function of the assessment (Stigler, 2010).

Data That Are Turned Into Information

If someone is told that 80 percent of the students in third grade in a particular school scored proficient or higher on the state assessment in language arts, would that person be in a position to make an informed judgment about the quality of that performance? If across the state only 40 percent of similar students were proficient, a school helping four out of five students to achieve that benchmark would represent an extraordinary achievement. If, however, 96 percent of similar students in the state scored proficient on the same assessment, educators in the school with 80 percent scoring proficient would certainly need to consider some fundamental changes to their program or practices. Data alone do not inform. To translate data into information typically requires a basis of comparison.

This same principle applies not only to a school but also to each teacher within a school. Most educators can teach their entire career and not know if they teach a skill or concept better or worse than a colleague in the room next door who is teaching the same subject or grade level. If an isolated teacher creates his or her own assessment and after initial instruction discovers 70 percent of students were able to demonstrate proficiency, is that a cause for celebration or concern? Who knows? All the teacher has are data. But if that same teacher administers a common assessment and discovers that all three of his teammates were able to help more than 90 percent of their students demonstrate proficiency, the teacher is informed. Two keys to improvement in any activity are information and support. Evidence of student learning from team-developed common formative assessments provides the information, and the collaborative team process can supply the support.

Results Vital to Providing Students With Access to an Effective System of Interventions

The results from frequent common formative assessments will reveal the specific needs of individual students. Instead of saying students need intervention because they are failing mathematics, the school is able to say, "These eight students need help with solving problems involving unit rates and constant speed, and these five students struggle with using ratio reasoning to convert measurement units." Common formative assessments are much better suited than standardized tests for identifying the specific, diagnostic support students require.

Common Formative Assessments: The Great Persuader

The biggest reason common formative assessments provide a powerful catalyst for school improvement is that they offer the most effective tool for persuading educators to change their professional practice. The key challenge and core problem in any substantive improvement effort is getting people to change long-standing behavior (Kotter & Cohen, 2002). The problem is exacerbated in education because of the high regard educators have for their existing knowledge and skills. In a comprehensive nationwide survey of teachers, 84 percent of those surveyed report that they are "very confident they had all the knowledge and skills necessary to enable all of their students to succeed academically" (Markow & Pieters, 2010, p. 33). The remaining 16 percent are somewhat confident. Why change when you already have all the necessary knowledge and skills to teach well?

The survey also reveals that educators attribute student failure to a lack of effort and ability on the part of students rather than any deficiencies in their professional practice. Only 36 percent of teachers and 51 percent of principals believe that all their students have the ability to succeed academically. Only 17 percent of elementary teachers and 5 percent of secondary teachers believe that all their students are motivated to succeed academically (Markow & Pieters, 2010).

So what might persuade educators to change their practice if they sincerely believe they already have all the prerequisite knowledge and skills? *The most powerful lever for changing professional practice is concrete evidence of irrefutably better results* (Elmore, 2004; Fullan, 2008; Patterson, Grenny, Maxfield, McMillan, & Switzler, 2008). As Richard Elmore (2010) writes, "Adult beliefs about what children can learn are changed by watching students do things that the adults didn't believe that they—the students—could do" (p. 8). Effective use of team-developed common assessments is the best strategy for providing that irrefutable evidence. Consider the teacher who has worked with colleagues to agree that learning a particular skill or concept is vital to a student's academic success. This same teacher then helps to create an assessment that he or she acknowledges is a valid way of determining whether or not the student has become proficient in that skill or concept. When the teacher learns that students in the room next door are consistently demonstrating higher levels of mastery than his or her own students, at some point, the teacher will become curious. As Kerry Patterson and colleagues (2008) note, "Nothing changes the mind like the hard, cold world hitting it with actual real-life data" (p. 51).

The other lever for persuading educators to change practice is the *power of positive peer pressure* that comes with being a member of a collaborative team. When people work interdependently to achieve a common goal for which all members are mutually accountable, the performance of each individual directly impacts the ability of the team to achieve its goal. Most educators don't want to let down either their students or their colleagues. If a team has set a SMART goal for the unit, but it fails to achieve the goal because one teacher's students are unable to demonstrate proficiency, and the problem recurs in the next unit, and the next, at some point, that teacher will look to either change practice or change professions (Chenoweth, 2009; Stigler, 2010).

So to be as explicit as possible, I assert the following five truths.

1. The key to the ability of schools to have a positive impact on student learning is the collective expertise of the educators within a school or district.

2. Improved student learning will require improved professional practice.

3. Improved professional practice will require educators to change some of their traditional practices and adopt new instructional practices.

4. Among the most powerful motivators for persuading educators to change their practice are (1) concrete evidence of irrefutably better results and (2) the positive peer pressure inherent in being a member of a collaborative team.

5. The best strategy for utilizing these motivators and improving professional practice is engaging members of a collaborative team in the individual and collective analysis of evidence of student learning from team-developed common formative assessments as part of the recursive teaching and learning process.

Overcoming Traditional Obstacles to Using Common Formative Assessments

Collaborative teams are likely to need training and support to increase their assessment literacy and create high-quality assessments. The biggest obstacle to the effective use of common formative assessments, however, is not a lack of expertise but rather traditional assessment practices and the assumptions behind them. Educators must address the traditions of teacher isolation, tracking, grading, and avoiding conversations that might create adult discomfort.

The Tradition of Teacher Isolation

Once again, individual autonomy and privacy of practice have been the entrenched cultural norms of schooling in the United States for more than a century. Educators who are accustomed to working alone, making decisions on their own, and having almost absolute power over how they manage their classrooms will need to embrace a new mindset that leads to fundamental changes in how they approach their work. Some of the cultural shifts include:

- *From* working in isolation *to* working as a member of a collaborative team

- *From* working independently *to* working interdependently

- *From* individual decisions about content *to* a collective commitment to provide students with a guaranteed and viable curriculum, unit by unit

- *From* a focus on curriculum coverage *to* a fixation with each student's learning

- *From* individually created summative assessments *to* team-developed common formative assessments with occasional team-developed summative assessments

- *From* viewing assessment as taking time away from instruction *to* recognizing good assessment is a vital element of good instruction

- *From* using assessments to assign grades *to* using assessments to respond to the needs of individual students and to inform and improve instructional practice

- *From* privacy of practice *to* open sharing of practice

- *From* "these are my kids" *to* "these are our kids"

Educators who are accustomed to working alone, making decisions on their own, and having almost absolute power over how they manage their classrooms will need to embrace a new mindset that leads to fundamental changes in how they approach their work.

- *From* making decisions on the basis of personal preference or traditional practice *to* making decisions on the basis of evidence of effective practice

It will not be easy to make these substantive cultural changes. The necessary cultural shifts are similar to the advice offered to Blackstone in the novel *Shogun* as he struggles to learn the customs and language of the Japanese: "It is all so simple, Anjin-san. Just change your concept of the world" (Clavell, 1975, p. 504). If schools are going to become places committed to high levels of learning for both students and adults, educators must change their concept of almost everything in the world in which they work.

The Tradition of Tracking

The impact of common formative assessments is diminished when schools track students into different groups based on perceptions of student ability. Sometimes the tracking is explicit, such as a high school that assigns students to gifted, college-preparatory, vocational, or remedial programs. Sometimes the tracking is less overt but equally apparent, such as an elementary school that assigns students into groups of bluebirds, robins, sparrows, and crows for each grade level. Even the youngest students recognize this for what it is: tracking.

In a school that uses this approach to assign students to classrooms, common formative assessments no longer inform. Students in the higher tracks are expected to achieve at higher levels than those in the lower tracks, and when that inevitability occurs, differences in results are attributed to differences in students rather than differences in instruction. When students are grouped heterogeneously, results from common assessments are comparing apples to apples, and educators are more likely to examine differences in achievement through the lens of differences in professional practice.

I will have more to say about tracking in the next chapter. For now, suffice it to say that tracking has minimal effects on learning outcomes and profoundly negative effects in terms of equity (Hattie, 2009). In his summary of more than three hundred studies of tracking, Hattie (2009) concludes that no group benefits from the practice and that educational opportunity, achievement, and life chances are severely limited for students in the low groups.

I am certainly not opposed to accelerating student learning, provided the opportunity for acceleration is available to all students. For example, high schools should provide students with access to a curriculum that moves beyond traditional high school courses and offers the equivalent of college-level work. Traditional tracking, however, has no place in a school committed to helping all students learn at high levels.

> Traditional tracking has no place in a school committed to helping all students learn at high levels.

Traditional Grading Practices

The idea that assessments should be used to gather evidence of student learning, identify students who need additional time and support, provide those students with access to systematic interventions, and give them additional opportunities to demonstrate their learning often makes educators—particularly secondary school educators—uncomfortable. One of their frequently expressed concerns is that giving some students additional chances to learn is "not fair" to the students who passed the first time. If the mission of a school is to identify students who learn fast and who learn the first time we teach it, this approach makes sense. But if the mission of the school is to ensure all students learn, it does not. One way to resolve this fairness question is to provide all students with additional opportunities to prove they have learned at a higher level. For example, students unable to demonstrate proficiency would be *required* to keep working and learning until they become proficient. Students who were proficient on the initial assessment who wanted to demonstrate advanced proficiency could qualify for the opportunity to do so if they completed some prerequisite assignments from their teachers that proved they, too, had put some extra time and effort into their learning. A school committed to helping all students learn at higher levels would look for ways to encourage all students to keep working and learning.

Another frequent argument against formative assessment is that providing students with these second chances won't prepare them for the harsh realities of the "real world" or the "sink or swim" environment of higher education, where students are expected to take full responsibility for their learning; requiring students to get additional help until they become proficient simply "enables" students to give less than their best effort.

Upon hearing these arguments, I have asked educators to consider these three questions.

1. Do you mean it when you say your mission is to help all students learn at high levels?

   Inevitably, educators answer this question in the affirmative.

2. Do you acknowledge that if *all* students are to learn at high levels, some will need more time and support than others?

Again, the answer to this question is a resounding "Yes!"

3. So have you created the systems that ensure students who struggle receive the additional time and support necessary to become proficient?

It is this third question that often creates discomfort among educators. The next chapter will address characteristics of effective systems of intervention, but many educators question not how to implement effective interventions but whether these systems are beneficial to students. After all, they argue, schools must teach more than content. They must teach responsibility and the importance of meeting deadlines. With the school taking on greater responsibility for student learning, student responsibility is diminished. Students must be allowed to fail in order to teach them accountability and responsibility.

Certainly, responsibility is a critical life skill, and just as certainly, not every student is innately blessed with a strong sense of responsibility. Therefore, the real question becomes, What is the best way to teach students responsibility and ensure high levels of learning for all students? I contend that the best way to teach students responsibility is to insist that students do what responsible people do. Responsible people do the work. Responsible people seek assistance when they are struggling to succeed.

> The best way to teach students responsibility is to insist that students do what responsible people do. Responsible people do the work. Responsible people seek assistance when they are struggling to succeed.

How does the traditional practice of allowing an irresponsible student who would rather take a zero than do the work teach that student to act responsibly? How does allowing a student to opt out of a program to provide him or her with assistance teach responsibility? If a student is truly going to enter a sink-or-swim situation in higher education, the best preparation is to teach the student to swim—to provide the student with the knowledge, skills, and habits essential to success in that situation—rather than allow the student to sink first in high school.

Educators in schools with high failure rates justify the failures by saying, "The students won't do their work." Clearly, doing the work is an essential skill for success in schools. If that is the case, schools must do more than bemoan the lack of this essential skill in students. They must teach the skill by creating systems that place students in an environment during the school day where their work is monitored closely until it is completed and they can demonstrate proficiency. Which school is more effective in teaching responsibility: one that allows students to ignore requirements and elect to fail or one that demands students do what is required to succeed?

There is virtually no research or evidence to suggest that higher incidents of failure in school produce higher levels of responsibility, greater academic achievement in college, or a higher likelihood of success in meeting the demands of adult life. In fact, we have more than a century of compelling evidence that passively allowing students to fail does not teach them to be responsible.

> Which school is more effective in teaching responsibility: one that allows students to ignore requirements and elect to fail or one that demands students do what is required to succeed?

Furthermore, the current system is not working even for those students who graduate from high school and enter college. The United States has the second-highest collegiate dropout rate in the industrialized world (Porter, 2013). Based on overwhelming evidence, advocating for our traditional "real world" approach to interventions is misguided at best and unethical at worst. If all students are to learn, educators must do more than invite students to learn; they must insist that students engage in the behaviors that lead to learning.

The Tradition of Avoiding Adult Discomfort

The cultural changes necessary to promote high levels of learning for all students are certain to create anxiety for educators as they move from the comfort zone of traditional practice to a fundamentally different way of approaching their work. This anxiety is an inevitable by-product of substantive change in any organization. But this discomfort often leads educators to seek to circumvent the PLC process and settle for "PLC lite." They may create a rubric for assessing the quality of student work but avoid the collaborative process of applying the rubric to actual evidence of student learning to ensure they have established the inter-rater reliability that results in consistent feedback to students from teacher to teacher. Instead of working together in their teams to develop common assessments, they use assessments created by others—the textbook authors, a district committee, or the writers of commercially prepared assessments. They forget that it is not the product—the actual test—that leads to greater adult learning, it is the *process* of exploring together the question of how to gather the best evidence of student learning that leads to greater insights.

> It is not the product—the actual test—that leads to greater adult learning, it is the *process* of exploring together the question of how to gather the best evidence of student learning that leads to greater insights.

When teams of teachers become more effective in creating high-quality assessments, it helps them to become more effective in their instruction. Their deeper understanding of the standards and stronger awareness of the kinds of tasks that prepare students for the assessments help them to design and deliver higher-quality learning experiences for their students (Darling-Hammond & Conley, 2015). Removing educators from the process removes them from the learning.

But the one activity that creates the greatest discomfort for educators is sharing the results from common formative assessments with their colleagues. Doing so lifts the veil of secrecy that has characterized classroom practice. Results may reveal that they have not been effective in teaching a vital concept. To avoid this potential for discomfort, they often will administer the common assessment but refrain from the transparent sharing of results. They will speak in generalities about student learning rather than explore which strategies seemed to be most effective. This failure to collect, analyze, and present evidence of student learning beyond self-reported anecdotes and the reluctance of educators to make their work public are among the greatest barriers to establishing effective PLCs (Annenberg Institute for School Reform, n.d.).

When educators stop short of using the results from team-developed common formative assessments to inform and improve their individual and collective professional practice, they circumvent the entire PLC process. All the other steps in that process—assigning educators to teams, clarifying the SMART goals they are pursuing and the commitments that will guide their work, establishing a guaranteed and viable curriculum for each unit, developing common assessments to monitor the achievement of each student—are intended to put educators in a position where they can use easily accessible and openly shared evidence of student learning to improve their instruction. This collective analysis and professional dialogue is the crux, the very essence, of the work. It brings student learning and instructional practice into the open. It is, in short, what real PLCs do. To fail to engage in this crucial element of the process is to fail to function as a PLC. If students are to learn at higher levels, educators must assign a higher priority to improving student achievement than they do to preserving tradition or avoiding discomfort. Districts and schools should make teacher-created common formative assessments the cornerstone of their assessment practices, and every professional educator should ensure that all students receive the benefit of this powerful, proven process to improve student learning.

Taking the Necessary Steps

There is no recipe or step-by-step manual for becoming a PLC, but there are some things that *must* be done as part of the process. Using evidence of student learning to inform and improve practice is one of those things, and schools that are sincere in their desire to create a PLC will act accordingly. In doing so, they will discover that despite the very best efforts of teachers, in virtually every unit, some students will be unable to demonstrate proficiency because not all students learn at the same rate and in the same way. The next chapter addresses how PLCs respond to that challenge.

CHAPTER 10

Ensuring Every Student Succeeds

If the goal of our nation's schools was to have *most* students grad-uate from high school while providing the opportunity for *many* to successfully transition into postsecondary educational oppor-tunities, there would be no need to improve our current system of education—a vast majority of schools across the country are currently achieving these outcomes. But because success in the K–12 system is essential for access to opportunities in our chang-ing global economy, our mission must be that *every* student will graduate with the academic skills, knowledge, and dispositions required to continue learning after high school.

I have asked thousands of educators if they concur with the following assertions.

- Every student does not learn the same way.

- Every student does not develop at the same speed.

- Some students lack the social and academic behaviors needed to succeed in school.

- Some students are intensely behind in foundational skills.

- Some students come from home environments that are unable to support or are counterproductive to success in school.

Not a single educator has challenged these assertions. They are, in fact, universal truths of our profession. Given these conditions, it is impossible for individual teachers to provide core instruction designed to meet the learning styles of each student, provide additional time when students don't master key concepts after initial teaching, successfully address the academic and social behavior needs of every student, provide intensive remediation for students on skills not mastered in previous years, extend learning for students who have already mastered grade-level curriculum, and compensate for home environments that are working against these outcomes.

Ensuring every student succeeds requires schools to develop highly effective, systematic interventions to provide students with additional time and support. *Interventions* are anything a school does above and beyond the core instruction that all students receive that helps students succeed in school. *Systematic* means that every learner who needs the help receives it, regardless of his or her assigned teacher (Buffum, Mattos, & Weber, 2012). *Effective* means that the interventions used are proven to be successful and are targeted to meet individual needs of each student.

Helping every student to succeed would be much easier if our educational system was purposely designed around this outcome. Unfortunately, our traditional model of education was never intended to help all students learn at high levels. It took more than two hundred years from the time the first schools were established in the American colonies before the K–12 system came into being, and even then, there was no expectation that even a majority of students would complete the education that system provided. Secondary schools were created as selective institutions "catering to the relatively few students who had the interest and the means to attend school past the primary grades"

(Rumberger, 2011, p. 21). As Harvard President Charles Eliot reported to Congress in 1893:

> Their main function [of high school] is to prepare for the duties of life that small proportion of all the children in the country—a proportion small in number, but very important to the welfare of the nation—who show themselves able to profit by an education prolonged to the eighteenth year, and whose parents are able to support them while they remain so long at school. (as cited in Dorn, 1996, p. 41)

Because only a select few were expected to advance beyond grammar school, providing interventions for students who struggled was not necessary. Differences in student achievement were considered desirable, as this variance helped identify the perceived "best and brightest" for promotion to the next level of education.

Only 14 percent of children fourteen to seventeen years old attended high school in 1900 (Rumberger, 2011). Since America's economy at that time was driven by farms and factories, those who dropped out of the educational system had access to entry-level jobs that rarely required more than the three Rs of reading, writing, and basic 'rithmetic to earn a living wage. Fifty years later, only 34 percent of the population aged twenty-five and older had earned a high school diploma. It wasn't until 1970 that the majority (52 percent) of Americans twenty-five and older had completed high school, but jobs in agriculture and industry continued to offer those who didn't finish high school access to the middle class (U.S. Census Bureau, n.d.).

Since so few students were expected to attend college, high schools created different tracks to prepare students for their anticipated destiny—advanced tracks for the college bound and vocational, general, or remedial tracks for all others. With this arrangement, there was no pressing need for schools to provide systematic interventions. If a student struggled in a higher track of learning, the solution wasn't to provide additional time and support but instead to lower the student's academic expectations and demote him or her to a lower track. Ultimately, if a student failed in the lowest tracks of school, then dropping out of school was acceptable—an option that is still legally permissible in most states beginning at the age of sixteen.

Once again, today, there is virtually no path to the middle class without some level of postsecondary education or training. As the American Diploma Project (2004), now known as the ADP Network, states:

> Successful preparation for both postsecondary education and employment requires learning the same rigorous English and mathematics content and skills. No longer do students planning to go to work after high school need a different and less rigorous curriculum than those planning to go to college. In fact, nearly all students will require some postsecondary education, including on-the-job training, after completing high school. Therefore, a college and workplace readiness curriculum should be a graduation requirement, not an option, for all high school students. (pp. 8–9)

Unfortunately, as Jeannie Oakes (2005) finds in her landmark study *Keeping Track*, the deep structure of tracking remains "uncannily robust" today (p. xi). Most schools still sort students based on judgments of student ability.

Special Education

The only nationally mandated systematic process in the United States to address the needs of students who are unsuccessful in school is special education. Currently, more than 6.5 million children receive services under the Individuals With Disabilities Education Improvement Act (IDEIA; U.S. Department of Education, n.d.), an increase of more than 50 percent since 1990

(National Center for Education Statistics, 2013). One of the reasons for the explosion in identified students is because, traditionally, schools have operated from the assumption that "failure to succeed in a general education program meant the student must, therefore, have a disability" (Prasse, n.d.).

The primary purpose of the original legislation that created special education—the Education for All Handicapped Children Act of 1975—was not to provide special needs students additional time and support to ensure they learn at high levels but instead to allow students with disabilities to attend public school at all. In 1970, most public schools denied enrollment to students with special needs, and only one in five students with disabilities was served in American public schools. While the legislation has been very effective at ensuring children with special needs have access to a free and appropriate public education, it is debatable if the education most special needs students receive is appropriate.

Unfortunately, special education has proven to be tragically insufficient and ineffective at helping students close their achievement gaps and secure the academic success necessary to adequately prepare them for life beyond special education. The graduation rate for special needs students was 61 percent in 2014—almost 20 percent lower than regular education students (Diament, 2014). Special needs students are also woefully underrepresented in postsecondary education (Samuels, 2010), but they are overrepresented in one arena—prison. Up to an estimated 50 percent of the U.S. prison population were identified as having special needs in school (National Center on Secondary Education and Transition [NCSET], 2002).

Minority students are much more likely to be identified as special needs. African American students make up only 16 percent of the student population but occupy as much as 32 percent of the seats in some special education programs. Those numbers are similar for Latino students (U.S. Department of Education, 2009b).

The failure of special education as an effective learning intervention is not due to ineffective special education teachers. Like virtually all educators, these highly trained and dedicated professionals work tirelessly each day on behalf of their students. The problem goes back to the original purpose of special education. The legislation was neither intended nor designed to be an academic intervention but instead was a civil rights issue. Subsequently, traditional special educational policies have allowed at-risk students to fall too far behind before receiving systematic help, have disengaged general education teachers from the intervention process, and have overwhelmed special education resources at the school site with far too many students to serve (Buffum et al., 2012).

> The failure of special education as an effective learning intervention is not due to ineffective special education teachers. Like virtually all educators, these highly trained and dedicated professionals work tirelessly each day on behalf of their students.

If there were the equivalent of a Truth in Lending Act in education, when educators recommended a student for special education, they would be required to inform parents of the following facts.

- If your child qualifies for special education, he or she will qualify for additional support that will be provided by highly trained staff who will work tirelessly on your child's behalf.

- Your child's individualized education program (IEP) goals will most likely be based on below-grade-level learning outcomes. So even if your child meets his or her goals, he or she will still fall further behind grade level.

- The longer your child is in special education, the more likely he or she will be removed from regular education classes.

- There is less than a 5 percent chance your child will catch up to a point that he or she will get out of special education.

- It is basically a coin toss if your student will graduate from high school.

- It is more likely your child will go to prison than college after high school.

- Please sign this initial IEP.

By almost any measure, traditional special education has failed miserably as an intervention, and it would be naïve to think that it will get significantly better results in the future without significant changes.

More Recent Efforts to Provide Interventions

Since the passage of NCLB, the punitive consequences of not meeting required levels of yearly progress have created a new level of urgency for schools to provide struggling students with additional support. Some of the most common efforts have included:

Utilizing Scientifically Research-Based Intervention Programs

NCLB and IDEIA advocate the use of interventions based on "research that involves the application of rigorous, systematic, and objective procedures to obtain reliable and valid knowledge relevant to educational activities and programs" (IDEIA, 2004). As a result, some districts have created lists of approved interventions that constitute the only programs that can be used by their schools, which, in turn, restrict a school's ability to creatively meet the individual needs of each child. Furthermore, outside of primary reading, there are a limited number of scientifically research-based interventions for each subject and grade level.

Other schools and districts have fallen into the trap of searching for the perfect product to buy that will help all their struggling readers, writers, or mathematics students. It would be great if there were a single program a school could purchase that ensured every student would learn how to read. Unfortunately, this product does not exist. At-risk readers don't all struggle for the same reason, so there is no one program that will address every child's unique needs. There *are* some very good, scientifically research-based products available that can become powerful, targeted tools in a school's intervention toolbox—but there is no silver bullet solution for struggling students.

Retention

The *Washington Post* reports that thirteen states have adopted laws that require schools to identify, intervene, and potentially retain students who fail to read proficiently by the end of third grade and that many more states are considering similar legislation (Layton, 2013). The research on the effectiveness of retention is abundant and conclusive: retention does not promote higher levels of learning, close achievement gaps, or increase an at-risk student's odds of future success in school. The most comprehensive meta-analysis on retention finds that being retained one year almost doubles a student's likelihood of dropping out, while being retained twice almost guarantees it (Hattie, 2009). There are also significant equity concerns regarding the use of retention. A comprehensive study from the Office for Civil Rights finds that retention rates are highest among traditionally disadvantaged minorities (West, 2012). Educators who continue to retain pupils at grade level do so despite cumulative research evidence showing that the potential for negative effects consistently outweighs positive outcomes. It would be difficult to find another educational practice for which the evidence is so unequivocally negative (Hattie, 2009).

Response to Intervention

Response to intervention (RTI), also referred to as response to instruction or a multitiered system of supports (MTSS), has been permissible and promoted by federal law since the reauthorization of the Individuals With Disabilities Education Improvement Act in 2004. RTI's underlying premise is that schools should not delay providing systematic help for struggling students until they fall far enough behind to qualify for special education but instead should provide timely, targeted, systematic interventions to all students who demonstrate the need (Buffum et al., 2012).

RTI is traditionally represented in the shape of a pyramid (see figure 10.1). The pyramid is wide at the bottom to represent the core instruction that all students receive. As students demonstrate the need, they receive additional layers of increasingly more targeted and intensive help. Fewer students should need the services offered at the upper levels, thus creating the tapered shape of a pyramid.

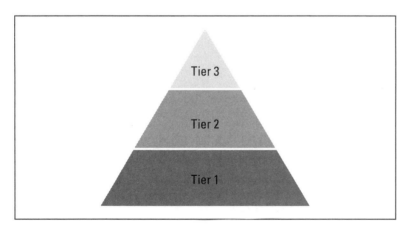

Figure 10.1: The RTI pyramid.

RTI has an astounding yearly impact rate of 1.08 standard deviations growth (Hattie, 2012). Unfortunately, most schools and districts are struggling to secure the student achievement results that RTI, when done well, can provide.

Many states, districts, and schools mistakenly view RTI as primarily a new process to qualify students for special education.

Many states, districts, and schools mistakenly view RTI as primarily a new process to qualify students for special education, making the tiers merely new hoops that a school must jump through prior to placing students into traditional special education services. Instead of providing students with multiple tiers of support, students are moved from tier to tier on the path to special education. Once qualified, students gain access to the failed practices previously described.

Observations on Typical Interventions

I have had the privilege of working with schools in all fifty states, comprising every level (elementary, middle, and high school), size, and demographic. I have seen firsthand what most schools are providing as interventions. The typical approach to intervention is as follows.

- Students are randomly assigned to a teacher for each grade or subject.

- Each teacher is responsible for basically meeting all the initial learning needs of every student assigned to him or her.

- The teacher provides daily instruction, typically in a whole-group setting.

- Instruction is provided within an instructional block or class period, predetermined by the school's master schedule.

- If a student has the prerequisite skills and knowledge for the subject, if the teacher's instructional style and methods match a student's learning style, and if the class period provides the student with enough time to learn, then the student will be successful in acquiring the intended outcome.

- There is no schoolwide, systematic plan to provide students with additional time and support prior to special education.

- Struggling students might receive additional time and support if assigned to a teacher with the desire and ability to come early, stay late, or give up lunch to provide extra help.

- The school will contact parents of struggling students to elicit their support. Regarding misbehavior, the initial parent contact will most likely be immediate, but communication regarding poor academic progress will usually come every six to nine weeks. If the student hasn't fallen too far behind by this point, if the parents have the means to help, and if the teacher's grading practices allow for students to correct their mistakes, then parental interventions might help the student to catch up.

- As students continue to struggle, they will be pulled from grade-level core instruction to receive remedial support. This instruction is usually provided by teachers lowest in seniority, teachers or instructional aides lacking expertise in the subject area, or a computer program.

- The students struggling the most will be retained or transferred to an alternative school setting.

- Once a student fails to such a point that there is a discrepancy of at least two standard deviations' difference between the student's perceived IQ and current level of achievement, the student is placed in special education, where he or she will have virtually no chance to ever catch up.

This scenario not only represents what occurs at most schools today but how schools have traditionally functioned for the past half century.

The reason efforts to provide interventions have so often failed is because schools don't have an intervention problem—they

> The reason efforts to provide interventions have so often failed is because schools don't have an intervention problem—they have a "what we do all day" problem.

have a "what we do all day" problem. Interventions cannot make up for a core instructional program defined by teacher isolation, a culture of "my students and your students," tracking students by perceived ability and demographic expectations, assessing students with archaic grading practices, and expecting parents and special education to be the primary solution for struggling students. As long as interventions are viewed as an appendage to a school's traditional instructional program, instead of an integral part of a school's collaborative efforts to ensure all students succeed, interventions will continue to be ineffective.

What We Must Do to Ensure High Levels of Learning for Every Student

To create a highly effective, systematic process to ensure success for every student, a school staff must restructure its assumptions and practices around the following essential outcomes (Mattos & Buffum, 2015).

- Because all students must leave high school with the skills, knowledge, and dispositions necessary to succeed in postsecondary education, all students must have access to grade-level, college-readiness curriculum. Schools will remove tracks of core instruction focused exclusively on below-grade-level expectations.

- Because all students do not learn the same way, develop at the same speed, enter school with the same prior knowledge, or have the same academic supports at home, students will be provided additional time and support to achieve these rigorous expectations.

- Because a single teacher could not possibly meet the diverse needs of all his or her students, schools will create a systematic intervention process to ensure struggling students get additional time and support for learning that goes beyond what an individual classroom teacher can provide. Achieving this goal will require staff members to work collaboratively and take collective responsibility for each student's success.

- Extra support will be available to all students who demonstrate the need. Because some students cannot come to school early or stay late, schools will embed this help during the school day, when students are required to be at school and all staff members are available to assist.

- Some students will need extra support on meeting essential grade-level standards, others will require intensive remedial help in foundational skills, and some students will need both. The school will create a master schedule where students can have access to this support without missing new essential core instruction.

- If given the choice, some students would prefer to opt out of this additional support. Because success or failure in school is life altering, students will not be given the option of failing. Interventions, when necessary, will be directive.

- Some students will enter school already meeting grade-level expectations. Additional time and support will not come at the expense of these students. Just as schools establish extra assistance to help at-risk students reach grade-level expectations, they will also provide all students with additional time and support to help them succeed in the most rigorous coursework.

Nondiscretionary Elements of Effective Systems of Intervention (What's Tight)

Because school demographics, student needs, staff expertise, state guidelines, and school resources vary greatly, implementing the essential elements of effective intervention is bound to look different from school to school. Educators must be insistent—*tight*—that specific critical elements of effective interventions are present at every school and then flexible—*loose*—on how each school implements these practices. Those tight elements include:

- Interventions must be provided in addition to effective, grade-level core instruction, not in place of it.

- An effective system of interventions starts with good initial teaching.

- There must be a systematic and timely process to identify students who need additional time and support.

- The master schedule must allocate time for supplemental and intensive interventions.

- Interventions must be targeted by student, by standard.

- Interventions must be provided by trained professionals.

- Interventions must be directive.

- Interventions must not come at the expense of students who succeed in core instruction.

> Educators must be insistent—*tight*—that specific critical elements of effective interventions are present at every school and then flexible—*loose*—on how each school implements these practices.

Let's consider each of these tight elements in more detail.

Interventions Must Be Provided in Addition to Effective, Grade-Level Core Instruction, Not in Place of It

Every student might not leave each school year having mastered *every* grade-level standard, but every student must master the learning outcomes that the school or district has deemed indispensable for future success. Anything less, and the student is already on a trajectory to be unable to graduate from high school.

Achieving this goal begins by collectively answering the first critical question of the PLC process: What do we expect students to learn? As discussed in chapter 8, educators must create a guaranteed and viable curriculum grade by grade, course by course, and unit by unit that represents the skills, content knowledge, and behaviors every student must master for future success. Equally important, they must then ensure students have access to this essential grade-level curriculum as part of their core instruction program. With the rare exception for those few students who are profoundly disabled, there should be no "track" of core instruction that focuses exclusively on below-grade-level skills.

> Every student must master the learning outcomes that the school or district has deemed indispensable for future success.

It is self-evident that students placed in a below-grade-level curriculum will end up below grade level at the end of the year. Yet this practice continues in schools that claim their mission is to ensure all students learn at high levels. When asked why, educators present the following reasons.

- **"We are differentiating and teaching students at their level."** As stated at the beginning of this chapter, all students don't learn the same way or at the same speed, so differentiating core instruction is needed to ensure all students learn. But it is the teaching methods that should be differentiated, *not* the essential learning expectations. When a third-grade collaborative team determines that a specific standard is essential, and agrees on the level of rigor required to meet proficiency, then this must be the expectation for all their students. What most schools call differentiation in core instruction is really tracking. The highest group is taught rigorous curriculum, the middle group is taught at grade level, and the lowest group gets modified curriculum—code word for remedial, watered-down expectations.

- **"We place these students into a remedial program to catch them up."** The logic behind pulling students from core curriculum to "catch them up" is baffling. Removing students from core instruction to provide remediation in foundational skills does not help students "catch up" to grade-level expectations. Every day, while these students are pulled from their classrooms, they miss new grade-level essential curriculum needed to succeed next year. It is the proverbial "one step forward—two steps back." Students do not need access to grade-level essential standards *or* remediation in prior skills—students need access to grade-level essential standards *and* interventions. This is how to close a student's achievement gap. To achieve this goal, a school's master schedule must be aligned to this outcome, a topic discussed later in this chapter.

- **"We have to follow the student's IEP."** I often hear educators say students must be pulled from grade-level instruction because their special education plan requires it. Again, this claim is perplexing. Who primarily writes each student's yearly IEP goals and service plan? The educators at the school! And these yearly plans are not chiseled in stone, with no further opportunity to revise them until next year. So if educators don't find a student's current IEP is ensuring his or her success, then they have both the authority and obligation to revise the plan to better meet the student's needs.

- **"Some students are just too low. They can't do it."** This is the most common answer regarding why some students are placed in remedial tracks of learning—and by far the most disturbing. All educators believe that their students can learn, but many feel how much a student can learn varies depending on his or her innate abilities and demographic background. This assumption goes back to our history of tracking students and creates a sliding scale of student expectations. These beliefs are not expressed formally in the school's mission statement or policies, but they are carried out in school practice every day. Across the United States, minority students, English learners, and economically disadvantaged students are disproportionately represented in special education (Brantlinger, 2006; Ferri & Connor, 2006; Skiba et al., 2008; Skiba, Poloni-Staudinger, Gallini, Simmons, & Feggins-Azziz, 2006) and underrepresented in gifted and honors programs (Donovan & Cross, 2003). A student's ethnicity, native language, and economic status do not reduce the child's innate capacity to learn. Yet, when we make assumptions on what we think students are capable of learning based upon these demographic factors, they become a self-fulfilling prophecy (Buffum et al., 2012).

Any school dedicated to ensuring all students learn at high levels must stop debating what they *think* students can or can't do and instead change the question to this: *How will we get every learner there?* But it is unlikely all school staff members will dedicate themselves to ensuring all students succeed when they begin with the assumption that some students can't do it in the first place.

> Any school dedicated to ensuring all students learn at high levels must stop debating what they *think* students can or can't do and instead change the question to this: *How will we get every learner there?*

An Effective System of Interventions Starts With Good Initial Teaching

A successful system of interventions is grounded in highly effective initial teaching. Thus, the key to effective intervention is to have more good teaching in more classrooms more of the time (DuFour & Mattos, 2013). This raises an important question: What is good teaching?

Effective teaching cannot be reduced to a single template, rubric, or checklist aligned to program fidelity because there is no such thing as a universally effective teaching strategy, methodology, or textbook series (DuFour & Mattos, 2013). Such an approach fails to provide teachers with the professional autonomy needed to practice the art of teaching.

Yet allowing the instructional pendulum to swing completely in the opposite direction by allowing each teacher total autonomy over his or her instructional decisions is equally ineffective. There are instructional practices that are proven to be more effective for most students and many that are not. Any school dedicated to ensuring all its students learn at high levels cannot assume that each faculty member has the knowledge, skills, and inclination to consistently use these proven practices in his or her classroom.

> Effective instruction requires both an expectation that all teachers use practices proven to have the greatest impact on student learning while simultaneously enabling teachers to infuse their own style and differentiate instruction for individual student needs.

Effective instruction requires both an expectation that all teachers use practices proven to have the greatest impact on student learning while simultaneously enabling teachers to infuse their own style and differentiate instruction for individual student needs. The key lies in identifying and leveraging the right practices that all students must receive, regardless of which teacher they are assigned to for core instruction. To this end, the research in our profession is abundantly clear: good teaching is a collaborative effort. Ensuring that all students succeed requires a school to embrace the following mantra: good teaching is not what *I* do *for* my students but instead what *we* do *with* our students.

The instructional practices that have the greatest impact on teaching include (Hattie, 2009):

- Teachers must work collaboratively rather than in isolation.
- Teachers must agree on the essential learning all students must acquire.

- Teachers must agree on how students will demonstrate their learning.

- Teachers must assess their individual and collective effectiveness on the basis of the evidence of student learning.

Hattie (2009) finds that when teacher teams determine a limited number of rigorous essential learning outcomes that all students must master, and agree on how students will demonstrate mastery of each, the yearly impact rate is 0.56 standard deviations. And when teacher teams use common formative assessments to both assess student progress and collectively reflect on the teaching practices, the impact is 0.90!

These outcomes align perfectly with the first two critical questions of the PLC process.

1. What do we expect students to learn?

2. How will we know they are learning it?

Answering these critical PLC questions during Tier 1 core instruction creates the instructional focus and ongoing assessment processes necessary to effectively respond when students need additional support.

There Must Be a Systematic and Timely Process to Identify Students Who Need Additional Time and Support

Every school has interventions, but very few have systematic interventions. A school has a systematic intervention process when it can make the following promise to every parent:

> It does not matter which teacher your student is assigned to at this school—if your child needs additional time and support, we guarantee he or she will receive it until he or she is learning at high levels. (Buffum et al., 2012, p. 159)

Failure to create a timely, systematic process to identify students in need of additional help leaves the question of interventions up to each teacher to resolve. If the mission of the school is to ensure high levels of learning for all students, all students are entitled to participate in a system that guarantees they will receive extra time and support whenever they struggle. The system would make it virtually impossible for a single student to slip through the cracks.

> If the mission of the school is to ensure high levels of learning for all students, all students are entitled to participate in a system that guarantees they will receive extra time and support whenever they struggle.

Identifying students who need interventions requires timely monitoring of student progress. Every school has a process for this—report cards. Unfortunately, traditional grading practices have numerous drawbacks as tools to identify students for additional help. One of the worst problems is the amount of time students are allowed to fail before teachers submit grades. Many schools have teachers submit student grades on a quarterly basis. That means one-fourth of the year passes before that information can be used to identify students in need of additional help.

Additionally, grades rarely give specific information regarding the reasons the student is struggling. Students fail courses for a multitude of reasons, each often requiring a very specific intervention. Finally, at most schools, the process by which student grades are determined varies greatly from teacher to teacher. Some teachers place a greater weight on effort, while others more on test scores. Some teachers include a student's behavior when determining a student's academic marks, while others don't. Because of this tremendous variance, it is problematic to use traditional report card practices as the primary way to identify students who need additional support.

I recommend the following three processes for timely monitoring of student learning.

Team-Developed Common Formative Assessments

Identifying students for additional time and support begins when teacher teams answer the question, How will we know students are learning? Before even beginning a unit of study that contains essential curriculum, the team has planned for how student progress will be measured. The information gained from these assessments will be more timely because the assessments are administered either during or immediately at the end of each unit. The information is also extremely targeted, providing insights into exactly which learning targets a specific student needs additional support to master. Common formative assessments developed by the team should be the primary anchor practice of an effective Tier 2 supplemental intervention process.

Staff Recommendations

While a common assessment aligned to essential standards is a powerful tool to identify students in need of interventions after core instruction, its use will not be sufficient to identify every struggling student. Common assessments measure a student's need for academic support, but not every student struggles at school for academic reasons. If a mathematics team identified "order of operations" as an essential standard and then administered an assessment on this topic, the information provided would be an outstanding way to identify students in need of additional instruction and practice at applying this skill. But this mathematics assessment would be ineffective at identifying a student who is having severe difficulties making friends or a child demonstrating aggressive behavior on the playground. Who might notice these student needs? The staff.

This staff recommendation process must be timely. Teacher input should be solicited at least every three weeks. Participation from all site educators must be required. If even one teacher is permitted to be excused from the process, then the students who are assigned to this teacher are much less likely to receive additional time and support. All staff members should start the year knowing when the identification process will take place, how the information will be gathered, and what criteria will be used for identifying students in need (Buffum et al., 2012). Finally, the process must be simple and efficient so as not to require an unreasonable amount of time on the part of teachers to participate in the process.

Universal Screening

The best intervention is prevention, and it is possible to identify students who need additional time and support *before* they fail. This is especially the case for students who enter a new school year with significant gaps in foundational skills. If an incoming eighth-grade student begins the year reading at a third-grade level, can the school predict this student will need support? In RTI, the process of proactively identifying students for intensive interventions is called *universal screening*.

> The best intervention is prevention, and it is possible to identify students who need additional time and support *before* they fail.

Traditionally, universal screening was accomplished by giving short, quick assessments to all students in foundational skills, such as reading, writing, and number sense. But universal screening does not have to be a test. Toward the end of each school year, staff can already begin to identify students who will return next fall needing intensive support. Additionally, schools could contact their feeder schools and proactively identify incoming students who will need extra help. The simple question, Which of your students will need us most? can reveal a wealth of information that allows a school to be proactive rather than reactive.

For example, at-risk ninth graders usually have a history of struggling in school long before entering high school, and predicting which incoming students are likely to need extra support is not difficult. High school educators should have a process to work with their eighth-grade counterparts to identify the students who will need them most well before those students enter the school as freshmen. Likewise, middle and junior high schools should have a process to work with elementary feeder schools, and elementary schools with preschools and parents to clearly define the necessary prerequisites for success. Through a universal screening process, the schools will be able to identify the incoming students who will need extra time and support to acquire the essential foundational knowledge and skills necessary for success at the next level.

When schools use frequent common assessments to monitor each student's mastery of essential standards, a staff recommendation process to identify students who are struggling with nonacademic issues, and universal screening to proactively address student needs, they can create systems that make it almost impossible for students to slip under a school's intervention radar screen.

The Master Schedule Must Allocate Time for Supplemental and Intensive Interventions

Even the most effective core instruction will not successfully meet the needs of every student. Every time a new essential standard is initially taught, a learning-focused school must anticipate that some students will not master it by the end of the unit. When a majority of students are successful, classroom teachers must move on to the next unit of study. But for students who have not mastered the previous unit's essential standards, the school will need to provide time for additional support on these standards without those students missing new initial core instruction. Additionally, students who enter the school year with significant gaps in foundational skills will need daily, intensive remediation in these skills while still having access to grade-level essential curriculum. Finally, it is likely that the students who need intensive help in remedial skills will also have difficulty with new core curriculum the first time it is taught. These students will need supplemental support in meeting grade-level essential curriculum, and intensive interventions in remedial skills, while still having access to new essential core instruction. The RTI pyramid, shown again in figure 10.2, visually captures this thinking.

The pyramid is visually separated into tiers (Buffum et al., 2012).

- Tier 1 represents a school's core instructional program, in which all students receive effective instruction on grade-level essential curriculum.

- Tier 2 is intended to provide timely, targeted supplemental academic and behavioral interventions to ensure that all students end each school year with the essential skills and knowledge needed to succeed the following year and beyond.

- Tier 3 ensures students who begin the school year with significant deficits in the universal skills of reading, writing, number sense, English language, and academic and social behaviors receive intensive academic and behavioral remediation in these foundational skills.

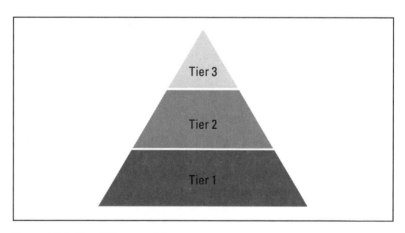

Figure 10.2: The RTI pyramid.

When applied properly, the tiers should be viewed as layers of support based on each student's learning needs. In other words, a school should not view the RTI process as moving students from one tier to another but instead as providing supplemental and intensive help in addition to core instruction. The most at-risk students will need effective Tier 1 core instruction on grade-level essential standards *and* Tier 2 supplemental support in meeting these critical outcomes *and* Tier 3 intensive instruction on foundational skills that should have been mastered years ago.

At Tier 2, schools should dedicate time in their master schedule at least once a week, but preferably more frequently, for students to receive additional time and support to master essential grade-level curriculum. This time should also be flexible and fluid, meaning students should be able to move into and out of the tier based on demonstrated mastery of the targeted learning outcomes.

Many schools try to find this time by extending the school day for interventions, offering extra help before school, at lunch, during recess, and after school. Unfortunately, these options have significant drawbacks. If students are required to forgo a social lunch or recess with their peers to receive interventions, the extra time and support are often perceived by the student to be punitive. Most schools cannot require a student to come early or stay late, especially if the learner is dependent on school transportation, must work to support the family, or is needed at home to tend to younger siblings. Also, before- and after-school interventions usually extend beyond teacher contract hours, which, in turn, requires additional site funds to pay teachers a stipend for this work. When these funds are not available, schools often utilize volunteers or classified employees to staff these programs. While volunteers and support staff can be helpful for some types of interventions, they rarely have any professional training in the areas in which they are tutoring.

Ultimately, for interventions to work best, they must be offered during a time when teachers are paid to be there and students are required to be there. Yet many educators tell us, "We would like to implement these ideas, but our master schedule just won't allow it." When asked why they cannot change the schedule, educators often respond that they don't have the authority to

> For interventions to work best, they must be offered during a time when teachers are paid to be there and students are required to be there.

make such changes due to state, district, and contractual restraints. Ironically, these same schools change their schedules often throughout the year—for pep rallies, assemblies, fine-arts events, state and district testing, holidays, parent conferences, and poor weather. If the schedule is a tool that reflects the school's priorities, many schools are assigning a higher priority to cheering for athletic teams than to providing struggling students with the time and support they need to succeed.

Another common explanation is that there is no time for interventions because there is already too much required curriculum to cover. As established previously, it is impossible to cover all the content in the curriculum American educators are asked to teach. Ensuring students learn what is essential must take priority over covering every standard. It is unacceptable to deny struggling students time for interventions simply to maintain the appearance that the school is covering every required state standard.

In reality, the most common reason for why most schools don't revise their master schedule is because key adults in the building don't want to change it. Too often, schools create their master schedule, from teacher assignments to course and subject offerings, based more on the needs and desires of the adults in the building and less on the needs of the students. Once a school embraces student learning as its mission, a myriad of scheduling options become available. Hundreds of schools throughout North America have successfully revised their master schedule to achieve the outcomes of core teaching and intervention time within existing state guidelines, contractual agreements, and site resources. To see examples of master schedules that provide time for

> Ensuring students learn what is essential must take priority over covering every standard.

intervention from model PLCs, visit the following resources on AllThingsPLC.

- Highland Elementary School Master Schedule (www .allthingsplc.info/files/uploads/schedule_examples _elementary.pdf)

- Middle and High School Intervention Examples (www.allthingsplc.info/files/uploads/middle_high _intervention_examples.pdf)

- See the Evidence (www.allthingsplc.info/evidence)

At Tier 3, intensive intervention focuses on the universal skills of learning: reading, writing, number sense, English language, attendance, and behavior. These skills can only be developed over time, so intensive interventions need to be provided for targeted students as part of their instructional day. At the elementary level, this is usually accomplished by extra support "pushing into" classrooms during guided or independent practice activities or "pulling" students during those times when new direct instruction on essential standards is not occurring so the struggling students can receive intensive remediation from highly skilled educators who know exactly which skills the students are lacking. For example, a strategy to provide intensive support for literacy skills is utilizing grade-level social studies and science curriculum. During time set aside for instruction in these subjects, one of the grade-level teachers, a reading specialist, or a special education teacher can provide support for students lacking literacy skills while using appropriate texts to teach the relevant social studies and science content. At the secondary level, intensive interventions are most commonly provided through designed courses. Again, the key is that these services must be provided *in addition to* a student's access to essential grade-level curriculum, not in place of it.

Interventions Must Be Targeted by Student, by Standard

To target interventions effectively, a school should consider two criteria. First, a school must target interventions by the student, by the standard. In other words, what specific essential skill or knowledge is this student lacking? This level of intervention specificity is why identifying essential standards is so vital. Unless a school has clearly identified the essential standards that every student must master and unwrapped the standards into specific student learning targets, it would be nearly impossible to have the curricular focus and specific assessment data necessary to target interventions to this level. In the end, educators need to continually ask, "What exactly do we want students to learn from this intervention?" The more specific the answer, the more targeted the intervention, and the more likely educators will hit the target.

Focusing efforts by the student, the standard, and the learning target is the first step in focused interventions, but there is a second, equally important consideration: Why didn't the student learn? We must address the cause of a student's struggles, not merely the symptoms (Buffum et al., 2012). Unfortunately, most schools' interventions are ineffective because they are too broad in focus and rarely address a student's individual learning needs. For example:

- Schools often offer interventions like study hall for all students with an F in a particular class. These students have earned Fs for a variety of reasons, yet one teacher is expected to address the numerous learning needs of the students in study hall. If the criterion for placement is having an F, then what is the target of the intervention? To "un-F" these students?

- Schools often use universal screening data to place students into reading interventions and then put all the learners who need intensive support into the same reading intervention. All these students may score in the intensive range on a universal screening assessment, but they certainly do not have the same reading needs. It would be impossible for one teacher to meet all their needs in the same intervention period.

- Some schools place students in interventions based on the prior year's state assessment results. For example, students who score below proficient on the state mathematics assessment are automatically placed in an intensive mathematics intervention program. Again, it is highly unlikely that all the students scored poorly on the state assessment for the same reasons.

Poor grades, disruptive behavior, and infrequent attendance are all symptoms. The more important questions are: Why is this student failing a class? What is causing this student to demonstrate disruptive behavior? Why did this student fail the exam? Why is this student chronically absent? When interventions get down to by student, by standard, by name, and by need, they become highly successful.

Interventions Must Be Provided by Trained Professionals

Douglas Reeves (2009) finds that one of a school's most effective learning strategies is to have highly trained teachers work with the students most at risk. Unfortunately, the vast majority of schools do the exact opposite. According to the National Partnership for Teaching in At-Risk Schools (2005), "Not only do the teachers of low-income students tend to be more poorly trained in the subject they teach, they also are far more likely to have significantly less teaching experience" (p. 3).

This approach is justified at most schools by a faculty seniority system in which more tenured teachers usually work with students who are high achieving, while new teachers must "pay their dues" with students who are more at risk. These practices are often protected by teacher contract language that limits the ability of site administration to reassign teacher positions or revise a teacher's course or grade-level teaching assignment. Even when not written into contractual agreements, this practice is frequently supported by school administrators because parents of the most successful students often complain if their child is assigned to an inexperienced teacher's class.

If there were no labels in education—regular ed, special ed, Title I, EL, gifted, accelerated—how would a school group students for interventions? Wouldn't it be based on students who have the same needs, such as:

- Students who still struggle with a consonant-vowel-consonant (CVC) blend
- Students who have difficulty multiplying exponents
- Students who are lacking organizational skills to keep track of assignments

And how would a school determine which staff members should lead each of these interventions? Wouldn't it be based on who has training and expertise in teaching CVC blends, algebra, or organizational skills? Although this approach is clearly logical, it is often not the norm, as many schools instead group students by labels tied to funding sources. Such decisions are justified with the claim "But the law does not allow us the flexibility to group students by need." Actually, there is now much more flexibility in federal law and in most state regulations. For example, the federal reauthorization of IDEIA in 2004 promotes early intervening services (EIS), which allow a percentage of special education resources to be used in preventive ways to support students not currently in special education.

Unless our most at-risk students have access to our most effective teachers, it is unlikely that any particular intervention strategy, practice, or program will prove effective.

Interventions Must Be Directive

Interventions *must* be mandatory. It is disingenuous for a school to claim that its mission is to ensure that all students learn at high levels yet allow its students to choose failure (Buffum et al., 2012). When help is optional, the students who are most likely to take advantage of this offer are the ones already succeeding at school, while the students least likely are those most at risk. There are students in every school who are not blessed with innate organizational skills, work ethic, grit, and motivation. If these students are to achieve at high levels, educators must commit to intentionally teaching these vital skills in their classrooms and through directive intervention rather than continuing the tradition of passively allowing students to fail.

> It is disingenuous for a school to claim that its mission is to ensure that all students learn at high levels yet allow its students to choose failure.

Interventions Must Not Come at the Expense of Students Who Succeed in Core Instruction

A common concern educators present regarding creating time for interventions during the school day is that it is unfair to students who excel during initial teaching. This is a very understandable concern, but it is based on a faulty premise that intervention time can only be used for reteaching and remediation. In reality, flexible time in a school's master schedule can be used for not only remediation and reteaching but also to extend learning and support for students in the most rigorous curriculum.

For example, in many high schools, when a student struggles in honors, advanced placement, or international baccalaureate curriculum, the approach of the school is not to provide extra help but to assume that the learner is not capable and remove him or her from the more rigorous coursework. Educators know that all students do not learn the same way or at the same speed—this universal truth applies to students in advanced physics just as it does to a student in grade-level curriculum. For this reason, flexible time and support should not come at the cost of any student's needs, as the very purpose of the time is to meet the individual needs of each student. In fact, schools that provide an effective system of interventions see an increase in the percentage of students succeeding in rigorous curriculum and scoring at advanced levels on standardized assessments.

The Challenge Ahead

As a general concept, creating a system of effective interventions is appealing to virtually all educators—who would not want to provide extra support for students in need? Interventions sound great . . . when someone else is providing them. But the enthusiasm quickly wanes when educators realize that creating processes to ensure all students succeed will require much more than purchasing a new remedial reading program, starting an after-school homework club, hiring an intervention teacher, or revising the master schedule to create an intervention period. Creating a highly effective, systemic intervention process requires a school staff to take collective responsibility for student success, collaborate regularly, agree on essential learning outcomes and pacing, abandon traditional teaching and assessment practices that were designed to create a bell-shaped curve of student success, and make significant revisions to the school's master schedule and resource allocations. This level of change is difficult—very difficult. In the end, many schools struggle because too many adults in the building

> Creating a highly effective, systemic intervention process requires a school staff to take collective responsibility for student success, collaborate regularly, agree on essential learning outcomes and pacing, abandon traditional teaching and assessment practices that were designed to create a bell-shaped curve of student success, and make significant revisions to the school's master schedule and resource allocations.

are unwilling to accept the level of temporary disequilibrium and discomfort required to significantly change what they do all day. The next chapter discusses the essential role that effective leadership plays in leading change and taking these powerful ideas from research to reality.

CHAPTER 11

The Principal
as Lead Learner

School leadership matters a lot! It is second only to teaching
among school-related factors that impact student achievement
(Leithwood, Louis, Anderson, & Wahlstrom, 2004). Furthermore,
the principal plays a vital role in cultivating the culture of a PLC
(Bryk et al., 2010; Huggins, Scheurich, & Morgan, 2011; Louis
& Wahlstrom, 2011; McREL, 2005; Wallace Foundation, 2012).
For better or worse, principals are the critical cog that can support
or inhibit both student and adult learning.

   In light of the importance of the position, it is troubling that
principals are feeling overwhelmed these days, and with good
reason. Throughout most of the 20th century, principals were
considered effective if students were well behaved, teachers were
happy, and parent complaints reaching the central office were
kept to a minimum. Today, they are asked to assume responsibility for twenty-one different areas of school improvement
(Marzano et al., 2005).

   Principals are pulled in one direction by those who view them
as middle managers who serve as a conduit between the central
office and the school's staff. In this view, principals are to ensure

policies created by others are implemented efficiently. This focus calls on principals to *do things right*: build the master schedule, oversee the budget, implement effective student discipline policies, complete the teacher evaluation process, and so on.

They are pulled in an entirely different direction by researchers who challenge them to serve not merely as managers but as *leaders* who *do the right things*—the things that have the greatest impact on student learning. But even the call to lead is muddied by mixed messages. Principals have been urged to function as instructional leaders, transformational leaders, servant leaders, strategic leaders, learning leaders, empowering leaders, participatory leaders, delegatory leaders, or moral leaders. Small wonder that 75 percent of principals report that their job has become too complex, a view shared by principals regardless of the school level, the school location, the proportion of low-income or minority students, or the proportion of students performing at or above grade level (Markow et al., 2013).

The complexity of the current principalship is compounded by the perception of principals themselves that although they face tremendous responsibilities, they have little influence over key elements of their schools. Nine in ten feel they are accountable for everything that happens to the students in their school, but only 42 percent feel they have control over removing an ineffective teacher or influencing curriculum and instruction (Markow et al., 2013). These findings are particularly troubling in light of research that has shown a strong relationship between a principal's self-efficacy and his or her effectiveness (Louis, Leithwood, Wahlstrom, & Anderson, 2010).

In the face of this increasing responsibility and diminishing control, half of principals feel under great stress several days a week, and principal job satisfaction plummeted from 76 percent in 2004 to 59 percent in 2013. In one survey, one-third of principals reported they were likely to leave their job and pursue a different occupation within the next five years (Markow et al., 2013).

The best advice I can offer to principals confronting these challenges is simple: no one person has the energy, expertise, and influence to fulfill all the responsibilities of your job successfully. If you try to do it all by yourself, you will fail. The only hope of meeting the demands of the contemporary principalship is dispersing leadership throughout the school (Bryk et al., 2010; DuFour & Marzano, 2011; Fullan, 2014; Marzano et al., 2005). By creating lots of leaders in the school, you can focus on two key elements of leading a PLC: establishing clarity and coherence throughout the staff and creating the conditions that allow teachers to succeed at what they are being asked to do.

This is not revolutionary advice. For decades, both the National Association of Elementary School Principals and the National Association of Secondary School Principals (NASSP) have urged their members to practice collaborative leadership (DuFour & DuFour, 2012; Farrace, 2012). As the NASSP (1996) reports, the command-and-control, run-a-tight-ship

> The only hope of meeting the demands of the contemporary principalship is dispersing leadership throughout the school.

leadership style that distinguished some principals in the past is ill suited to the collaborative leadership necessary for significant school improvement. Principals who share leadership are consistently found in strong PLCs because the "many tasks of transforming schools require many leaders" (Louis & Wahlstrom, 2011, p. 52).

Dispersing Leadership

Principals don't need to have all the answers about improving their schools, but they must ask the right questions and create a variety of structures and processes to engage the staff in the consideration of those questions. One of those structures is a guiding coalition of influential staff members to help identify, advocate for, and ultimately guide the key improvement strategies for the school. Others refer to this structure as the *leadership team* (Marzano et al., 2005), *guiding team* (Kotter & Cohen, 2002), or simply getting the right people on the bus (Collins, 2005). Although the terms may vary, the underlying premise does not: even the most competent leaders will struggle to bring about substantive change without the support of allies who are willing to serve as champions for that change. A principal who is unable to win the support of a small cadre of key people to support the change has little chance of persuading the entire staff to do so. Failure to create a guiding coalition is one of the most neglected steps in the change process (Kotter & Cohen, 2002).

> Even the most competent leaders will struggle to bring about substantive change without the support of allies who are willing to serve as champions for that change.

Most organizations have approximately 15 percent of their members who are so respected and connected that if they support a proposal, the majority of their peers are likely to support it as well (Patterson et al., 2008). These "opinion leaders" may not be among the early adopters who are prone to support new initiatives, but principals should be sure to include some of them on the guiding coalition.

Another strategy for dispersing leadership is the collaborative team process itself. That process empowers teams to make critical decisions: what to teach, how to teach, how to pace content, how to gather evidence of student learning, what criteria members will use in assessing the quality of student work, and which SMART goals they will pursue. With this increase in authority comes an increase in responsibility. Empowered teams are less likely to cite the decisions of others as the core of their problems because they are making the decisions. People tend to advocate for and support what they help create.

Designating leaders for the collaborative teacher team process is another strategy for promoting shared leadership. Principals can take different approaches to assigning team leaders. Generally, the principal should recruit particular individuals as team leaders based on the respect of their peers or perceived leadership potential. A new principal might ask the team to select its leader within clearly defined parameters. Still others may encourage small teams with three or fewer members to operate as collaborative groups in which responsibilities such as team leader, recorder, or timekeeper rotate among members of the team each year. The way in which team leaders are selected can vary, but leaderless teams do not work well. Someone on the team must be responsible for serving as a liaison to the principal and helping the team move forward with the PLC process.

When a team leader structure is in place, principals can work through those leaders to help promote the success of the team. For example, imagine a principal in a K–5 elementary school who recognizes the importance of every team establishing a quality SMART goal to guide its collaborative efforts. Rather than trying to work with the entire faculty all at once in the goal-setting process, the principal could work with the six grade-level team leaders to train them to lead that process. He or she could explain why SMART goals are such a significant aspect of the PLC process, provide team leaders with tools and resources to help their teams write good goals, encourage questions, and model how the leaders might work with their teams. In short, the principal would be developing the capacity, competence, and confidence of team leaders for each step on the PLC journey.

Even with a designated team leader, the collaborative team process, when done well, generates opportunities for situational leadership. If a team discovers that one of its members is helping students achieve exceptional results on a particular skill, that member is in a position to take the lead in explaining the instructional strategies impacting those results. Leadership opportunities emerge based on evidence of expertise rather than a designated title.

Finally, principals can convene task forces to explore a particular aspect of the school that warrants attention. The task force is given a charge to:

- Clarify the problem
- Gather resources for addressing the problem
- Develop shared knowledge with the rest of the staff about the problem and alternative strategies for addressing it
- Recommend a solution
- Build consensus for supporting the solution

Examples of topics for a site-based task force might include creating a schedule that allows for both collaboration and intervention, grading practices that support student learning, and strategies for increasing parent involvement in the education of their children. Creating a task force is directly aligned to a fundamental tenant of a PLC—building shared knowledge prior to making decisions.

Unlike the other structures, task forces are short term, focused, and disbanded when they have completed their charge. But membership in a task force that improves some aspect of the school can be a very satisfying leadership experience.

Leading a PLC is never a solo act. An excellent way to assess the effectiveness of a principal is the number of other leaders he or she is developing and nurturing.

Creating Clarity and Coherence

Researcher Marcus Buckingham (2005) concludes that the one thing leaders of any organization must know in order to be effective is the importance of clarity—communicating clearly and consistently the purpose of the organization, the future it is attempting to create, the specific actions members can take immediately to achieve its purpose and long-term goals, and the indicators of progress it will track. If the principal and guiding coalition have worked with staff to establish a common mission, a shared vision, collective commitments, and mutual goals, they have laid the foundation of a PLC and provided a degree of clarity. If they have established the structures that support a collaborative culture, they have addressed an essential prerequisite for an effective PLC. But if, at that point, the educators in the building are not clear about the right work or do not focus their collaborative efforts on that work, there will be no gains in student achievement. One of the most important responsibilities of a principal in leading the PLC process is to ensure all staff members are clear on the nature of the work to be done and demonstrate the discipline to focus their collective efforts on that work. To paraphrase W. Edwards Deming, it is not enough to work hard; you must clarify the right work and then work hard. Effective leaders at all levels will ensure there is agreement on the right work.

> One of the most important responsibilities of a principal in leading the PLC process is to ensure all staff members are clear on the nature of the work to be done and demonstrate the discipline to focus their collective efforts on that work.

One of the important ways in which principals and guiding coalitions contribute to clarity and coherence is by establishing a culture that is *simultaneously loose and tight*. In some aspects of the school, members of the faculty are empowered to make important decisions and have the autonomy to execute those decisions. These areas represent the *loose* aspect of the culture and include such things as teams establishing their own goals, collective commitments, guaranteed and viable curriculum, pacing, instructional practices, and common assessments.

There are other aspects of the school culture, however, that are *tight*. These six elements of the culture are nondiscretionary, and every member of the faculty is expected to honor and observe these core practices of a PLC, which include the following.

1. Educators work collaboratively rather than in isolation and have clarified the commitments they have made to each other about how they will work together.

2. The fundamental structure of the school becomes the collaborative team in which members work inter-dependently to achieve common goals for which all members are mutually accountable.

3. The team establishes a guaranteed curriculum, unit by unit, so all students have access to the same knowledge and skills, regardless of which teacher they are assigned.

4. The team develops common formative assessments to frequently gather evidence of student learning.

5. The school creates systems of intervention to ensure students who struggle receive additional time and support for learning in a way that is timely, directive, diagnostic, and systematic.

6. The team uses evidence of student learning to inform and improve the individual and collective practices of its members.

Note that each of these elements is essential to the PLC process. A staff cannot pick three or four of these conditions to implement in their school and claim to be a PLC. If the process is to generate improved results, all the characteristics must be tight.

Once a guiding coalition has established what is tight, it must communicate the importance of these aspects of the school to staff "clearly, repeatedly, enthusiastically, and repeatedly (that's not a typo). When it comes to reinforcing clarity, there is no such thing as too much communication" (Lencioni, 2012, p. 15).

This level of clarity demands more than memos and speeches; it requires congruence between articulated priorities and the day-to-day work of the school. It requires systems to ensure that every process and program reminds the staff what is really important. It requires a consistent, sustained focus and direction. It requires monitoring and modeling on the part of the guiding coalition. The most effective principals will not attempt to attend to twenty-one different responsibilities but will instead work with the guiding coalition to provide crystal clarity about the few things that matter most in terms of improving student and adult learning.

Servant Leadership and Reciprocal Accountability

In the simultaneous loose-tight culture described in the previous section, educators are held accountable for focusing on critical elements of the PLC process and demonstrating high quality in the work they produce. It is, therefore, incumbent on the principal and guiding coalition to view their role as providing teams with everything they need to succeed in what they are being asked to do. They should think of their leadership not as positional authority to impose their will but as servant leadership to meet the needs of others. They should constantly ask, "What must we do to fulfill our responsibility to support others?" and "What support can we provide that will enable our staff to accomplish what needs to be accomplished?"

For each essential aspect of the PLC process, the principal and guiding coalition should anticipate the questions that may arise as teams work through the process. The leaders should then attempt to provide the assistance and support to help answer those questions. For example, consider a team that has been asked to develop common formative assessments for each unit its members teach. Seven questions likely to arise from this task are as follows.

1. **Why questions:** Why should we develop common formative assessments? Can you present a rationale as to why we should engage in this work? Why can't we use assessments created by others rather than create our own? What evidence is there to suggest that creating our own common formative assessments is more desirable and effective than what we have traditionally done?

2. **What questions:** What is the exact meaning of common assessment, of formative assessment? What resources, tools, templates, materials, and examples can you provide us to assist in our work? Is there a succinct article that can guide us as we create our assessments? Will you provide us with access to high-quality assessments as models? Can we have access to professional development on how to create good assessments?

3. **How questions:** How do we proceed? Is there a preferred process for writing high-quality assessments? Is there a sequence we should follow?

4. **When questions:** When will you give us time to develop common formative assessments? When do you expect us to complete the task? What is the timeline?

5. **Guiding questions:** Which questions are we attempting to answer with this task? Which questions will help us stay focused on the right work?

6. **Quality questions:** What criteria can we use to judge the quality of our common formative assessments? How will we know when we have done good work?

7. **Assurance questions:** What suggestions can you offer to increase the likelihood of our success? What cautions can you alert us to? Where do we turn when we struggle?

A guiding coalition committed to servant leadership will be prepared to answer these questions for each of the essential elements of the PLC process. *Learning by Doing, Second Edition* (DuFour et al., 2010) is designed as a tool to help the guiding coalition address this aspect of its responsibility for every step on the PLC journey.

Monitoring the Work of Teams

The principal and guiding coalition must also have a process to monitor the work of each collaborative team in order to provide support for a team that struggles to succeed in the task at hand. One team may lack clarity about the elements of SMART goals. Another team may be experiencing conflict. A third may need help in coordinating schedules to provide time for collaboration. In every case, however, servant leaders can't provide effective support to a team unless they are aware of the obstacles and challenges the team is facing.

Leaders often create a false dichotomy when it comes to monitoring the work of others. They choose between micromanaging every detail and laissez-faire leadership, where they turn people loose and hope for the best. The first strategy fails to create ownership in the process or build the capacity of the staff. The second makes it impossible to support a team that is experiencing difficulty or to learn from a team that is accomplishing great things. Furthermore, one of the important ways that leaders communicate priorities is what they pay attention to. Leaders who are inattentive to the work of teams send the message that the work is unimportant.

The best solution to this challenge is for the principal to work with the guiding coalition and team leaders to establish clarity regarding (1) the products teams will generate as a result of the collaborative team process and (2) timelines for when those products will be completed. Assuming a team is provided with time to meet on a regular basis, the timeline for specific products might look like the following.

1. After two meetings, present your team's collective commitments.

2. After three meetings, present your team's SMART goal.

3. After five meetings, present the essential outcomes for the unit you are about to teach.

4. After seven meetings, present your team-developed common formative assessment for the unit.

5. After nine meetings, present your analysis of student achievement for that unit, your insights as to what worked and what didn't, and your strategies for improving your effectiveness in teaching the essential outcomes.

Note that these products represent the natural output of a collaborative team that is focused on the right work in the PLC process. A collaborative team that is clear on its collective commitments and its essential outcomes will have no difficulty in presenting copies of these products to the guiding coalition. Note also that the timeline and products are established collaboratively rather than dictated by the administration.

> One of the important ways that leaders communicate priorities is what they pay attention to. Leaders who are inattentive to the work of teams send the message that the work is unimportant.

A "best evidence synthesis" of leadership behaviors that impact student achievement finds "leading teacher learning and development" is twice as powerful as any other factor (Robinson, 2011). Ranking a distant second is ensuring teacher quality. But, once again, attempting to influence teacher quality by micromanaging and supervising one teacher at a time is "ineffective and counterproductive" and almost certain to result in a "bloody disaster" (Fullan, 2014, pp. 34, 88). One longitudinal study of principals attempting to improve instruction through informal classroom walk-throughs finds the practice is negatively associated with learning and school improvement (Grissom, Loeb, & Master, 2013). Once again, the best way for principals to foster teacher development and improve teacher quality is not by engaging in these high-time, low-yield strategies but by using the PLC process to ensure adult learning aligned to essential student learning is embedded in the routine practices of the school. The current focus on instruction is misplaced. Our nation needs schools that make learning—for students and adults—the central focus of the school and principals who see themselves as lead learners.

Building Consensus and Responding to Resistance

Chapter 6 addressed the importance of building the solid foundation of a PLC—*shared* mission, vision, collective commitments, and goals. The foundation will be a powerful aspect of the PLC process only to the extent that it reflects the hopes and goals of the entire staff rather than the dictates of the central office or principal. All staff members should have an opportunity for input and to have their questions asked and answered.

Too often, however, principals fail to move from this important dialogue to even more important *action* because not every staff member approves of the proposed direction. As mentioned in chapter 5, some district collective bargaining contracts specify the exact percentage of staff members who must approve of a proposal for it to go forward. Most districts do not, however, and the assumption is that decisions in those schools will be reached through consensus. A problem arises when there is no consensus on the term *consensus*.

Principals who equate consensus with unanimity set an impossibly high bar for taking action. If every member of the staff is given

> Not all decisions should be made by consensus, but when they are, the guiding coalition has an obligation to ensure all staff members have the evidence they need to make an informed decision.

veto power over taking action, action will never occur. If every member of the staff must get on board the school improvement train before that train begins to roll, it is unlikely to ever leave the station. Waiting for universal support for a decision is almost certain to lead to paralysis, delay, and frustration (Lencioni, 2005).

Not all decisions should be made by consensus, but when they are, the guiding coalition has an obligation to ensure all staff members have the evidence they need to make an informed decision. Therefore, in attempting to build consensus for implementing the PLC process, principals should work with their guiding coalition to:

- Build shared knowledge regarding the current reality of their school, the elements of the PLC process, and the research base supporting the benefits of the process

- Engage in dialogue with staff to identify and address concerns and questions

- Encourage dissent and invite all staff to present contradictory research and evidence that suggest the PLC process is detrimental to student learning

- Seek to understand the perspectives of those who are opposed to taking action by asking them to share their thought processes and assumptions

- Articulate your thought process and assumptions, search for areas of agreement, and acknowledge areas of disagreement

- Demonstrate a willingness to compromise on some of the specifics of implementation, provided those compromises do not violate the big ideas of the PLC process

Once the guiding coalition has met these obligations, I recommend a two-part standard for consensus for moving forward with implementation.

1. All points of view have not only been heard but solicited.

2. The will of the group is evident even to those who most oppose it.

If that standard is met, all members of the staff should be expected and must be required to act in accordance with the will of the group. The deepest understanding about the PLC process will not occur until the staff begins to do what PLCs do. So the principal and the leadership team must move quickly to make the structural changes that support collaborative work, help clarify the specific work that needs to be done, and provide the support that enables the staff members to succeed at what they are being asked to do. One of the biggest leadership mistakes principals make is the failure to move a staff from learning about PLCs, thinking about PLCs, and talking about PLCs to doing what PLCs do. As Admiral Hyman Rickover (1982) writes, "Knowing is easy; it is the doing that is difficult. The critical issue is not what we know but what we do with what we know. The great end of life is not knowledge, but action" (pp. 8–9).

> The deepest understanding about the PLC process will not occur until the staff begins to do what PLCs do.

The Importance of a Willingness to Confront

In moving the staff to action, it is likely that a principal will discover that, despite all efforts to build consensus and support for moving forward, there will be some members of the staff who will resist. Some of that resistance will be overt, as in "I won't do this, and you can't make me!" Much is likely to be covert, as in "I'm on board," but the person closes the classroom door and continues to do what he or she has always done. How principals address this resistance will have a major impact in determining whether or not the PLC process will succeed or fail in the school.

The entire PLC process depends on collective responsibility and collective commitments. When staff members do not fulfill their responsibilities and do not honor their commitments to their teammates, principals *must* be prepared to confront these violations of the process. I have stressed the importance of clear communication in this chapter. There is nothing more damaging to organizational clarity than incongruity between what the principal claims are priorities and his or her personal behavior. The unwillingness to address an obvious problem and a reluctance to hold people accountable severely weaken the PLC process. The prerequisite loose and tight culture of PLCs is impossible to establish in a school with a principal who is unwilling to be tight about collective commitments and core practices.

> There is nothing more damaging to organizational clarity than incongruity between what the principal claims are priorities and his or her personal behavior. The unwillingness to address an obvious problem and a reluctance to hold people accountable severely weaken the PLC process.

It is certainly preferable to have staff members engage in the PLC process out of commitment rather than compliance. It is almost inevitable, however, that at some point on the PLC journey, a principal must conduct a crucial conversation with a staff member to insist that the person change his or her behavior in order to contribute to the process. When that conversation becomes necessary, principals should consider the following seven guidelines.

1. Conduct the conversation in private.

2. Express specific concerns regarding the *behavior* of the individual. Avoid generalities ("You are having a negative impact on your team") or judgments about attitudes

("You seem very unhappy"). Stick to behaviors ("You have missed two of your last three meetings, you did not contribute to developing your team's common formative assessment, and you have not shared your students' results from the assessment with your colleagues").

3. Contrast the individual's behavior with the collective commitments the staff has made to better achieve the mission of the school ("As you know, we have made collective commitments to help us in our efforts to ensure high levels of learning for all students. Those commitments include attending all team meetings and contributing to the work of the team"). Remind the individual that these commitments were created by the entire faculty and that he or she had a voice in this process.

4. Invite the individual to explain his or her behavior in light of the commitments. Look for areas of agreement and common ground. Be prepared to share specific research and evidence that support why the requested behaviors are desirable and necessary.

5. Clarify the very specific behaviors that you will require of the individual. For example, the principal might say, "There are three things I need you to begin doing immediately. First, you *must* attend all your team meetings. Second, you *must* honor each of the collective commitments your team has established regarding how members will fulfill their responsibilities and relate to one another. Third, you *must* provide me with specific evidence each week that you are (1) teaching your students the essential learning outcomes agreed on by your team and (2) preparing your students to demonstrate their attainment of those outcomes on the common assessments created by the team. We can discuss different ways you might provide me with such evidence.

To ensure that there are no misunderstandings, I will provide you with a written directive detailing these expectations."

6. Invite the individual to suggest any support, training, or resources he or she may need to comply with the directive.

7. Clarify the specific consequences that will occur if the individual does not comply with the directive. Failure to comply with a specific directive is considered insubordination in almost all school districts, and there are policies outlining the escalating consequences for someone deemed insubordinate.

Following the crucial conversation, it is essential that the principal monitor the staff member's *behavior* rather than his or her attitude. A principal cannot require reluctant staff members to be happy about participating in the PLC process, but a principal can require their full participation. Attempts to talk a person into a new attitude are often unproductive. New attitudes typically result from new experiences that, in turn, are the result of engaging in new behaviors (Achor, 2010; Fullan, 2011a; Pfeffer & Sutton, 2000). The biggest breakthroughs in resistance come from new "seeing is believing" experiences (Ferguson, Hackman, Hanna, & Ballantine, 2010, p. 32). If the PLC process proves beneficial to students, provides resistant staff with a positive experience, and leads to better results, changes in beliefs and higher levels of commitment are likely to follow.

> If the PLC process proves beneficial to students, provides resistant staff with a positive experience, and leads to better results, changes in beliefs and higher levels of commitment are likely to follow.

Having the courage to confront does not ensure a positive outcome with the individual, but it is an essential element of clear communication with the rest of the staff. When principals describe certain processes and behaviors as vital to the PLC but fail to confront those who blatantly disregard them, the staff learns those processes and behaviors aren't so vital after all. Furthermore, failure to confront undermines trust in the principal (Bryk et al., 2010). As DuFour and Fullan (2013) note:

> The most powerful form of accountability in a loose-tight culture is peer-to-peer accountability, rather than traditional top-down supervision. But ironically, the only way to develop this lateral accountability is for leaders to demonstrate a willingness to address the situation when people do not honor core values and practices. In high-trust schools and districts, leaders are more—not less—likely to confront those who demonstrate a lack of commitment to their students and their colleagues. (pp. 58–59)

It's difficult to look up to a leader who always has his or her ear to the ground rather than standing for something. Effective leaders of PLCs recognize that the willingness to confront is a powerful way to demonstrate what their school stands for.

Celebration as Communication

Celebration is the flip side of the confrontation coin, and effective principals recognize that both represent powerful ways to remind everyone in the organization of priorities and what is valued. The most powerful motivator for knowledge workers is making progress in meaningful work (Amabile & Kramer, 2011). Therefore, principals must be vigilant in seeking out and publicly celebrating incremental progress on the PLC journey.

Researchers from both inside and outside of education who have examined the question of how effective leaders help people throughout the organization maintain the focus of their improvement efforts offer remarkably consistent advice: "Plan for short-term wins" (Amabile & Kramer, 2011; Elmore & City, 2007; Fullan, 2011a; Heath & Heath, 2010; Kotter & Cohen,

2002). I have emphasized throughout this book that the PLC process is a journey rather than an event, but most people won't continue on that journey unless, early on, they see evidence that it is taking them where they want to go. The identification and celebration of short-term wins provide that evidence.

> The PLC process is a journey rather than an event, but most people won't continue on that journey unless, early on, they see evidence that it is taking them where they want to go.

Planning for short-term wins is very different from *hoping* for short-term wins. Effective principals translate the complex PLC process into a series of incremental, doable steps and publicly acknowledge when those steps have been completed. When every team has established a SMART goal and clarified its commitments regarding how it will work together, celebrate! When teams have administered their first common formative assessment, celebrate! Call attention to the team that has recognized a significant deficit in student learning and created an action plan for addressing it. Tell stories of individual students who have moved from failure to success because of the collective efforts of staff members engaged in the school's system of interventions. Constantly search for evidence that students are learning at higher levels, call attention to the progress, and seek every opportunity to express appreciation and admiration for the individual and collective efforts that are contributing to that progress. This attention to the celebration of short-term wins helps people throughout the organization believe in their collective ability "to solve the next problem *because they have done it so many times before*" (Fullan, 2011a, p. 108).

Effective principals will not wait for monumental accomplishments before celebrating. They don't look for milestones; they look for "inch pebbles" (Heath & Heath, 2010, p. 136). These principals also recognize that achieving short-term wins will not fuel momentum if people are unaware of them. They may send notes of thanks and appreciation to individual staff members or teams; however, they also celebrate progress in a very public way through forums such as faculty meetings, small-group dialogues, newsletters, parent meetings, and bulletins.

The idea that schools should make a concerted attempt to recognize and celebrate the effort of individuals, teams, and the faculty runs counter to long-standing practice. The excessively egalitarian culture of traditional schooling has worked against meaningful celebration other than the generic "You are the best damn faculty in the state." The prevailing attitude that "We are all good teachers here, so publicly acknowledging any one of us somehow belittles the rest of us" has led school leaders to drastically undercommunicate sincere, positive appreciation and admiration of individuals and teams. Yet a fifty-year longitudinal study of what employees value most reveals that "feeling appreciated" is their top priority (Kouzes & Posner, 2003, p. 13). A survey of twelve thousand white-collar employees finds that workers are vastly more satisfied and productive when they feel valued and appreciated for their contributions to meaningful, purpose-driven work. Feeling appreciated by their supervisor has a more significant impact on their sense of trust than any other leadership behavior (Schwartz & Porath, 2014).

Attempting to create a culture that celebrates honoring collective commitments and incremental progress may initially lead to objections from some staff members. Nevertheless, principals must remember that an excellent predictor of the future behavior of any organization is to examine the people and events it elects to honor (Buckingham, 2005). So principals and leadership teams should press forward with celebration, even in the face of initial resistance, and follow these four guidelines adapted from *Learning by Doing, Second Edition* (DuFour et al., 2010).

1. **Explicitly state the purpose of celebration.** Remind staff that celebration is an important way to reinforce core values and priorities and to sustain momentum for moving forward on the PLC journey.

2. **Make celebration everyone's responsibility.** Although principals must help to create the conditions to support public recognition and celebration in their schools, they should not be solely responsible for determining who and what is to be celebrated. Initially, the guiding coalition or a specific task force might take on this responsibility. The ultimate goal, however, is to have all members of the staff contribute to a collective effort to recognize, appreciate, and applaud their colleagues as they progress on the PLC journey.

3. **Establish a clear link between the recognition and the behavior or commitment to be reinforced.** Celebration will have little impact "if a staff believes recognition is presented randomly, that each person deserves to be honored regardless of his or her contribution to the improvement effort, or that rewards are given for factors unrelated to the goal of creating a professional learning community" (DuFour & Eaker, 1998, p. 145). The answer to the question, What behavior or commitment are we attempting to encourage with this recognition? should be readily apparent. Recognition should always be accompanied by a story relating the contribution of the individual or team back to the school's foundation of mission, vision, collective commitments, and goals. In that way, the recognition not only expresses admiration and appreciation but also provides others with a model they can emulate.

4. **Create opportunities to have many winners.** An effective celebration process will convince every member of the staff that he or she can be a winner and that his or her efforts can be noted and appreciated. Frequent public acknowledgments for a job well done and a wide distribution of small symbolic gestures of appreciation and admiration are far more powerful tools for

communicating priorities than infrequent "grand prizes" that create a few winners and many losers. In fact, celebration can be disruptive and detrimental if there is a perception that recognition and reward are reserved for an exclusive few. Establishing artificial limits on appreciation—such as "We honor no more than five individuals per meeting" or "Only those with five or more years of experience are eligible"—lessens the impact celebration can have on a school or district. Developing a PLC requires creating systems specifically designed not only to provide celebrations *but also to ensure that there are many winners.*

Can celebration be overdone? Absolutely. The most important criterion for assessing the appropriateness of recognition for a team or individual should be the sincerity with which the recognition is given. A commendation should represent genuine and heartfelt appreciation and admiration. As long as the recognition meets that criterion, principals need not worry about being too appreciative because "extraordinary achievements never bloom in barren and unappreciative settings" (Kouzes & Posner, 2006, p. 44).

The Role of the Principal

When Becky and I were asked to write on the role of the principal in school improvement for the National Association of Elementary School Principals (DuFour & DuFour, 2012), we could have simply stated, "Build the capacity of your staff to create a high-performing PLC." Although this response would have been entirely accurate, it would have also been much too generic to be of use to principals. So we offered the following specific list of responsibilities to guide the work of principals (DuFour & DuFour, 2012).

- Clarify the purpose, vision, collective commitments, and goals that define your school.

- Create a culture that is simultaneously loose and tight, and clearly communicate the purpose and priorities of your school.

- Use the collaborative team as the fundamental structure of your school, and put systems in place to facilitate and support the collaborative team process.

- Ensure that students have access to a guaranteed and viable curriculum unit by unit.

- Monitor each student's learning through an ongoing assessment process that includes multiple team-developed common formative assessments.

- Provide every teacher and every team with access to ongoing evidence of student learning, and ensure they use that evidence to inform and improve their individual and collective practices.

- Provide students who struggle with additional time and support for learning in a way that is timely, directive, precise, and systematic, and provide students who are proficient with opportunities for extension and enrichment.

- Demonstrate reciprocal accountability by providing staff members with the time, resources, and support that enable them to succeed at what you are asking them to do.

- Disperse leadership throughout the school, and build such a strong collaborative culture that those other leaders can continue the PLC journey long after you have left the school.

- Persevere in the face of obstacles and setbacks, and never lose faith that your efforts and the collective efforts of the staff can overcome those challenges and ultimately lead to higher levels of student achievement.

- Stay the course.

This is the role of the principal, a role that is daunting but doable. While this chapter has focused on the role of the principal, these leadership behaviors are equally relevant and important for leaders at the district level. A coordinated team approach between the central office and building principal increases the likelihood of success in this most challenging of jobs.

It is certainly easier for principals to merely manage the building, preserve the status quo, and avoid creating discomfort. For too long, too many principals have chosen the easier path. But if we are to create schools committed to helping all students learn at higher levels, American schools need principals who have the courage to move beyond managing to leading and developing the leadership capacity of many others, principals who can build consensus for substantive change and work through the inevitable discomfort, and principals who accept there will be times when they must settle for less than universal affection from their staff. Those who take this path less chosen will embrace and articulate the moral imperative of ensuring high levels of learning for all students and will acknowledge that creating the conditions for addressing that imperative lies within their sphere of influence.

The Greatest Generation of Educators

In the first part of this book, I asserted that the educators in our schools today are the "greatest generation" of educators our nation has ever seen. There is no question that they have helped more students learn at higher levels than ever before in our history. They have been able to do so in spite of an ill-advised, punitive, sanction-driven reform agenda that has not proven successful anywhere in the world, including the United States.

Despite their unprecedented achievements, they continue to be characterized unfairly by harsh critics, many of whom champion the privatization of schooling and call for the demise of public education. Educators have been accused of caring little about their students. Yet two different independent surveyors of retailers confirm that 92 percent of teachers spend $1.6 billion (or about $500 per teacher) out of their own pockets to provide their students with classroom supplies (Leinbach-Reyhle, 2014; Shepard, 2014). These figures do not include the lunches, field trips, coats, and necessities teachers routinely purchase for their needy students. Nine out of ten students say their teachers are willing to give them extra help when needed. Facts like these do not support the premise that educators don't care about their students.

Teachers have been described as lazy, and their jobs have been dismissed as easy. I am certain, however, that at 8:00 p.m. on a weeknight in America, there are still more teachers working on behalf of those they serve—coaching, supervising, grading papers, preparing lessons, contacting parents—than all the other professions combined. American educators deserve far better than the incessant criticism they continue to hear. It is my sincere hope that policymakers will consider the information in this book and rethink our nation's approach to improving schools.

> American educators deserve far better than the incessant criticism they continue to hear. It is my sincere hope that policymakers will consider the information in this book and rethink our nation's approach to improving schools.

I applaud America's educators for wringing the last few drops of student success from a system that was never designed to accomplish what they are now being asked to do—to ensure all students learn at high levels. Further meaningful progress will require fundamental changes to that system, and educators must lead and embrace those changes rather than cling to the vestiges of traditional structures and cultures that are ill suited to the needs of contemporary students.

It will take a critical mass of educators willing to accept responsibility for leading the change if this transformation is to occur. Educators must recognize that they have—within their sphere of influence—the ability to create vastly improved conditions for teaching and learning. Rather than waiting for others to improve their schools and districts, they must do so themselves. Rather than looking out the window for help, they must look in the mirror and acknowledge that there are important things that they can do now to begin the transformation.

Author Terry Pratchett (1997) captures this tendency to assign responsibilities to others when he writes:

> It is so much easier to blame it on Them. It was bleakly depressing to think it might be Us. If it was Them, then nothing was anyone's fault. If it was Us, well I am one of Us. I've certainly never thought of myself as one of Them. No one ever thinks of himself as one of Them. We are always one of Us. It is Them that do the bad things. (p. 206)

It is certainly true that part of the problem in American education is that we have taken good people—teachers and principals—and put them in a bad system that was never intended to help all students learn. It is equally certain, however, that those same teachers and principals must play a critical role in changing that system. As the ancient Persian poet Rumi (n.d.) once wrote in the thirteenth century, "Yesterday I was clever, so I wanted to change the world. Today I am wise, so I am changing myself." It is time for our profession to become wise. It is time for its members to begin changing themselves.

The candidness of this book and the unequivocal approach to its recommendations might offend some readers. My purpose is neither to place blame nor to challenge the motives or integrity of

It is certainly true that part of the problem in American education is that we have taken good people—teachers and principals—and put them in a bad system that was never intended to help all students learn. It is equally certain, however, that those same teachers and principals must play a critical role in changing that system.

educators. The fact is, however, that they live in a day and time in which providing a good education to most students is no longer acceptable—they must provide a great education for every student. Moving from good to great requires a willingness to look at the brutal facts (Collins, 2005). Until educators are willing to examine and acknowledge that our traditional assumptions and beliefs about their work are outdated and detrimental to the challenges of today, they will never get better results for students.

I also suspect many readers will agree with most of the recommendations but will claim those recommendations are not realistic or possible at their school. They will refer to state regulations, contractual agreements, and financial constraints that create insurmountable barriers to these desired outcomes. To this, I say, "It is being done." While there is a compelling level of research to support what is proposed in this book, the research is not theory to me. I have personally witnessed traditional elementary, middle, and high schools led to record levels of student achievement. In each case, the staffs accomplished these outcomes without violating legal regulations and within union contractual agreements.

I have worked with schools in every state that are successfully implementing these practices. There are examples of schools as small as a one-room schoolhouse to exceedingly large comprehensive high schools and from traditional brick-and-mortar buildings to virtual schools. There is not "something in the water" at these schools that makes them different from all others. What is different is they moved from viewing themselves as victims of their circumstances to masters of their own fate. They stopped focusing on what they could not control and instead took responsibility for what they could. They embraced the fact that the average student spends more than 30 percent of his or her waking hours from age five to eighteen at school and that they could use this time to make a significant impact on the lives of learners. Insisting that improving student learning is beyond the reach of educators is not based on fact but rather represents justification for inactivity and acceptance of the status quo.

So superintendents, don't wait for more enlightened state and federal policy to help implement the PLC process in schools throughout your district. Read *Cultures Built to Last* (DuFour & Fullan, 2013), which describes in detail how to implement the PLC process across an entire system. Then take personal responsibility for working effectively with others to ensure that process is guiding the work in every school. Principals, don't wait for the central office to champion the PLC process. Take personal responsibility for creating the guiding coalition and faculty consensus to bring the process to life in your school. You can become the model that leads to district transformation. Teachers, don't wait for your principals to lead you on the PLC journey. Lead them! Take personal responsibility for developing such a powerful collaborative team that your results cause the principal and the rest of the staff to sit up and take notice. All educators are in a position to lead this process because leadership capacity is not reserved for the elite few. The ability to lead is widely distributed throughout the general population and "accessible to anyone who has a passion and purpose to change the way things are" (Kouzes & Posner, 2010, p. 5). We need a critical mass of educators with passion and purpose who are committed to doing the right work.

The driving force for these changes will not be fear but love. I have never seen a great principal who had contempt for

> All educators are in a position to lead this process because leadership capacity is not reserved for the elite few.

his or her faculty. Great principals *love* their staff. I have never seen a great teacher who had disdain for his or her students. Great teachers *love* their students. Greatness in our field is always a labor of love—of our students, our colleagues, our work, our subjects, and our purpose. Love can be the primary driver in our profession if it can be channeled into a new definition of what schools must become to prepare students for a world in which the ability to continue learning beyond the K–12 system is vital to their success and well-being.

The journey is certainly not easy. To extend the journey analogy, it is easier to lie in anchor and accept things as they are. It is easier to simply drift from fad to fad. It is difficult to stay the course when buffeted by the inevitable ill winds of frustration and mistakes. But for those who stay the course with a firm resolve to succeed, the intrinsic rewards far outweigh the costs.

I have seen firsthand the energy, the enthusiasm, and the joy generated by educators engaged in a successful collective endeavor. I have witnessed how their sense of belonging, of accomplishment, and of being successful in significant, purpose-driven work appealed to their fundamental human needs. They would never go back to working in isolation. Every educator should have this experience.

> If there is one undeniable reality for every educator every year, it is that we are going to work hard. The real question is this: Will we work hard and succeed or work hard and fail?

The journey will undoubtedly require hard work. But if there is one undeniable reality for every educator every year, it is that we are going to work hard. The real question is this: Will we work hard and succeed or work hard and fail? Working tirelessly and failing creates despair and drives good, talented people out of our profession. But working hard and seeing the fruits of our efforts—seeing more students learn and succeed—are what draw people to this profession.

And without question, this journey will require educators to demonstrate courage. In *Harry Potter and the Sorcerer's Stone*, J. K. Rowling (1998) writes, "It takes a great deal of bravery to stand up to our enemies, but just as much to stand up to our friends" (p. 221). Sadly, the greatest obstacle to transforming many schools does not lie outside the building but rather within it. Some educators will claim it is unfair to hold educators accountable for student learning and "unprofessional" to relinquish any of their personal classroom autonomy. Others will not openly question a learning-focused mission and collaboration as general principles but will instead resist the specific actions necessary to make these outcomes a reality. Unless we are willing to demonstrate the courage to professionally confront our resistant colleagues and passionately advocate for what is ethically right for the students we serve, it is unlikely any substantial change will ever take root.

Courage is needed not merely to launch the PLC journey but to sustain it. As William Faulkner writes, "You cannot swim for new horizons until you have the courage to lose sight of the shore." This courage, this willingness to leave the shore in pursuit of a better future, has been an essential attribute to America's success and prosperity. It took courage for the Pilgrims to leave their homes in pursuit of the New World. It took courage for settlers to harness a wagon and travel west in hopes of a better future. It took courage for three astronauts to board the Apollo 11 spacecraft, hoping to take a giant leap for mankind. Today, the greatest generation of educators is being called on to summon the courage to take a giant leap of their own in order to secure a better life for our children and our nation.

So of every reader, I ask:

- "Do you believe it is desirable that schools function as PLCs?"

- "Do you believe that it is feasible that you and your colleagues can help your school become a high-performing PLC?"

- "Will you act with a sense of urgency, as if the very lives of your students depend on your action, because in a very literal sense, more so than at any other time in American history, they do?"

If your answer to these questions is "yes," then we must ask the most important question of all.

- "What are you personally prepared to do to bring the PLC process to life in your school or district?"

Thankfully, the greatest generation of American educators is on hand to take on this challenge.

References and Resources

Achor, S. (2010). *The happiness advantage: The seven principles of positive psychology that fuel success and performance at work*. New York: Crown Business.

ACT. (2013). *2012 retention/completion summary tables*. Accessed at www.act.org /research/policymakers/pdf/12retain_trends.pdf on August 19, 2013.

Adler, M. (2014, April). *Review of* Measuring the Impacts of Teachers. Boulder, CO: National Education Policy Center. Accessed at http://nepc.colorado .edu/files/ttr-chetty-teachimpacts_0.pdf on January 2, 2015.

Altschuler, G. C., & Blumin, S. M. (2009). *The GI bill: A new deal for veterans*. New York: Oxford University Press.

Alvarez, L. (2014, November 9). States listen as parents give rampant testing an F. *New York Times*. Accessed at www.nytimes.com/2014/11/10/us/states-listen -as-parents-give-rampant-testing-an-f.html on November 15, 2014.

Amabile, T., & Kramer, S. (2011). *The progress principle: Using small wins to ignite joy, engagement, and creativity at work*. Boston: Harvard Business Review Press.

American Bar Association. (2013). *2011 survey on lawyer discipline systems (S.O.L.D.)*. Accessed at www.americanbar.org/content/dam/aba/administrative/professional _responsibility/2011_sold_final_report.authcheckdam.pdf on March 21, 2015.

American Diploma Project. (2004). *Ready or not: Creating a high school diploma that counts*. Washington, DC: Achieve. Accessed at www.achieve.org/files /ReadyorNot.pdf on March 5, 2014.

American Psychological Association. (2012). *Facing the school dropout dilemma*. Washington, DC: Author. Accessed at www.apa.org/pi/families/resources /school-dropout-prevention.pdf on March 25, 2015.

American Statistical Association. (2014, April 8). *ASA statement on using value-added models for educational assessment*. Accessed at www.amstat.org/policy /pdfs/ASA_VAM_Statement.pdf on April 8, 2015.

Annenberg Institute for School Reform. (n.d.). *Professional learning communities: Professional development strategies that improve instruction*. Providence, RI: Author. Accessed at http://annenberginstitute.org/pdf/proflearning.pdf on March 23, 2015.

Arcuri, S. C. (2015, January 13). Letter of the day: School vouchers harm public schools. *Tampa Tribune*. Accessed at http://tbo.com/list/news-opinion -letterday/letter-of-the-day-school-vouchers-harm-public-schools-20150113 on April 8, 2015.

Barber, M., & Mourshed, M. (2007, September). *How the world's best-performing school systems come out on top*. New York: McKinsey. Accessed at www .mckinseyonsociety.com/downloads/reports/Education/Worlds_School _Systems_Final.pdf on January 1, 2010.

Barber, M., & Mourshed, M. (2009, July). *Shaping the future: How good education systems can become great in the decade ahead* (Report on the International Education Roundtable). New York: McKinsey. Accessed at www.mckinsey .com/locations/southeastasia/knowledge/Education_Roundtable.pdf on December 20, 2010.

Barth, R. S. (1991). Restructuring schools: Some questions for teachers and principals. *Phi Delta Kappan, 73*(2), 123–128.

Bendor, J., Bordoff, J., & Furman, J. (2007, February). *An education strategy to promote opportunity, prosperity, and growth*. Washington, DC: Brookings Institution. Accessed at www.brookings.edu/~/media/research/files/papers /2007/2/14%20education%20bendor/200702education.pdf on April 8, 2015.

Berliner, D. (2014). Exogenous variables and value-added assessments: A fatal flaw. *Teacher College Record, 116*(1). Accessed at www.tcrecord.org/content.asp ?contentid=17293 on March 23, 2015.

Black, P., Harrison, C., Lee, C., Marshall, B., & Wiliam, D. (2004). Working inside the black box: Assessment for learning in the classroom. *Phi Delta Kappan, 86*(1), 8–21.

Blanchard, K. (2007). *Leading at a higher level: Blanchard on leadership and creating high performing organizations*. Upper Saddle River, NJ: Pearson/ Prentice Hall.

Board on Testing and Assessment. (2009). *Letter report to the U.S. Department of Education on the Race to the Top fund*. Washington, DC: National Academies Press. Accessed at www.nap.edu/openbook.php?record_id=12780&page=1 on April 8, 2015.

Bohrnstedt, G. W., & Stecher, B. M. (Eds.). (2002, August). *What we have learned about class size reduction in California* [Prepublication copy]. Sacramento, CA: California Department of Education. Accessed at www.classize.org /techreport/CSR_Capstone_prepub.pdf on February 22, 2015.

Boston Consulting Group. (2014, December). *Teachers know best: Teachers' views on professional development*. Seattle, WA: Gates Foundation. Accessed at http:// collegeready.gatesfoundation.org/sites/default/files/Gates-PDMarketResearch -Dec5.pdf on February 20, 2015.

Bracey, G. W. (2006, July/August). Put to the test: Believing the worst. *Stanford Magazine*. Accessed at www.stanfordalumni.org/news/magazine/2006 /julaug/features/nclb.html on March 23, 2015.

Brantlinger, E. A. (Ed.). (2006). *Who benefits from special education?: Remediating (fixing) other people's children*. Mahwah, NJ: Erlbaum.

Braun, H. I. (2005, September). *Using student progress to evaluate teachers: A primer on value-added models.* Princeton, NJ: Educational Testing Service. Accessed at www.ets.org/Media/Research/pdf/PICVAM.pdf on March 20, 2015.

Breslow, J. M. (2012, September 12). *By the numbers: Dropping out of high school.* Accessed at www.pbs.org/wgbh/pages/frontline/education/dropout-nation /by-the-numbers-dropping-out-of-high-school on March 23, 2015.

Broad Foundation. (n.d.). *Our public education system is in deep distress.* Accessed at http://broadeducation.org/about/crisis_stats.html on August 20, 2013.

Brokaw, T. (1998). *The greatest generation.* New York: Dell.

BruinKid. (2011, March 1). *Jon Stewart defends teachers* [Blog post]. Accessed at www.dailykos.com/story/2011/03/01/951283/-Jon-Stewart-defends-teachers on April 22, 2015.

Bryk, A. S., Sebring, P. B., Allensworth, E., Luppescu, S., & Easton, J. Q. (2010). *Organizing schools for improvement: Lessons from Chicago.* Chicago: University of Chicago Press.

Buckingham, M. (2005). *The one thing you need to know . . . about great managing, great leading, and sustained individual success.* New York: Free Press.

Buffum, A., Mattos, M., & Weber, C. (2012). *Simplifying response to intervention: Four essential guiding principles.* Bloomington, IN: Solution Tree Press.

Bush, G. H. W. (1989, February 9). *Address before a joint session of Congress.* Accessed at http://millercenter.org/president/bush/speeches/speech-3420 on March 1, 2015.

Bushaw, W. J., & Calderon, V. J. (2014). Try it again, Uncle Sam: The 46th annual PDK/Gallup poll of the public's attitudes toward the public schools. *Phi Delta Kappan, 96*(1–2), 8–20, 48–59. Accessed at www.pdkmembers .org/members_online/publications/GallupPoll/kpoll_pdfs/pdkpoll46_2014 .pdf on April 8, 2015.

Bushaw, W. J., & Lopez, S. J. (2011). Betting on teachers: The 43rd annual Phi Delta Kappa/Gallup poll of the public's attitudes toward the public schools. *Phi Delta Kappan, 93*(1), 8–26. Accessed at www.pdkmembers .org/members_online/publications/archive/pdf/PDK_93_1/8pdk_93_1.pdf on April 8, 2015.

Bushaw, W. J., & McNee, J. A. (2009). Americans speak out: Are educators and policy makers listening?—The 41st annual Phi Delta Kappa/Gallup poll of the public's attitudes toward the public schools. *Phi Delta Kappan, 91*(1), 8–23.

Carey, K. (2015, January 24). A quiet revolution in helping lift the burden of student debt. *New York Times.* Accessed at www.nytimes.com/2015/01/25 /upshot/a-quiet-revolution-in-helping-lift-the-burden-of-student-debt.html ?nlid=65639414&src=recpb&abt=0002&abg=1 on April 8, 2015.

Carini, R. M., Powell, B., & Steelman, L. C. (2000). Do teacher unions hinder educational performance?: Lessons learned from state SAT and ACT scores. *Harvard Educational Review, 70*(4), 437–466.

Carnevale, A. P., Jayasundera, T., & Hanson, A. R. (2012, September). *Career and technical education: Five ways that pay along the way to the B.A.* Washington, DC: Center on Education and the Workforce. Accessed at https://cew .georgetown.edu/wp-content/uploads/2014/11/CTE.FiveWays.FullReport .pdf on February 23, 2015.

Carnevale, A. P., Smith, N., & Strohl, J. (2010, June). *Help wanted: Projections of jobs and education requirements through 2018.* Washington, DC: Center on Education and the Workforce. Accessed at https://cew.georgetown.edu /wp-content/uploads/2014/12/fullreport.pdf on April 8, 2015.

Carnevale, A. P., Smith, N., & Strohl, J. (2013, June). *Recovery: Job growth and education requirements through 2020.* Washington, DC: Center on Education and the Workforce. Accessed at https://cew.georgetown.edu/wp-content /uploads/2014/11/Recovery2020.FR_.Web_.pdf on April 8, 2015.

Center for Media and Democracy. (2014). *Exposed: America's highest paid government workers.* Madison, WI: Author. Accessed at www.prwatch.org /files/americas_highest_paid_government_workers.pdf on March 20, 2015.

Center for Research on Education Outcomes. (2009). *Multiple choice: Charter school performance in 16 states* [Executive summary]. Stanford, CA: Author. Accessed at http://credo.stanford.edu/reports/MULTIPLE_CHOICE _EXECUTIVE%20SUMMARY.pdf on May 2, 2010.

Center on International Education Benchmarking. (n.d.a). *Finland overview.* Accessed at www.ncee.org/programs-affiliates/center-on-international -education-benchmarking/top-performing-countries/finland-overview on March 21, 2015.

Center on International Education Benchmarking. (n.d.b). *Singapore overview.* Accessed at www.ncee.org/programs-affiliates/center-on-international -education-benchmarking/top-performing-countries/singapore-overview on March 21, 2015.

Chenoweth, K. (2009). It can be done, it's being done, and here's how. *Phi Delta Kappan, 91*(1), 38–43.

Childress, S. (2012, September 25). *Apollo 20: One man's plan to fix failing schools.* Accessed at www.pbs.org/wgbh/pages/frontline/education/dropout-nation /apollo-20-one-mans-plan-to-fix-failing-schools on March 30, 2015.

Chingos, M. M. (2012, November). *Strength in numbers: State spending on K–12 assessment systems.* Washington, DC: Brookings Institution. Accessed at www.brookings.edu/~/media/research/files/reports/2012/11/29%20cost %20of%20assessment%20chingos/11_assessment_chingos_final.pdf on April 8, 2015.

Clavell, J. (1975). *Shogun: A novel of medieval Japan.* New York: Dell.

College Board. (2008, December). *Coming to our senses: Education and the American future.* New York: Author. Accessed at http://professionals .collegeboard.com/profdownload/coming-to-our-senses-college-board-2008 .pdf on March 23, 2015.

College Board. (2013, February). *The 9th annual AP report to the nation.* New York: Author. Accessed at http://media.collegeboard.com/digitalServices /pdf/ap/rtn/9th-annual/9th-annual-ap-report-single-page.pdf on March 21, 2015.

College Board. (2014, February). *The 10th annual AP report to the nation.* New York: Author. Accessed at http://media.collegeboard.com/digitalServices/pdf /ap/rtn/10th-annual/10th-annual-ap-report-to-the-nation-single-page.pdf on March 20, 2015.

Collins, J. C. (2005). *Good to great and the social sectors: A monograph to accompany* Good to Great. New York: HarperBusiness.

Collins, J. C., & Porras, J. I. (1994). *Built to last: Successful habits of visionary companies.* New York: HarperBusiness.

Commission on No Child Left Behind. (2007). *Beyond NCLB: Fulfilling the promise to our nation's children.* Washington, DC: Aspen Institute.

Conley, D. T. (2007, March). *Redefining college readiness.* Eugene, OR: Educational Policy Improvement Center. Accessed at www.aypf.org/documents /RedefiningCollegeReadiness.pdf on March 23, 2015.

Consoletti, A. (2011, December). *The state of charter schools: What we know—and what we do not—about performance and accountability.* Washington, DC: Center for Education Reform. Accessed at www.edreform.com/wp-content /uploads/2011/12/StateOfCharterSchools_CER_Dec2011-Web-1.pdf on April 8, 2015.

Covey, S. R. (1990). *The 7 habits of highly effective people: Powerful lessons in personal change.* New York: Simon & Schuster.

Cremata, E., Davis, D., Dickey, K., Lawyer, K., Negassi, Y., Raymond, M. E., et al. (2013). *National charter school study, 2013.* Stanford, CA: Center for Research on Education Outcomes. Accessed at http://credo.stanford.edu /documents/NCSS%202013%20Final%20Draft.pdf on March 20, 2015.

Darling-Hammond, L., & Conley, D. T. (2015). Assessment systems for deeper learning. In J. A. Bellanca (Ed.), *Deeper learning: Beyond 21st century skills* (pp. 235–271). Bloomington, IN: Solution Tree Press.

de la Torre, M., & Gwynne, J. (2009, October). *When schools close: Effects on displaced students in Chicago public schools.* Chicago: Consortium on Chicago School Research. Accessed at https://ccsr.uchicago.edu/sites/default/files /publications/CCSRSchoolClosings-Final.pdf on April 8, 2015.

Delaware Department of Education. (2013, August). *Professional learning community (PLC) participant survey report (2012–2013).* Dover, DE: Author. Accessed at www.doe.k12.de.us/cms/lib09/DE01922744/Centricity/domain/184 /tleu%20reports%20and%20presentations/2013PLCSurveyReport_FINAL .pdf on March 21, 2015.

Deming, W. E. (2000). *Out of the crisis*. Cambridge, MA: Massachusetts Institute of Technology Press.

Diament, M. (2014, April 29). *Graduation rates fall short for students with disabilities*. Accessed at www.disabilityscoop.com/2014/04/29/graduation -rates-disabilities/19317 on April 8, 2015.

Dinan, S. (2014, October 6). An eye-popping 20% of U.S. residents abandon English at home. *Washington Times*. Accessed at www.washingtontimes.com/news/2014 /oct/6/one-in-five-in-us-dont-speak-english-at-home-repor/?page=all on March 20, 2015.

Dolton, P., & Marcenaro-Gutierrez, O. (2013, October). *2013 global teacher status index*. London: Varkey GEMS Foundation. Accessed at https://varkeygemsfoundation .org/sites/default/files/documents/2013GlobalTeacherStatusIndex.pdf on March 21, 2015.

Donaldson, M. L., & Johnson, S. M. (2011). Teach for America teachers: How long do they teach? Why do they leave? *Phi Delta Kappan, 93*(2), 47–51.

Donovan, M. S., & Cross, C. T. (Eds.). (2003). *Minority students in special and gifted education*. Washington, DC: National Academies Press.

Dorn, S. (1996). *Creating the dropout: An institutional and social history of school failure*. Westport, CT: Praeger.

Driskell, N. (2015, January 30). *Global perspectives: How top performers are measuring 21st century skills*. Accessed at www.ncee.org/2015/01/global-perspectives -how-top-performers-are-measuring-21st-century-skills on February 5, 2015.

Drucker, P. F. (2006). *Classic Drucker: Essential wisdom of Peter Drucker from the pages of* Harvard Business Review. Boston: Harvard Business Review Press.

Duffett, A., Farkas, S., Rotherham, A. J., & Silva, E. (2008, May). *Waiting to be won over: Teachers speak on the profession, unions, and reform*. Washington, DC: Education Sector. Accessed at www.educationsector.org/usr_doc /WaitingToBeWonOver.pdf on April 8, 2015.

DuFour, R., & DuFour, R. (2012). *The school leader's guide to Professional Learning Communities at Work*. Bloomington, IN: Solution Tree Press.

DuFour, R., DuFour, R., & Eaker, R. (2008). *Revisiting Professional Learning Communities at Work: New insights for improving schools*. Bloomington, IN: Solution Tree Press.

DuFour, R., DuFour, R., Eaker, R., & Many, T. (2010). *Learning by doing: A handbook for Professional Learning Communities at Work* (2nd ed.). Bloomington, IN: Solution Tree Press.

DuFour, R., & Eaker, R. (1998). *Professional Learning Communities at Work: Best practices for enhancing student achievement*. Bloomington, IN: Solution Tree Press.

DuFour, R., & Fullan, M. (2013). *Cultures built to last: Systemic PLCs at Work*. Bloomington, IN: Solution Tree Press.

DuFour, R., & Marzano, R. J. (2011). *Leaders of learning: How district, school, and classroom leaders improve student achievement*. Bloomington, IN: Solution Tree Press.

DuFour, R., & Mattos, M. (2013). How do principals really improve schools? *Educational Leadership, 70*(7), 34–40.

Editorial Board. (2014, June 11). A new battle for equal education. *New York Times*. Accessed at www.nytimes.com/2014/06/12/opinion/in-california-a-judge-takes-on-teacher-tenure.html on March 23, 2015.

EdLeader21. (n.d.). *The professional learning community for 21st century education leaders*. Accessed at www.edleader21.com/index.php on March 23, 2015.

Edsall, T. B. (2012, March 12). The reproduction of privilege [Blog post]. *New York Times*. Accessed at http://campaignstops.blogs.nytimes.com/2012/03/12/the-reproduction-of-privilege/?nl=todaysheadlines&emc=edit_th_20120312 on March 23, 2015

Education Next. (2014). Program on education policy and governance—Survey 2014. Accessed at http://educationnext.org/files/2014ednextpoll.pdf on April 8, 2015.

Education Week. (2014, June 5). Diplomas count 2014: Motivation matters—Engaging students, creating learners. Accessed at www.edweek.org/ew/toc/2014/06/05/index.html on January 19, 2015.

Eichenwald, K. (2012, August). Microsoft's lost decade. *Vanity Fair*. Accessed at www.vanityfair.com/news/business/2012/08/microsoft-lost-mojo-steve-ballmer on March 21, 2015.

Elmore, R. F. (2004). *School reform from the inside out: Policy, practice, and performance*. Cambridge, MA: Harvard Education Press.

Elmore, R. F. (2010). "I used to think . . . and now I think . . .": Reflections on the work of school reform. *Harvard Education Letter, 26*(1), 7–8.

Elmore, R. F., & City, E. (2007). The road to school improvement: It's hard, it's bumpy, and it takes as long as it takes. *Harvard Education Letter, 23*(3). Accessed at www.hepg.org/hel/article/229#home on March 23, 2015.

FairTest. (2015, January 19). *Independent test results show NCLB fails*. Accessed at www.fairtest.org/independent-test-results-show-nclb-fails on March 21, 2015.

Farhi, P. (2012, April/May). Flunking the test. *American Journalism Review*. Accessed at http://ajrarchive.org/Article.asp?id=5280 on March 20, 2015.

Farrace, B. (2012, March 8). The common elements of school transformation [Blog post]. *Education Week*. Accessed at http://blogs.edweek.org/edweek/transforming_learning/2012/03/the_common_elements_of_school_transformation.html?cmp=ENL-EU-VIEWS2 on April 8, 2015.

Ferguson, R. F., Hackman, S., Hanna, R., & Ballantine, A. (2010, June). *How high schools become exemplary: Ways that leadership raises achievement and narrows gaps by improving instruction in 15 public high schools* (2009 Achievement Gap Initiative Conference Report). Cambridge, MA: Achievement Gap Initiative at Harvard University. Accessed at www.agi.harvard.edu/events/2009Conference /2009AGIConferenceReport6-30-2010web.pdf on March 23, 2015.

Ferri, B. A., & Connor, D. J. (2006). *Reading resistance: Discourses of exclusion in desegregation and inclusion debates.* New York: Lang.

Flynn, K., & Hill, J. (2005, December). *English language learners: A growing population* [Policy brief]. Denver, CO: Mid-continent Research for Education and Learning. Accessed at www.inet-migrant.org/resources/2013/educational /policyBrief_ELL.pdf on April 8, 2015.

Forum for Education and Democracy. (2008). *Democracy at risk: The need for a new federal policy in education.* Amesville, OH: Author.

Fryer, R. G. (2011, March). *Teacher incentives and student achievement: Evidence from New York City public schools* (NBER Working Paper No. 16850). Cambridge, MA: National Bureau of Economic Research. Accessed at www .nber.org/papers/w16850 on November 5, 2012.

Fullan, M. (2005). *Leadership and sustainability: System thinkers in action.* Thousand Oaks, CA: Corwin Press.

Fullan, M. (2007). *The new meaning of educational change* (4th ed.). New York: Teachers College Press.

Fullan, M. (2008). *The six secrets of change: What the best leaders do to help their organizations survive and thrive.* San Francisco: Jossey-Bass.

Fullan, M. (2010). *All systems go: The change imperative for whole system reform.* Thousand Oaks, CA: Corwin Press.

Fullan, M. (2011a). *Change leader: Learning to do what matters most.* San Francisco: Jossey-Bass.

Fullan, M. (2011b). *The moral imperative realized.* Thousand Oaks, CA: Corwin Press.

Fullan, M. (2014). *The principal: Three keys to maximizing impact.* San Francisco: Jossey-Bass.

Fulton, K., & Britton, T. (2011, June). *STEM teachers in professional learning communities: From good teachers to great teaching.* Washington, DC: National Commission on Teaching and America's Future. Accessed at http://nctaf .org/wp-content/uploads/2012/01/1098-executive-summary.pdf on April 8, 2015.

Fulton, K., Yoon, I., & Lee, C. (2005, August). *Induction into learning communities.* Washington, DC: National Commission on Teaching and America's Future. Accessed at http://nctaf.org/wp-content/uploads/NCTAF _Induction_Paper_2005.pdf on March 23, 2015.

Gallimore, R., Ermeling, B. A., Saunders, W. M., & Goldenberg, C. (2009). Moving the learning of teaching closer to practice: Teacher education implications of school-based inquiry teams. *Elementary School Journal, 109*(5), 537–553.

Gerber, S. (2014, June 2). Here's the real problem with America's educational system. *Time.* Accessed at http://time.com/2806663/american-education on March 20, 2015.

Goldstein, D. (2014a). *The teacher wars: A history of America's most embattled profession.* New York: Doubleday.

Goldstein, D. (2014b, June 11). Will California's ruling against teacher tenure change schools? *The Atlantic.* Accessed at www.theatlantic.com/education /archive/2014/06/california-rules-teacher-tenure-laws-unconstitutional /372536 on March 23, 2015.

Goleman, D., Boyatzis, R., & McKee, A. (2004). *Primal leadership: Learning to lead with emotional intelligence.* Boston: Harvard Business Review Press.

Goodlad, J. I. (1984). *A place called school: Prospects for the future.* New York: McGraw-Hill.

Great Schools Partnership. (2013). *Value-added measures.* Accessed at http:// edglossary.org/value-added-measures on March 20, 2015.

Green, E. (2014, July 23). Why do Americans stink at math? *New York Times.* Accessed at www.nytimes.com/2014/07/27/magazine/why-do-americans -stink-at-math.html on April 8, 2015.

Greenberg, J., McKee, A., & Walsh, K. (2013a, December). *Teacher prep review: A review of the nation's teacher preparation programs.* Washington, DC: National Council on Teacher Quality. Accessed at www.nctq.org/dmsView /Teacher_Prep_Review_2013_Report on April 8, 2015.

Greenberg, J., McKee, A., & Walsh, K. (2013b). *Teacher prep review: A review of the nation's teacher preparation programs* [Executive summary]. Washington, DC: National Council on Teacher Quality. Accessed at www.nctq.org /dmsView/Teacher_Prep_Review_executive_summary on January 22, 2015.

Greenstone, M., Looney, A., Patashnik, J., & Yu, M. (2013, June). *Thirteen economic facts about social mobility and the role of education.* Washington, DC: Brookings Institution. Accessed at www.brookings.edu/research /reports/2013/06/13-facts-higher-education on April 8, 2015.

Grissom, J. A., Loeb, S., & Master, B. (2013). *Effective instructional time use for school leaders: Longitudinal evidence from observations of principals.* Accessed at http:// cepa.stanford.edu/sites/default/files/effective%20instructional%20time%20use .pdf on February 22, 2014.

Gurria, A. (2011). Editorial: Fifty years of change in education. In *Education at a glance 2011: OECD indicators* (pp. 13–20). Paris: Organisation for Economic Co-operation and Development. Accessed at www.oecd.org /dataoecd/37/45/48642586.pdf on March 15, 2012.

Haertel, E. H. (2013). *Reliability and validity of inferences about teachers based on student test scores.* Princeton, NJ: Education Testing Service. Accessed at http://www.ets.org/Media/Research/pdf/PICANG14.pdf on June 11, 2014.

Hanover Research. (2011, June). *A survey of Race to the Top teacher evaluation systems.* Washington, DC: Author. Accessed at www.shaker.org/Downloads/A%20Survey%20of%20Race%20to%20the%20Top%20Teacher%20Evaluation%20Systems%20-%20Membership.pdf on April 8, 2015.

Hanushek, E. A., Peterson, P. E., & Woessmann, L. (2013). *Endangering prosperity: A global view of the American school.* Washington, DC: Brookings Institution Press.

Hanushek, E. A., & Rivkin, S. G. (2006). Teacher quality. In E. A. Hanushek & F. Welch (Eds.), *Handbook of the economics of education* (Vol. 2, pp. 1051–1078). Amsterdam, Netherlands: Elsevier.

Hanushek, E. A., & Rivkin, S. G. (2012). The distribution of teacher quality and implications for policy. *Annual Review of Economics, 4*(1), 131–157. Accessed at http://hanushek.stanford.edu/sites/default/files/publications/Hanushek%2BRivkin%202012%20AnnRevEcon%204.pdf on April 8, 2015.

Hargreaves, A., & Fullan, M. (2012). *Professional capital: Transforming teaching in every school.* New York: Teachers College Press.

Harrigan, J. R., & Davies, A. (2012, August 28). Public high schools are not doing their jobs. *U.S. News and World Report.* Accessed at www.usnews.com/opinion/blogs/economic-intelligence/2012/08/28/public-high-schools-are-not-doing-their-jobs on March 20, 2015.

Hattie, J. (2009). *Visible learning: A synthesis of over 800 meta-analyses relating to achievement.* New York: Routledge.

Hattie, J. (2012). *Visible learning for teachers: Maximizing impact on learning.* New York: Routledge.

Heath, C., & Heath, D. (2010). *Switch: How to change things when change is hard.* New York: Broadway Books.

Herman, J., & Linn, R. (2013, January). *On the road to assessing deeper learning: The status of Smarter Balanced and PARCC assessment consortia* (CRESST Report No. 823). Los Angeles, CA: National Center for Research on Evaluation, Standards, and Student Testing. Accessed at www.cse.ucla.edu/products/reports/R823.pdf on April 8, 2015.

Hewlett Foundation. (2012). *Hewlett Foundation 2012 annual report.* Accessed at www.hewlett.org/2012-annual-report on June 11, 2015.

Hirsch, E. D., Jr. (1996). *The schools we need and why we don't have them.* New York: Anchor Books.

Hollingsworth, B. (2013, November 7). *Nation's Report Card: Only a third of 8th graders can read, compute at grade level.* Accessed at http://cnsnews.com/news/article/barbara-hollingsworth/nations-report-card-only-third-8th-graders-can-read-compute-grade on March 20, 2015.

Holmes Group. (1990). *Tomorrow's schools: Principles for the design of professional development schools.* East Lansing, MI: Author.

Holmes Group. (1995). *Tomorrow's schools of education: A report of the Holmes Group*. East Lansing, MI: Author. Accessed at http://files.eric.ed.gov /fulltext/ED399220.pdf on April 8, 2015.

Hoover Institution. (2011). *Best and worst in American education, 2011*. Accessed at www.hoover.org/research-teams/k-12-task-force/research-themes/best -and-worst-american-education-2011 on January 19, 2015.

Hout, M., & Elliott, S. W. (Eds.). (2011). *Incentives and test-based accountability in education*. Washington, DC: National Academies Press.

Hout, M., Frueh, S., & Elliott, S. W. (2013). Do high-stakes tests improve learning? *Issues in Science and Technology, 29*(1). Accessed at http://issues .org/29-1/michael on March 21, 2015.

Huffington Post. (2012, October 16). 'Rubber rooms' in New York schools cost city $22 million a year for teachers awaiting hearings. Accessed at www .huffingtonpost.com/2012/10/16/rubber rooms in new york city 22 million _n_1969749.htmlork on March 23, 2015.

Huggins, K. S., Scheurich, J. J., & Morgan, J. R. (2011). Professional learning communities as a leadership strategy to drive math success in an urban high school serving diverse, low-income students: A case study. *Journal of Education for Students Placed at Risk, 16*(2), 67–88.

Indiana Public School Superintendent. (2005, November 28). *Gerald Bracey's letter to the* NY Times [Blog post]. Accessed at www.thesupersblog.blogspot .com/2005/11/gerald-braceys-letter-to-ny-times.html on March 20, 2015.

Individuals With Disabilities Education Improvement Act of 2004, Pub. L. No. 108–446 § 300.115 (2004).

Ingersoll, R. M. (2007, February). *A comparative study of teacher preparation and qualifications in six nations* [Policy brief]. Philadelphia: Consortium for Policy Research in Education. Accessed at www.cpre.org/sites/default/files /policybrief/887_rb47.pdf on March 21, 2015.

Inskeep, S. (2010, March 2). *Former 'No Child Left Behind' advocate turns critic* [Audio file]. Accessed at www.npr.org/templates/story/story.php ?storyId=124209100 on May 20, 2014.

Kahlenberg, R. D., & Potter, H. (2014, October 28). Ensuring equity in charter schools. *Education Week*. Accessed at www.edweek.org/ew/articles/2014 /10/29/10kahlenberg.h34.html?cmp=ENL-EU-NEWS2 on April 8, 2015.

Kanter, R. M. (2004). *Confidence: How winning streaks and losing streaks begin and end*. New York: Crown Business.

Katzenbach, J. R., & Smith, D. K. (2006). *The wisdom of teams: Creating the high-performance organization* (Reprint ed.). New York: HarperBusiness.

Kegan, R., & Lahey, L. L. (2001). *How the way we talk can change the way we work: Seven languages for transformation*. San Francisco: Jossey-Bass.

Kena, G., Aud, S., Johnson, F., Wang, X., Zhang, J., Rathbun, A., et al. (2014, May). *The condition of education 2014* (NCES 2014-083). Washington, DC: National Center for Education Statistics. Accessed at http://nces.ed.gov /pubs2014/2014083.pdf on April 8, 2015.

Kenny, C. (2012, August 19). The real reason America's schools stink. *Businessweek.* Accessed at www.bloomberg.com/bw/articles/2012-08-19/the-real-reason -americas-schools-stink on March 20, 2015.

Kildeer Countryside School District 96. (n.d.). *Curriculum frameworks 2014– 2015.* Accessed at www.kcsd96.org/curriculum/curriculum-frameworks.cfm on April 8, 2015.

King, M. L., Jr. (2001). Beyond Vietnam. In C. Carson & K. Shepard (Eds.), *A call to conscience: The landmark speeches of Dr. Martin Luther King, Jr.* (pp. 133–164). New York: Warner Books.

Kirp, D. L. (2000). *Comment by David L. Kirp.* Accessed at http://muse.jhu.edu /journals/brookings_papers_on_education_policy/v2000/2000.1schwartz _comment02.html on July 15, 2012.

Klein, J. (2011, June 26). The failure of American schools. *The Atlantic.* Accessed at www.theatlantic.com/magazine/archive/2011/06/the-failure-of-american -schools/308497 on March 20, 2015.

Kotter, J. P., & Cohen, D. S. (2002). *The heart of change: Real-life stories of how people change their organizations.* Boston: Harvard Business School Press.

Kouzes, J. M., & Posner, B. Z. (2003). *Encouraging the heart: A leader's guide to rewarding and recognizing others.* San Francisco: Jossey-Bass.

Kouzes, J. M., & Posner, B. Z. (2006). *A leader's legacy.* San Francisco: Jossey-Bass.

Kouzes, J. M., & Posner, B. Z. (2010). *The truth about leadership: The no-fads, heart-of-the-matter facts you need to know.* San Francisco: Jossey-Bass.

Layton, L. (2013, March 10). More states requiring third-graders to pass reading test to advance. *Washington Post.* Accessed at www.washingtonpost.com /local/education/more-states-requiring-third-graders-to-pass-reading-test-to -advance/2013/03/10/edcafb5e-76ec-11e2-aa12-e6cf1d31106b_story.html on April 8, 2015.

Leinbach-Reyhle, N. (2014, August 19). Teachers spend their own money on back to school supplies. *Forbes.* Accessed at www.forbes.com/sites /nicoleleinbachreyhle/2014/08/19/teachers-spend-own-money-school-supplies on March 17, 2015.

Leithwood, K., Louis, K. S., Anderson, S., & Wahlstrom, K. (2004). *How leadership influences student learning.* New York: Wallace Foundation. Accessed at www .wallacefoundation.org/knowledge-center/school-leadership/key-research /Documents/How-Leadership-Influences-Student-Learning.pdf on March 23, 2015.

Lencioni, P. (2005). *Overcoming the five dysfunctions of a team: A field guide.* San Francisco: Jossey-Bass.

Lencioni, P. (2012). *The advantage: Why organizational health trumps everything else in business.* San Francisco: Jossey-Bass.

Levine, A. (2006, September). *Educating school teachers.* Washington, DC: Education Schools Project. Accessed at www.edschools.org/pdf/educating_teachers_report .pdf on April 8, 2015.

Levine, A. (2013, June 21). Fixing how we train U.S. teachers. *Hechinger Report.* Accessed at http://hechingerreport.org/fixing-how-we-train-u-s-teachers on January 31, 2015.

Lezotte, L. W. (n.d.). *Revolutionary and evolutionary: The effective schools movement.* Accessed at www.effectiveschools.com/images/stories/RevEv.pdf on March 23, 2015.

Lieberman, A. (1995). Restructuring schools: The dynamics of changing practice, structure, and culture. In A. Lieberman (Ed.), *The work of restructuring schools: Building from the ground up* (pp. 1 17). New York: Teachers College Press.

Linn, R. L., Koretz, D. M., Baker, E. L., & Burstein, L. (1991). *The validity and credibility of the achievement levels for the 1990 National Assessment of Educational Progress in Mathematics* (CSE Technical Report No. 330). Los Angeles, CA: National Center for Research on Evaluation, Standards, and Student Testing. Accessed at www.cse.ucla.edu/products/reports/R330.pdf on January 20, 2015.

Little, J. W. (1990). The persistence of privacy: Autonomy and initiative in teachers' professional relations. *Teachers College Record, 91*(4), 509–536.

Little, J. W., & Bartlett, L. (2010). The teacher workforce and problems of educational equity. *Review of Research in Education, 34*(1), 285–328.

Little, J. W., Gearhart, M., Curry, M., & Kafka, J. (2003). Looking at student work for teacher learning, teacher community, and school reform. *Phi Delta Kappan, 85*(3), 184–192.

Looney, J. (2005). *Formative assessment: Improving learning in secondary classrooms.* Paris: Organisation for Economic Co-operation and Development.

Lortie, D. C. (1975). *Schoolteacher: A sociological study.* Chicago: University of Chicago Press.

Louis, K. S., Leithwood, K., Wahlstrom, K. L., & Anderson, S. E. (2010, July). *Investigating the links to improved student learning: Final report of research findings.* St. Paul, MN: Center for Applied Research and Educational Improvement. Accessed at www.wallacefoundation.org/knowledge-center /school-leadership/key-research/Documents/Investigating-the-Links-to -Improved-Student-Learning.pdf on April 8, 2015.

Louis, K. S., & Wahlstrom, K. (2011). Principals as cultural leaders. *Phi Delta Kappan, 92*(5), 52–56.

Lu, A. (2013, July 1). Parents revolt against failing schools. *USA Today.* Accessed at www.usatoday.com/story/news/nation/2013/07/01/stateline-parent-trigger -laws/2479347 on March 20, 2015.

Markow, D., Macia, L., & Lee, H. (2013, February). *The MetLife survey of the American teacher: Challenges for school leadership.* New York: MetLife. Accessed at www.metlife.com/assets/cao/foundation/MetLife-Teacher -Survey-2012.pdf on March 20, 2015.

Markow, D., & Pieters, A. (2010, April). *The MetLife survey of the American teacher: Collaborating for student success.* New York: MetLife. Accessed at http://files.eric.ed.gov/fulltext/ED509650.pdf on April 8, 2015.

Markow, D., & Pieters, A. (2012, March). *The MetLife survey of the American teacher: Teachers, parents and the economy.* New York: MetLife. Accessed at www.metlife.com/assets/cao/foundation/MetLife-Teacher-Survey-2011.pdf on February 6, 2013.

Martin, M. O., Mullis, I. V. S., Foy, P., & Stanco, G. M. (2012). *TIMSS 2011 international results in science.* Chestnut Hill, MA: Trends in International Mathematics and Science Study and Progress in International Reading Literacy Study International Study Center. Accessed at http://timssandpirls.bc.edu /timss2011/downloads/T11_IR_Science_FullBook.pdf on March 20, 2015.

Marzano, R. J. (2003). *What works in schools: Translating research into action.* Alexandria, VA: Association for Supervision and Curriculum Development.

Marzano, R. J. (2009). Setting the record straight on "high-yield" strategies. *Phi Delta Kappan, 91*(1), 30–37.

Marzano, R. J., Kendall, J. S., & Gaddy, B. B. (1999). What should students know? *American School Board Journal, 186*(3), 47–48, 60.

Marzano, R. J., Waters, T., & McNulty, B. A. (2005). *School leadership that works: From research to results.* Alexandria, VA: Association for Supervision and Curriculum Development.

Masterson, K. (2008, March 31). Worst teachers promised $10,000 by lobbyist. *Chicago Tribune.* Accessed at http://articles.chicagotribune.com/2008-03-31 /news/0803300194_1_bad-teachers-teachers-unions-center-for-union-facts on March 20, 2015.

Mattos, M., & Buffum, A. (2015). *It's about time: Planning interventions and extensions in secondary school.* Bloomington, IN: Solution Tree Press.

McCaffrey, D. F., Lockwood, J. R., Koretz, D. M., & Hamilton, L. S. (2003). *Evaluating value-added models for teacher accountability.* Santa Monica, CA: RAND. Accessed at www.rand.org/pubs/monographs/2004/RAND _MG158.pdf on March 20, 2015.

McCaffrey, D. F., Sass, T. R., & Lockwood, J. R. (2008). *The intertemporal stability of teacher effect estimates* (Working Paper No. 2008-22). Nashville, TN: National Center on Performance Incentives.

McDonald, J. P., Mohr, N., Dichter, A., & McDonald, E. C. (2007). *The power of protocols: An educator's guide to better practice* (2nd ed.). New York: Teachers College Press.

Mehta, J. (2013, May/June). Why American education fails: And how lessons from abroad could improve it. *Foreign Affairs.* Accessed at www.foreignaffairs.com /articles/139113/jal-mehta/why-american-education-fails on April 8, 2015.

Mehta, J. (2014, July 16). Five inconvenient truths for reformers [Blog post]. *Education Week.* Accessed at http://blogs.edweek.org/edweek/learning _deeply/2014/07/five_inconvenient_truths_for_reformers.html on December 20, 2014.

Mid-continent Research for Education and Learning. (2005, November). *Final report: High-needs schools—What does it take to beat the odds?* Denver, CO: Author. Accessed at www.mcrel.org/~/media/Files/McREL/Homepage /Products/01_99/prod57_BeatTheOdds.ashx on April 8, 2015.

Miron, G., Mathis, W., & Welner, K. (2015, February). *Review of* Separating Fact and Fiction. Boulder, CO: National Education Policy Center. Accessed at http://nepc.colorado.edu/thinktank/review-separating-fact-and-fiction on April 8, 2015.

Miron, G., Urschel, J. L., Mathis, W. J., & Tornquist, E. (2010, February). *Schools without diversity: Education management organizations, charter schools, and the demographic stratification of the American school system.* Boulder, CO: Education and the Public Interest Center and Education Policy Research Unit. Accessed at http://epicpolicy.org/publication/schools-without-diversity on March 20, 2015.

Moe, T. M. (2011). *Special interest: Teachers unions and America's public schools.* Washington, DC: Brookings Institution Press.

Mullis, I. V. S., Martin, M. O., Foy, P., & Arora, A. (2012). *TIMSS 2011 international results in mathematics.* Chestnut Hill, MA: Trends in International Mathematics and Science Study and Progress in International Reading Literacy Study International Study Center. Accessed at http://timssandpirls .bc.edu/timss2011/downloads/T11_IR_Mathematics_FullBook.pdf on March 20, 2015.

Murphy, J., Hallinger, P., & Heck, R. H. (2013). Leading via teacher evaluation: The case of the missing clothes? *Educational Researcher, 42*(6), 349–354.

National Association of Colleges and Employers. (2011, November). *Job outlook 2012.* Bethlehem, PA: Author. Accessed at www.uwsuper.edu/career/students /upload/Job-Outlook-2012-Member-Version-1.pdf on March 23, 2015.

National Association of Colleges and Employers. (2014, November 12). *Job outlook: The candidate skills/qualities employers want, the influence of attributes.* Accessed at www.naceweb.org/s11122014/job-outlook-skills-qualities -employers-want.aspx on March 23, 2015.

National Association of Secondary School Principals. (1996). *Breaking ranks: Changing an American institution* (ERIC Document Reproduction Service No. ED393205). Reston, VA: Author.

National Center for Education Statistics. (2011, November). *The Nation's Report Card: Mathematics 2011* (NCES 2012-458). Washington, DC: Institute of Education Sciences, U.S. Department of Education. Accessed at http://nces .ed.gov/nationsreportcard/pdf/main2011/2012458.pdf on March 20, 2015.

National Center for Education Statistics. (2012a, May). *The Nation's Report Card: Science 2011* (NCES 2012-465). Washington, DC: Institute of Education Sciences, U.S. Department of Education. Accessed at http://nces.ed.gov /nationsreportcard/pdf/main2011/2012465.pdf on March 20, 2015.

National Center for Education Statistics. (2012b). *The status of achievement levels.* Accessed at http://nces.ed.gov/nationsreportcard/achlevdev.aspx on April 8, 2015.

National Center for Education Statistics. (2013). *Table 203.50: Enrollment and percentage distribution of enrollment in public elementary and secondary schools, by race/ethnicity and region: Selected years, fall 1995 through fall 2023.* Accessed at http://nces.ed.gov/programs/digest/d13/tables/dt13_203.50.asp on March 20, 2015.

National Center for Education Statistics. (2014a). *NAEP overview.* Accessed at http://nces.ed.gov/nationsreportcard/about on March 20, 2015.

National Center for Education Statistics. (2014b). *Selected statistics from the public elementary and secondary education universe: School year 2012–13.* Accessed at http://nces.ed.gov/pubs2013/2014098/tables.asp on April 8, 2015.

National Center for Education Statistics. (2015). *The NAEP glossary of terms.* Washington, DC: Institute of Education Sciences, U.S. Department of Education. Accessed at http://nces.ed.gov/nationsreportcard/glossary.aspx #achievement_levels on March 22, 2015.

National Center on Secondary Education and Transition. (2002, March). *Promoting effective parent involvement in secondary education and transition: Parent brief.* Minneapolis, MN: PACER Center. Accessed at www.ncset.org /publications/parent/NCSETParent_Mar02.pdf on April 8, 2015.

National Commission on Excellence in Education. (1983, April). *A nation at risk: The imperative for educational reform.* Washington, DC: U.S. Department of Education.

National Commission on Teaching and America's Future. (1996, September). *What matters most: Teaching for America's future.* New York: Author. Accessed at www.namodemello.com.br/pdf/tendencias/whatmattersmost .pdf on March 23, 2015.

National Council on Teacher Quality. (2010, February). *Teacher layoffs: Rethinking "last-hired, first-fired" policies.* Accessed at www.nctq.org/dmsView /Teacher_Layoffs_Rethinking_Last-Hired_First-Fired_Policies_NCTQ _Report on March 23, 2015.

National Governors Association Center for Best Practices & Council of Chief State School Officers. (n.d.). *Development process.* Accessed at www .corestandards.org/about-the-standards/development-process on March 15, 2015.

National Governors Association Center for Best Practices & Council of Chief State School Officers. (2008). *Benchmarking for success: Ensuring U.S. students receive a world-class education.* Accessed at www.corestandards.org /assets/0812BENCHMARKING.pdf on March 23, 2015.

National Governors Association Center for Best Practices & Council of Chief State School Officers. (2010). *Common Core State Standards for English language arts and literacy in history/social studies, science, and technical subjects.* Washington, DC: Author. Accessed at www.corestandards.org/assets/CCSSI _ELA%20Standards.pdf on April 8, 2015.

National Partnership for Teaching in At-Risk Schools. (2005). *Qualified teachers for at-risk schools: A national imperative.* Washington, DC: Author. Accessed at www.learningpt.org/pdfs/tq/partnership.pdf on April 8, 2015.

National Science Board. (2004). *Science and engineering indicators 2004.* Accessed at www.nsf.gov/statistics/seind04/c1/c1h.htm on March 25, 2015.

Nelson, H. (2013, July). *Testing more, teaching less: What America's obsession with student testing costs in money and lost instructional time.* Washington, DC: American Federation of Teachers. Accessed at www.aft.org/sites/default/files /news/testingmore2013.pdf on March 20, 2015.

North Central Regional Educational Laboratory. (1994). *Summary of goals 2000: Educate American Act.* Accessed at www.ncrel.org/sdrs/areas/issues /envrnmnt/stw/sw0goals.htm on March 21, 2015.

Oakes, J. (2005). *Keeping track: How schools structure inequality* (2nd ed.). New Haven, CT: Yale University Press.

Odden, A. R., & Archibald, S. J. (2009). *Doubling student performance . . . and finding the resources to do it.* Thousand Oaks, CA: Corwin Press.

O'Neill, J., & Conzemius, A. (with Commodore, C., & Pulsfus, C.). (2006). *The power of SMART goals: Using goals to improve student learning.* Bloomington, IN: Solution Tree Press.

Ontario Focused Intervention Partnership. (n.d.). *The OFIP journey: 2003-04–2013-14.* Accessed at https://ofip1415.files.wordpress.com/2014/10 /ofip-journey_2003_2013.pdf on March 21, 2015.

Organisation for Economic Co-operation and Development. (2005, November). *Formative assessment: Improving learning in secondary classrooms* [Policy brief]. Paris: Author. Accessed at www.oecd.org/edu/ceri/35661078.pdf on April 8, 2015.

Organisation for Economic Co-operation and Development. (2009, December). *21st century skills and competencies for new millennium learners in OECD countries* (EDU Working Paper No. 41). Paris: Author. Accessed at www .oecd.org/officialdocuments/publicdisplaydocumentpdf/?cote=EDU /WKP(2009)20&doclanguage=en on March 30, 2015.

Organisation for Economic Co-operation and Development. (2010a). Finland: Slow and steady reform for consistently high results. In *Strong performers and successful reformers in education: Lessons from PISA for the United States* (pp. 117–135). Paris: Author. Accessed at www.oecd.org/pisa /pisaproducts/46581035.pdf on March 21, 2015.

Organisation for Economic Co-operation and Development. (2010b). Singapore: Rapid improvement followed by strong performance. In *Strong performers and successful reformers in education: Lessons from PISA for the United States* (pp. 159–176). Paris: Author. Accessed at www.oecd.org/countries /singapore/46581101.pdf on March 21, 2015.

Organisation for Economic Co-operation and Development. (2011a). Financial and human resources invested in education. In *Education at a glance 2011: OECD indicators* (pp. 203–223). Paris: Author. Accessed at www.oecd.org /education/skills-beyond-school/48630868.pdf on January 29, 2015.

Organisation for Economic Co-operation and Development. (2011b). Lessons for the United States. In *Strong performers and successful reformers in education: Lessons from PISA for the United States* (pp. 227–256). Paris: Author. Accessed at www.oecd.org/pisa/46623978.pdf on April 8, 2015.

Organisation for Economic Co-operation and Development. (2012a). *Education at a glance 2012: OECD indicators*. Paris: Author. Accessed at www.oecd.org /edu/EAG%202012_e-book_EN_200912.pdf on February 5, 2013.

Organisation for Economic Co-operation and Development. (2012b). *Education at a glance: OECD indicators 2012, country note: United States*. Accessed at www.oecd.org/unitedstates/CN%20-%20United%20States.pdf on January 29, 2015.

Organisation for Economic Co-operation and Development. (2013a). How the quality of the learning environment is shaped. In *What makes schools successful?: Resources, policies and practices* (Vol. 4, pp. 165–188). Paris: Author. Accessed at www.oecd.org/pisa/keyfindings/Vol4Ch5.pdf on November 6, 2014.

Organisation for Economic Co-operation and Development. (2013b). Policy implications of school management and practices. In *What makes schools successful?: Resources, policies and practices* (Vol. 4, pp. 189–194). Paris: Author. Accessed at www.oecd.org/pisa/keyfindings/Vol4Ch6.pdf on March 20, 2015.

Organisation for Economic Co-operation and Development. (2013c). *Results from TALIS 2013: Country note—United States of America*. Accessed at www.oecd .org/unitedstates/TALIS-2013-country-note-US.pdf on March 23, 2015.

Organisation for Economic Co-operation and Development. (2014a). *CO2.2: Child poverty*. Accessed at www.oecd.org/els/soc/CO2_2_ChildPoverty _Jan2014.pdf on March 30, 2015.

Organisation for Economic Co-operation and Development. (2014b). *Education at a glance 2014: Country note—United States*. Accessed at www.oecd.org /edu/United%20States-EAG2014-Country-Note.pdf on April 8, 2015.

Organisation for Economic Co-operation and Development. (2014c). *Education at a glance 2014: OECD indicators*. Paris: Author. Accessed at www.oecd.org /edu/Education-at-a-Glance-2014.pdf on March 21, 2015.

Orland, M., & Anderson, J. (2013, April). *Assessment* for *learning: What policymakers should know about formative assessment.* San Francisco: WestEd. Accessed at www.wested.org/wp-content/files_mf/1370911288resource13062.pdf on April 8, 2015.

Paine, S. L., & Schleicher, A. (2011). *What the U.S. can learn from the world's most successful education reform efforts* (Policy Paper). New York: McGraw-Hill Research Foundation. Accessed at www.mcgraw-hillresearchfoundation .org/wp-content/uploads/pisa-intl-competitiveness.pdf on March 20, 2015.

Partanen, A. (2011, December 29). What Americans keep ignoring about Finland's school success. *The Atlantic.* Accessed at www.theatlantic.com /national/archive/2011/12/what-americans-keep-ignoring-about-finlands-school -success/250564 on April 8, 2015.

Partnership for 21st Century Schools. (2009). *P21 framework definitions.* Accessed at www.p21.org/storage/documents/P21_Framework_Definitions.pdf on April 8, 2015.

Patterson, K., Grenny, J., Maxfield, D., McMillan, R., & Switzler, A. (2008). *Influencer: The power to change anything.* New York: McGraw-Hill.

Pearlstine, N. (2011, October 13). How to fix the education crisis. *Businessweek.* Accessed at www.bloomberg.com/bw/magazine/how-to-fix-the-education -crisis-10132011.html on April 8, 2015.

Pellegrino, J. W., & Hilton, M. L. (Eds.). (2012). *Education for life and work: Developing transferable knowledge and skills in the 21st century.* Washington, DC: National Academies Press.

Pellegrino, J. W., Jones, L. R., & Mitchell, K. J. (Eds.). (1999). *Grading the Nation's Report Card: Evaluating NAEP and transforming the assessment of educational progress.* Washington, DC: National Academies Press.

Pfeffer, J., & Sutton, R. I. (2000). *The knowing-doing gap: How smart companies turn knowledge into action.* Boston: Harvard Business School Press.

Pfeffer, J., & Sutton, R. I. (2006). *Hard facts: Dangerous half-truths and total nonsense—Profiting from evidence-based management.* Boston: Harvard Business School Press.

Phi Delta Kappa. (2014). *PDK/Gallup polls of the public's attitudes toward the public schools.* Accessed at www.pdkmembers.org/members_online/publications /GallupPoll/k_q_quality_1.htm#506 on March 20, 2015.

Pink, D. H. (2009). *Drive: The surprising truth about what motivates us.* New York: Riverhead Books.

Popham, W. J. (2008). *Transformative assessment.* Alexandria, VA: Association for Supervision and Curriculum Development.

Popham, W. J. (2013, January 8). Waving the flag for formative assessment. *Education Week.* Accessed at www.edweek.org/ew/articles/2013/01/09/15popham .h32.html?tkn=LMSFalVt%2FzHY2790%2FCNw88VfniWfZ8Aa8EIS &cmp=ENL-EU-NEWS2 on February 23, 2015.

Porter, E. (2013, June 25). Dropping out of college, and paying the price. *New York Times*. Accessed at www.nytimes.com/2013/06/26/business/economy /dropping-out-of-college-and-paying-the-price.html on March 23, 2015.

Prasse, D. P. (n.d.). *Why adopt an RTI model?* Accessed at www.rtinetwork.org /learn/what/whyrti on April 8, 2015.

Pratchett, T. (1997). *Jingo: A novel of Discworld*. New York: Harper.

President's Council of Economic Advisers. (2014, December). *The economics of early childhood investments*. Accessed at www.whitehouse.gov/sites/default /files/docs/early_childhood_report1.pdf on March 22, 2015.

Ravitch, D. (2011, September/October). American schools in crisis. *Saturday Evening Post*. Accessed at www.saturdayeveningpost.com/2011/08/16/in-the -magazine/trends-and-opinions/american-schools-crisis.html on March 20, 2015.

Ravitch, D. (2012, May 14). *What do NAEP scores mean?* Accessed at http:// dianeravitch.net/2012/05/14/what-do-naep-scores-mean on March 20, 2015.

Ravitch, D. (2014). *Reign of error: The hoax of the privatization movement and the danger to America's public schools*. New York: Vintage Books.

Rebell, M. A., & Wolff, J. R. (2012, January 17). We can overcome poverty's impact on school success. *Education Week*. Accessed at www.edweek.org/ew /articles/2012/01/18/17rebell.h31.html on January 29, 2015.

Reeves, D. B. (2002). *The leader's guide to standards: A blueprint for educational equity and excellence*. San Francisco: Jossey-Bass.

Reeves, D. B. (2004). *Accountability for learning: How teachers and school leaders can take charge*. Alexandria, VA: Association for Supervision and Curriculum Development.

Reeves, D. B. (2007). Challenges and choices: The role of educational leaders in effective assessment. In D. B. Reeves (Ed.), *Ahead of the curve: The power of assessment to transform teaching and learning* (pp. 227–251). Bloomington, IN: Solution Tree Press.

Reeves, D. B. (2009). In education, standards aren't enough. *The Hill, 16*(82). Accessed at www.leadandlearn.com/sites/default/files/articles/090714-the -hill-in-education-standards-arent-enough.pdf on April 8, 2015.

Resmovits, J. (2011, December 21). Charter schools rarely closed for academic performance: Report. *Huffington Post*. Accessed at www.huffingtonpost .com/2011/12/21/charter-schools-closure_n_1164104.html on April 8, 2015.

Resmovits, J. (2014, September 24). Bill Clinton: Charter schools must be held to 'the original bargain.' *Huffington Post*. Accessed at www.huffingtonpost .com/2014/09/24/bill-clinton-charter-schools_n_5878084.html on April 8, 2015.

Rice, J. K. (2010, August). *The impact of teacher experience: Examining the evidence and policy implications* (Brief No. 11). Washington, DC: National Center for Analysis of Longitudinal Data in Education Research. Accessed at www .urban.org/uploadedpdf/1001455-impact-teacher-experience.pdf on March 21, 2015.

Rich, M. (2012, July 6). 'No Child' law whittled down by White House. *New York Times*. Accessed at www.nytimes.com/2012/07/06/education/no-child -left-behind-whittled-down-under-obama.html on March 20, 2015.

Rickover, H. G. (1982). *Thoughts on man's purpose in life*. New York: Council on Religion and International Affairs. Accessed at www.carnegiecouncil .org/publications/archive/morgenthau/763.html/_res/id=sa_File1/763 _2ndMML-H.G.Rickover.pdf on March 10, 2013.

Rippa, S. A. (1971). *Education in a free society: An American history* (2nd ed.). New York: McKay.

Robinson, P. (2015). Endangering prosperity. *Hoover Digest, 2015*(1), 117–125. Accessed at www.hoover.org/research/endangering-prosperity on March 20, 2015.

Robinson, V. (2011). *Student-centered leadership*. San Francisco: Jossey-Bass.

Roosevelt, F. D. (1938, September 27). *Message for American Education Week* (G. Peters & J. T. Woolley, Eds.). American Presidency Project. Accessed at www.presidency.ucsb.edu/ws/?pid=15545%23ixzz1vcCJrE42 on January 30, 2015.

Rosenholtz, S. (1986). Organizational conditions of teacher learning. *Teaching and Teacher Education, 2*(2), 91–104.

Rotberg, I. C. (2014). Charter schools and the risk of increased segregation. *Phi Delta Kappan, 95*(5), 26–30. Accessed at www.pdkmembers.org/members _online/publications/archive/pdf/PDK_95_5/26pdk_95_5.pdf on January 30, 2015.

Rothman, R. (2011, July). *Assessing deeper learning* [Policy brief]. Washington, DC: Alliance for Excellent Education. Accessed at http://all4ed.org/wp -content/uploads/2013/06/AssessingDeeperLearning.pdf on April 8, 2015.

Rowling, J. K. (1998). *Harry Potter and the sorcerer's stone*. New York: Levine Books.

Rumberger, R. W. (2011). *Dropping out: Why students drop out of high school and what can be done about it*. Cambridge, MA: Harvard University Press.

Rumi. (n.d.). *"Yesterday I was clever, so I wanted to change the world. Today I am wise, so I am changing myself."* Accessed at www.goodreads.com/quotes /551027-yesterday-i-was-clever-so-i-wanted-to-change-the on March 23, 2015.

Sahlberg, P. (2013, May 15). What if Finland's great teachers taught in U.S. schools? *Washington Post*. Accessed at www.washingtonpost.com/blogs/answer -sheet/wp/2013/05/15/what-if-finlands-great-teachers-taught-in-u-s-schools -not-what-you-think on May 15, 2013.

Samuels, C. A. (2010). Learning-disabled enrollment dips after long climb. *Education Week, 30*(3), 1, 14–15.

Samuels, C. A. (2015, January 2). Consensus on early ed. value, but policy questions remain. *Education Week*. Accessed at www.edweek.org/ew/articles /2015/01/08/consensus-just-the-starting-point-on-early-ed.html?cmp=ENL -CM-NEWS2 on April 8, 2015.

Saphier, J. (2005). *John Adams' promise: How to have good schools for all our children, not just for some.* Acton, MA: Research for Better Teaching.

Sarason, S. B. (1971). *The culture of the school and the problem of change.* Boston: Allyn & Bacon.

Sarason, S. B. (1996). *Revisiting "the culture of the school and the problem of change."* New York: Teachers College Press.

Sawchuk, S. (2010, September 21). Merit pay found to have little effect on achievement. *Education Week.* Accessed at www.edweek.org/ew/articles /2010/09/21/05pay_ep.h30.html on April 8, 2015.

Schmidt, W. H., & Houang, R. T. (2007). Lack of focus in the mathematics curriculum: Symptom or cause? In T. Loveless (Ed.), *Lessons learned: What international assessments tell us about math achievement* (pp. 65–84). Washington, DC: Brookings Institution Press.

Schochet, P. Z., & Chiang, H. S. (2010, July). *Error rates in measuring teacher and school performance based on student test score gains* (NCEE 2010- 4004). Washington, DC: National Center for Education Evaluation and Regional Assistance. Accessed at http://ies.ed.gov/ncee/pubs/20104004 /pdf/20104004.pdf on March 20, 2015.

Scholastic. (2012). *Primary sources: 2012—America's teachers on the teaching profession.* Seattle, WA: Gates Foundation. Accessed at www.scholastic.com /primarysources/pdfs/Gates2012_full.pdf on April 8, 2015.

Scholastic. (2014). *Primary sources: America's teachers on teaching in an era of change* (3rd ed.). Seattle, WA: Gates Foundation. Accessed at www.scholastic .com/primarysources/PrimarySources3rdEditionWithAppendix.pdf on January 22, 2015.

Schwartz, T., & Porath, C. (2014, May 30). Why you hate work. *New York Times.* Accessed at www.nytimes.com/2014/06/01/opinion/sunday/why-you-hate-work .html on March 23, 2015.

Sergiovanni, T. J. (1994). *Building community in schools.* San Francisco: Jossey-Bass.

Sergiovanni, T. (2005). *Strengthening the heartbeat: Leading and learning together in schools.* San Francisco: Jossey-Bass.

Shepard, N. (2014, May 8). Teachers spending out of pocket for supplies, projects and field trips. *Deseret News.* Accessed at http://national.deseretnews.com /article/1440/teachers-spending-out-of-pocket-for-supplies-projects-and-field -trips.html on March 23, 2015.

Shyamalan, M. N. (2013). *I got schooled: The unlikely story of how a moonlighting movie maker learned the five keys to closing America's education gap.* New York: Simon & Schuster.

Simon, S. (2013, February 15). *Special report: Class struggle—How charter schools get students they want.* Accessed at www.reuters.com/article/2013/02/15/us -usa-charters-admissions-idUSBRE91E0HF20130215 on February 15, 2013.

Singapore Ministry of Education. (2010, April 26). *Teach less, learn more.* Accessed at www.moe.gov.sg/media/parliamentary-replies/2010/04/teach -less-learn-more.php on November 15, 2014.

Sinquefield, R. (2013, September 20). Public schools are failing, and that's a healthy sign for good teachers. *Forbes.* Accessed at www.forbes.com/sites /rexsinquefield/2013/09/20/public-schools-are-failing-and-thats-a-healthy -sign-for-good-teachers on March 20, 2015.

Skiba, R. J., Poloni-Staudinger, L., Gallini, S., Simmons, A. B., & Feggins-Azziz, R. (2006). Disparate access: The disproportionality of African American students with disabilities across educational environments. *Exceptional Children, 72*(4), 411–424.

Skiba, R. J., Simmons, A. B., Ritter, S., Gibb, A. C., Rausch, M. K., Cuadrado, J., et al. (2008). Achieving equity in special education: History, status, and current challenges. *Exceptional Children, 74*(3), 264–288.

Southern Education Foundation. (2015). *A new majority research bulletin: Low income students now a majority in the nation's public schools.* Accessed at www.southerneducation.org/Our-Strategies/Research-and-Publications/New -Majority-Diverse-Majority-Report-Series/A-New-Majority-2015-Update -Low-Income-Students-Now on March 20, 2015.

Sparks, S. D. (2011). Panel finds few learning benefits in high-stakes exams. *Education Week, 30*(33), 1, 14.

Sparks, S. D. (2013, July 29). Dropout indicators found for 1st graders. *Education Week.* Accessed at www.edweek.org/ew/articles/2013/07/29/37firstgrade .h32.html?tkn=YRXFxf2U7fneiqZz7tQQsojrJgXCEYZRzZxk&cmp=ENL-EU -NEWS1 on March 25, 2015.

Steinberg, L. (2014, February 11). What's holding back American teenagers? *Slate.* Accessed at www.slate.com/articles/life/education/2014/02/high _school_in_america_a_complete_disaster.html on March 20, 2015.

Stewart, V. (2012). *A world-class education: Learning from international models of excellence and innovation.* Alexandria, VA: Association for Supervision and Curriculum Development.

Stiggins, R. (2004). New assessment beliefs for a new school mission. *Phi Delta Kappan, 86*(1), 22–27.

Stiggins, R. (2007). Assessment *for* learning: An essential foundation of productive instruction. In D. B. Reeves (Ed.), *Ahead of the curve: The power of assessment to transform teaching and learning* (pp. 59–76). Bloomington, IN: Solution Tree Press.

Stiggins, R. (2014). *Defensible teacher evaluation: Student growth through classroom assessment.* Thousand Oaks, CA: Corwin Press.

Stigler, J. W. (2010, June 4). Needed: Fresh thinking on teacher accountability. *Education Week.* Accessed at www.edweek.org/ew/articles/2010/06/09 /33stigler_ep.h29.html on March 23, 2015.

Stigler, J. W., & Hiebert, J. (2009). Closing the teaching gap. *Phi Delta Kappan*, *91*(3), 32–37.

Strauss, V. (2010, October 25). The real effect of teachers union contracts [Blog post]. *Washington Post*. Accessed at http://voices.washingtonpost.com /answer-sheet/guest-bloggers/how-states-with-no-teacher-uni.html on March 22, 2015.

Strauss, V. (2012, March 12). The war on teachers: Why the public is watching it happen [Blog post]. *Washington Post*. Accessed at www.washingtonpost.com /blogs/answer-sheet/post/the-war-on-teachers-why-the-public-is-watching -it-happen/2012/03/11/gIQAD3XH6R_blog.html on January 21, 2015.

Strong American Schools. (2008). *Diploma to nowhere*. Washington, DC: Author. Accessed at www.broadeducation.org/asset/1128-diploma%20to %20nowhere.pdf on April 8, 2015.

Tavernise, S. (2012, February 9). Education gap grows between rich and poor, studies say. *New York Times*. Accessed at www.nytimes.com/2012/02/10 /education/education-gap-grows-between-rich-and-poor-studies-show .html on February 10, 2012.

The New Teacher Project. (2014, September). *Rebalancing teacher tenure: A post-Vergara guide for policymakers*. Brooklyn, NY: Author. Accessed at http:// tntp.org/assets/documents/TNTP_RebalancingTenure_2014.pdf on April 8, 2015.

Thomas, E. (2010, March 5). Why we must fire bad teachers. *Newsweek*. Accessed at www.newsweek.com/why-we-must-fire-bad-teachers-69467 on March 20, 2015.

Time. (2014, November 3). *Rotten apples* [Blog post]. Accessed at http:// timemagazine.tumblr.com/post/100742401579/times-new-cover-rotten -apples-its-nearly on March 20, 2015.

Timperley, H. (2009). *Using assessment data for improving teaching practice*. Accessed at http://research.acer.edu.au/cgi/viewcontent.cgi?article=1036 &context=research_conference on March 23, 2015.

Timperley, H., & Alton-Lee, A. (2008). Reframing teacher professional learning: An alternative policy approach to strengthening valued outcomes for diverse learners. *Review of Research in Education*, *32*(1), 328–369.

Tomlinson, C. A., & McTighe, J. (2006). *Integrating differentiated instruction and understanding by design*. Alexandria, VA: Association for Supervision and Curriculum Development.

Toppo, G. (2007, January 8). How Bush education law has changed our schools. *USA Today*. Accessed at www.usatoday.com/news/education/2007-01-07 -no-child_x.htm on March 23, 2015.

Treu, R. M. (2014, August 27). *Vergara v. State of California et al.: Tentative decision* (Case No. BC484642). Accessed at http://studentsmatter.org /wp-content/uploads/2014/08/SM_Final-Judgment_08.28.14.pdf on March 20, 2015.

Tucker, M. S. (2011, May). *Standing on the shoulders of giants: An American agenda for education reform*. Washington, DC: National Center on Education and the Economy. Accessed at www.ncee.org/wp-content/uploads/2011/05 /Standing-on-the-Shoulders-of-Giants-An-American-Agenda-for-Education -Reform.pdf on April 8, 2015.

Tucker, M. S. (2012). A different role for teachers unions. *Education Next, 12*(1), 16–20. Accessed at http://educationnext.org/a-different-role-for-teachers -unions on March 15, 2015.

Tucker, M. S. (2014). *Fixing our national accountability system*. Washington, DC: National Center on Education and the Economy. Accessed at www.ncee.org /wp-content/uploads/2014/08/FixingOurNationalAccountabilitySystemWebV4 .pdf on March 21, 2015.

USA Today. (2008, May 6). Teachers agree: Bad teachers with tenure too tough to fire. Accessed at www.usatoday.com/news/education/2008-05-06-teachers -tenure_N.htm on March 23, 2015.

USA Today. (2011, December 15). Report: Half of U.S. schools fail federal standards. Accessed at http://usatoday30.usatoday.com/news/education/story/2011-12 -15/schools-federal-standards/51949126/1 on March 20, 2015.

U.S. Census Bureau. (n.d.). *United States educational attainment of the population 25 years and over: 1940 to 2000*. Accessed at www.census.gov/hhes/socdemo /education/data/census/half-century/files/US.pdf on March 25, 2015.

U.S. Department of Education. (n.d.). *Building the legacy: IDEA 2004*. Accessed at http://idea.ed.gov on April 27, 2015.

U.S. Department of Education. (2003). *Fact sheet on the major provisions of the conference report to H.R. 1, the No Child Left Behind Act*. Accessed at www2 .ed.gov/nclb/overview/intro/factsheet.html on March 20, 2015.

U.S. Department of Education. (2009a). *Race to the Top program* [Executive summary]. Washington, DC: Author. Accessed at www2.ed.gov/programs /racetothetop/executive-summary.pdf on March 20, 2015.

U.S. Department of Education. (2009b, January). *28th annual report to Congress on the implementation of the Individuals With Disabilities Education Act, 2006* (Vol. 1). Washington, DC: Office of Special Education and Rehabilitative Services. Accessed at www2.ed.gov/about/reports/annual/osep/2006/parts -b-c/28th-vol-1.pdf on April 8, 2015.

U.S. Department of Education. (2010, May). *Race to the Top application for initial funding* (CFDA No. 84.395A). Washington, DC: Author. Accessed at www2.ed.gov/programs/racetothetop/application.doc on April 8, 2015.

U.S. General Accounting Office. (1993, June). *Educational achievement standards: NAGB's approach yields misleading interpretations* (Report to Congressional Requesters). Washington, DC: Author. Accessed at www.gao.gov/assets /160/153485.pdf on April 8, 2015.

Walker, T. (2013, December 18). A U.S. teacher in Finland: Teaching less, collaborating more [Blog post]. *Education Week*. Accessed at http://blogs .edweek.org/teachers/teaching_ahead/2013/12/how_does_finland_ support_teachers.html on December 19, 2013.

Wallace Foundation. (2012, January). *The school principal as leader: Guiding schools to better teaching and learning.* New York: Author. Accessed at www .wallacefoundation.org/knowledge-center/school-leadership/effective-principal -leadership/Documents/The-School-Principal-as-Leader-Guiding-Schools-to -Better-Teaching-and-Learning.pdf on January 7, 2012.

Welner, K. G., & Mathis, W. J. (2015, February). *Reauthorization of the Elementary and Secondary Education Act: Time to move beyond test-focused policies* [Policy memo]. Boulder, CO: National Education Policy Center. Accessed at http://nepc.colorado.edu/files/nepc-policymemo-esea.pdf on February 17, 2015.

West, M. R. (2005, December). *No Child Left Behind: How to give it a passing grade* [Policy brief]. Washington, DC: Brookings Institution. Accessed at www .brookings.edu/papers/2005/12education_west.aspx on March 23, 2015.

West, M. R. (2012, August). *Is retaining students in the early grades self-defeating?* (CCF Brief No. 49). Washington, DC: Brookings Institution. Accessed at www .brookings.edu/research/papers/2012/08/16-student-retention-west on April 8, 2015.

White House. (n.d.a). *Higher education.* Accessed at www.whitehouse.gov/issues /education/higher-education on March 22, 2015.

White House. (n.d.b). *No Child Left Behind.* Accessed at http://georgewbush -whitehouse.archives.gov/news/reports/no-child-left-behind.html on April 8, 2015.

Wiliam, D. (2011). *Embedded formative assessment.* Bloomington, IN: Solution Tree Press.

Wilson, R. (2014, December 17). Fresh attacks on Common Core ahead after GOP wave [Blog post]. *Washington Post.* Accessed at www.washingtonpost .com/blogs/govbeat/wp/2014/12/17/fresh-attacks-on-common-core-ahead -after-gop-wave on February 15, 2015.

Wolfe, S. M., Williams, C., & Zaslow, A. (2012). *Public citizen's health research group ranking of the rate of state medical boards' serious disciplinary actions, 2009–2011.* Accessed at www.citizen.org/documents/2034.pdf on March 21, 2015.

Yoshikawa, H., Weiland, C., Brooks-Gunn, J., Burchinal, M. R., Espinosa, L. M., Gormley, W. T., et al. (2013, October). *Investing in our future: The evidence base on preschool education.* Ann Arbor, MI: Society for Research in Child Development. Accessed at http://fcd-us.org/sites/default/files /Evidence%20Base%20on%20Preschool%20Education%20FINAL.pdf on February 7, 2015.

Zavis, A., & Barboza, T. (2010, September 28). Teacher's suicide shocks school. *Los Angeles Times.* Accessed at http://articles.latimes.com/2010/sep/28/local /la-me-south-gate-teacher-20100928 on January 25, 2015.

Zhao, E. (2012, April 25). New York City teacher ratings: Teacher data reports publicly released amid controversy. *Huffington Post.* Accessed at www .huffingtonpost.com/2012/02/24/new-york-city-teacher-rat_n_1299837 .html on March 20, 2015.

Index

Learning by Doing (2nd Edition)
Richard DuFour, Rebecca DuFour, Robert Eaker, and Thomas Many
This book is an action guide for closing the knowing-doing gap and transforming schools into PLCs. It includes seven major additions that equip educators with essential tools for confronting challenges.
BKF416

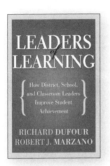

Leaders of Learning
Richard DuFour and Robert J. Marzano
Together, the authors focus on district leadership, principal leadership, and team leadership and address how individual teachers can be most effective in leading students—by learning with colleagues how to implement the most promising pedagogy in their classrooms.
BKF455

Cultures Built to Last
Richard DuFour and Michael Fullan
Take your professional learning community to the next level! Discover a systemwide approach for re-envisioning your PLC while sustaining growth and continuing momentum on your journey. You'll move beyond pockets of excellence while allowing every person to be an instrument of lasting cultural change.
BKF579

Are We a Group or a Team?
Mike Mattos
Build a powerful PLC to meet the needs of every student. Based on Mike Mattos's 1-5-10 team-evaluation activity, this unscripted video will give your team the step-by-step process they need to transition from a low-performing team to a high-performing team.
DVF065

Solution Tree | Press

a division of

Solution Tree

Visit solution-tree.com or call 800.733.6786 to order.

"Tremendous, tremendous, tremendous!

The speaker made me do some very deep internal reflection about the **PLC process** and the personal responsibility I have in making the school improvement process work **for ALL kids**."

—Marc Rodriguez, teacher effectiveness coach, Denver Public Schools, Colorado

PD Services

Our experts draw from decades of research and their own experiences to bring you practical strategies for building and sustaining a high-performing PLC. You can choose from a range of customizable services, from a one-day overview to a multiyear process.

Book your PLC PD today!
888.763.9045

Solution Tree